THE CATALOGUE OF CATALOGUES

THE COMPLETE GUIDE TO WORLD-WIDE SHOPPING BY MAIL

THE COMPLETE GUIDE TO WORLD-WIDE SHOPPING BY MAIL

THE CATALOGUE OF CATALOGUES

THE COMPLETE GUIDE TO WORLD-WIDE SHOPPING BY MAIL

MARIA ELENA DE LA IGLESIA

RANDOM HOUSE
NEW YORK

Library of Congress Cataloging in Publication Data

De La Iglesia, Maria Elena.
The catalogue of catalogues.

1. Mail-order business—Directories. I. Title.
HF5466.D45   380.1'025   72-1817
ISBN 0-394-46130-4 (trade)
ISBN 394-70781-8 (paper)

Design: Charles Schmalz

Manufactured in the United States of America
98765
First Edition

The articles listed below, which are depicted on part-title pages, are available at the following stores:

The chair on page 11, *at Martin F. Dodge.*
The front car, UV 24, on page 37, *at Halfway Garages.*
The pipes on page 45, at *Shannon Free Airport.*
Similar raincoats to the ones on page 47, at *Burberrys Ltd.*
The matchbox labels on page 63, at *H. S. Labels.*
The dishcloths on page 67, at the *Irish Linen Shop.*
The wine label on page 71, at *Wyatt Druid.*
The goods on page 75, at *Obéron* and *Stockmann.*
The cookie molds on page 81, at *Holland Handicrafts.*
The "Clubman" furniture on page 103, at *Pace Furniture Ltd.*
The jewelry on page 135, at *David Anderson.*
The harpsichord on page 143, at *Firma Kurt Wittmayer.*
The cameras on page 151, at *Quelle, Inc.*
The Mannoy tableware for the disabled is manufactured by *Melaware Ltd.,*
   Commerce Road, Brentford, Middlesex, England.
The camping equipment on page 161, at *Fjällräven SE-AB.*
The record player on page 167, at *Havemanns.*
The toy train on page 171, at *Obletter Spielwaren.*
The watches on page 179, at *Heldwein.*

Contents

Introduction

I started buying by mail from abroad the way many people do—by writing to shops I had visited in other countries and asking for things I had seen and liked but not bought because of being in a hurry, overpacked or simply indecisive. After a trip to Sweden I wrote and ordered some blankets; after Denmark, some lamps; after France, perfume; after England, toys, glassware, pottery and yet more blankets; after Spain a leather couch and a carpet. Everything worked out so well that by this time I was hooked. I was also spending so much time giving out addresses to friends and friends of friends, and listening to people's stories about the odd things they buy from abroad (children's underwear from London and feather pillows from Geneva), that it occurred to me it would be very useful to have a list of all the shops abroad that sell by mail to other countries.

When I started writing to shops I wondered how many of them would be organized to sell efficiently by mail. I discovered, rather to my surprise, that there was a whole underground movement of mail-order shoppers busily at work. In fact, it seems that so many Americans returning from abroad have written back that they have caused the shops to produce catalogues and start an overseas mail-order business. Each country's enterprises have mushroomed in whatever the country does well—Italy, for instance, has masses of shops selling kid gloves by mail, but none for toys; Germany has toys galore but no furniture; Denmark has furniture but no perfume, and so on.

One of the great advantages of doing your own importing is that you get a tremendous choice of exotic, well-designed and useful objects that you just can't buy in America. Every section of this book, almost every catalogue listed, has goods that have never been imported (and many more that are available only in big cities). And even with things that are popular imports, you can get a much wider choice by writing to the source. When American shops import, they obviously have to restrict themselves to a few of the most popular models in each line—sweaters, for instance, available in four colors in New York are available in fifteen in Scotland.

The other great advantage to buying directly from abroad is all the money you save. Of the things I ordered, the Swedish blankets, the perfume, the leather couch and the carpet cost half of what they would have cost in New York *after* shipping costs and duty were paid. When American shops import, they pay duty, and also often pay exporters, importers and distributors as well. And on top of that they raise prices; there are many lines on which shops expect to make a 100-percent profit, and others where they expect to charge "what the market will bear."

But although by buying directly from abroad you nearly always save money, it's not automatically the case. In a few categories American prices are so low that it is not worth buying from abroad—for instance, certain less expensive wines. In other cases it would not be to your advantage to buy a single object (such as a coffee table or a doll house) which is too large to mail, though it might be worthwhile as part of a larger shipment. So when you are buying from abroad only to save money, always check local prices first and remember to allow for shipping costs and duty.

Another good thing about shopping from abroad is that it is very easy. The large shops with special export departments and catalogues in English are so efficient that it is almost less trouble to buy from them than to cross town and brave a crowded department store. Buying from small shops that sell one-of-a-kind handicrafts, pictures, antiques, etc., is obviously more of an adventure and more of an effort, as you have to write and ask about sizes, prices, shipping costs, etc. Nervous beginners should stick to shops which sell mass-produced articles and have catalogues in English with prices given in dollars.

The one real disadvantage to mail order from abroad is that there is no instant gratification—you have to wait for catalogues, and then you have to wait for the goods. And while small parcels can be air-mailed and received immediately, others take longer, occasionally leaving the worried shopper imagining that they will never arrive (this has never happened in my experience).

The addresses in this book were originally taken from independent and reputable shopping guides to the specific areas, a few addresses were taken from government lists, and others were recommended by friends who had used them, (and I would be very pleased to hear about other shops that ought to be included in future editions). I wrote to over two thousand selected shops asking to see their catalogues. If the catalogues looked good, I sent a letter saying I was compiling a book, and asking various questions about how they sell to customers abroad and whether they can answer complicated letters in English (most can; there are warnings in the text about the exceptions). To many of the shops I then sent another irritating questionnaire asking for more details about prices of catalogues, when available, etc. From the shops answering these questions I chose those which seemed of most interest and included them in the book—there is no charge of any sort for being listed, of course. So all in all I hope that I have done everything possible to make sure that the listings are reliable. However, the book is intended as a guide to these shops, not an endorsement of them, and my descriptions are intended to give just an idea of the prices and the goods. Both of these are likely to change, so it is important to write for a catalogue or to check with the shop before ordering anything.

If, heaven forbid, the dollar should be devalued again, the goods in this book will go up in price; however, the same imported goods will go up in America too, so the price difference will usually stay the same.

Finally, the shops marked with crowns are royal warrant holders. Each crown means that the shop has supplied a member of the royal family with goods for at least two years and is allowed to boast about it—a handy indication that the shop is very reputable, but possibly expensive.

M.E.I.
March 1972

How to Buy

CATALOGUES

When there is a charge for a catalogue, the easiest, if riskiest, way to pay it is to *tape* coins onto a letter. If you prefer you can get international reply coupons at the post office, or you can pay with an ordinary check. When you make out the check (as with all amounts under $10 paid by personal check) you must add 50 cents for the bank charges that the shop will have to pay. Most of the catalogues listed as free will come by surface mail and take three weeks or more to arrive.

Some of the catalogue listings in this book include publication months; this is for shops which change a large part of their stock seasonally and allow their brochures to go out of print while the next one is being prepared. If you write just as a catalogue has run out, you may have to wait a couple of months before receiving an up-to-date one.

Most of the catalogues are in English; the exceptions are marked. Obviously foreign-language brochures are a nuisance if you don't know the language, as you have to write for more details, but for people who don't mind extra correspondence, they are very worthwhile, that is why I have included some.

ORDERING

When ordering from a shop whose description includes "prices in $" you will of course have no problem. For other shops the conversion tables at the back of this book should be a rough guide. At the time you want to send in an order and need to know the exact price in dollars, you can get the official exchange rate from a newspaper or bank, or buy up-to-date conversion tables from Perera, 636 Fifth Avenue, New York, N.Y. 10020. Or you can write to the shop and ask the price and shipping costs in dollars of what you are interested in. Don't forget to mention whether you want surface or air mail, and whether you want insurance.

Most of the shops will exchange things but this is troublesome, so when ordering, be obsessively specific about color, size, number, design, and so on. Be sure to keep the receipt for any duty you have paid, because if you do want to return a purchase, you will need it for the duty refund. I also find it very useful to keep copies of my orders to check dates, prices, reorders, etc., later on.

PAYING

PERSONAL CHECK

This is the method that I always use because it is by far the easiest—you simply make out one of your personal checks, exactly as you would if you were paying an American firm, and mail it to the shop. The disadvantage of this method is that it is much slower than any of the others; most shops wait until their bank has cleared the check with your bank, which can take up to four weeks but is usually done in two weeks. If the amount you are paying is less than $10, don't forget to add the 50 cents which the shop has to pay in bank charges. If the check is for more than $10, shops usually pay the bank charges themselves.

BANK DRAFT

Although banks use the same methods of sending money abroad, they have their own names and charges for each method, so your bank may call "bank draft" something different. If you don't mind going to the bank and filling out a form, buy an international certified check there, made out to the shop you are dealing with, and air-mail it yourself so that the money reaches the shop within a few days. The charge at my bank for this is $1.20 for any amount under $300.

CABLE AND MAIL TRANSFERS

By these methods the bank air-mails or cables the money to the shop's bank, and the shop is immediately notified. If you don't know what bank the shop uses, your bank will choose a bank near the shop, and the shop will be told to collect the money. The advantage of a cable transfer is of course speed; it's the fastest method. My bank charges $1.90 for an air-mail transfer, and $1.70, plus the cost of a cable, for a cable transfer.

LETTER OF CREDIT

If a large sum of money is involved, you can pay with a letter of credit so that the money is guaranteed, but the letter is not given to the shop until the shop has shown certain documents to a bank. Decide first, with the shop, as to what documents are important—they could be the invoice stating exactly what you have bought and the bill of lading to show that it has been shipped, and a time limit can also be included in the agreement. Most shops want the credit to be "irrevocable," then the customer can't suddenly decide he doesn't want the goods while the order is being prepared. Any bank will arrange a letter of credit, but charges vary.

INTERNATIONAL MONEY ORDER

At the post office you buy an international money order made out to the shop you are dealing with, and mail it yourself. At the moment the charges are: 45 cents for amounts under $10, 65 cents between $10 and $50, and 75 cents between $50 and $100.

SHIPPING

MAIL

Most parcels can be delivered exactly like domestic parcels, and if there is any duty it is paid to the mailman, along with a 70-cent handling charge, which the post office calls "postage due." However, there is a limit on the size and weight of a parcel that can be shipped by mail—it must not weigh more than 22 lbs., and the combined length and circumference of the parcel must not add up to more than 72". This means that the length of the parcel is measured in the usual way, but the width is measured with the tape right around the parcel.

AIR FREIGHT

This is used mainly for single objects which are too large to go by mail—framed pictures, large carpets, small pieces of furniture. Cargo of any size can be sent by air freight, and it is charged according to weight, volume and distance. Very roughly it works out at $1.20 to $1.70 a pound, and there is a minimum charge ($22 from Europe). The goods arrive at the airport nearest your address that has customs facilities, and you are notified of the arrival. You then go with identification and the bill from the shop (for customs) to the airport during office hours and see the parcel through customs (storage is charged if you don't go within five working days). If you want to employ a broker to get the parcel through customs, the airline can give you a list of firms.

SEA FREIGHT

This is only for large items such as furniture. Some of the shops in this book will arrange to have furniture delivered to your door by an agency, others just deliver to your nearest port. If furniture is delivered to a port, the steamship company will tell you when it arrives. You can then call a firm such as REA Express (formerly Railway Express) to see it through customs and deliver to your door, or you can save the flat fee of about $40 and get the furniture through customs yourself. If you do it yourself, you take the bill of lading and the bill for the furniture, both of which the shop will have sent you, and go to the steamship company to have the bill of lading stamped, then go to the customs house. Your crate will probably be opened, inspected and closed again, and you pay the duty. Then, with a certificate of clearance, you can take the goods away. If the package is too large, call someone experienced, like the REA people, who can tell you the exact cost of a job before they take it on; they charge by weight and distance. A few years ago I bought a couch from Spain and asked a small trucking firm to bring it over from the New Jersey docks to Manhattan. They charged by the hour, and as they were inexperienced, they kept arriving when the dock was closing, or at rush hour (and then consoling themselves with coffee breaks). I had to pay them $30 more than I would have paid REA. Big trucking firms such as REA are usually customs brokers too and take care of everything.

CUSTOMS DUTY

Duty isn't as high as you may think; for one thing, it is usually charged on the wholesale value of the goods (about 33 percent less than the retail value), for another, duty has been sharply reduced over the last few years and will probably remain at a new low level that was reached in January 1972. Gifts worth less than $10 are exempt from duty altogether, but only when bought by someone who is outside the country, so the very common practice of asking shops to mark parcels "Gift" is in fact illegal. However, I have found customs officers to be pretty lenient with small parcels—only one out of about ten toy or record parcels seems to be charged.

There is a guide to various rates of duty at the end of this book, but the rules for applying them are sometimes complicated, so you can't be sure what the exact charge will be until you receive the goods. If you ever think you have been overcharged, either refuse the parcel and write a protest to your postmaster, or accept the parcel, pay the duty, but send copies of the receipt for the duty and the shop's bill to the address given on the receipt. In both cases you may get a refund, though not of the 70 cents post office handling charge called "postage due." If you ever want to return goods you have bought from abroad, write to the address on the receipt for duty to see whether and how you can get a refund.

Antiques

The shops in the Fine Arts section (below) are listed strictly for people looking for "significant examples of important styles in good condition"—"important pieces," as the shops call them. At these levels, prices in England are no lower than American prices; there are simply more pieces available.

If, however, you are simply looking for handsome pieces of antique furniture to furnish a house, then, in addition to having a wider choice, you should be able to find things at lower prices in the Furniture and General section than you can locally.

But except for one or two of the mail-order specialists, don't expect the same service from the small and personal antique shops that you get from the stores in the other sections. They can only answer requests for specific items, and if you don't get an answer you must assume that the store didn't have what you wanted.

No duty is charged for anything that is over a hundred years old.

CARPETS

Perez, 112 Brompton Road, London S.W.3, England
An excellent London shop specializing in fine, old, antique and expensive Oriental carpets and rugs, old tapestries, needlework and Aubussons. Their wares are too sought-after ever to reach the stage of being listed; but private collectors write from all over the world describing what they are looking for. When Perez finds something possible, they send photographs and a full description for the customer's approval.

CLOCKS

Strike One, 1a Camden Walk, London N.1, England
Descriptive list, free. Photographs on request.

"Clocks for decoration, interest and investment," Strike One says enticingly. Their specialty is an ongoing responsibility for their clocks even after the clocks are ticking away in the new owners' homes. Everything is thoroughly overhauled and sold in perfect working order with a one-year guarantee (you can mail them back to be fixed); a record is kept of key sizes, so that lost keys can be replaced by mail; a comprehensive repair service covers not only clockwork mechanisms, but also cases, dials, hands, weights—all the things that most repair shops refuse to handle. And mail-order customers are given a very good five-page booklet on how to set up and look after their clocks.

Some of the clocks are quite old; a seventeenth-century, one-handed lantern clock has a square brass dial decorated and signed "Thomas Parker" in beautiful copperplate writing. A Black Forest cuckoo clock in the earliest style has roses painted around the face, and the cuckoo pops out from a bouquet of flowers. All sorts of clocks are sold—wall, shelf and long-case—and prices are usually well over $200.

CURIOS

Edward Golemberski, 95A Whitemore Road, Nottingham NG6 OHJ, England
Eight 28-page lists (published irregularly). Eight consecutive issues, $1.56 surface mail; $3.60 air mail.

An antique-and-curio catalogue (not illustrated) guaranteed to delight anyone looking for inexpensive, campy Victoriana to decorate their house or themselves. These are the things we were throwing out a few years ago, but with the rise of pop art have learned to love. For a mere $3.50 you can walk around wearing a large silver leaf-shaped pin saying "Mother," or hang on your wall an 1887 sampler with eight lines of religious quotation. For about $16, buy a rare nineteenth-

1
Strike One Very early Black Forrest cuckoo clock. $246.

2
Strike One Eight-day American shelf clock in rosewood and gilt by Seth Thomas, Plymouth Hollow. Recently sold for $104.

century Staffordshire group in perfect condition of two girls asleep below a guardian angel; or a lidded tobacco jar inscribed with the owner's name and decorated with sprigged scenes of men smoking and drinking. There is blue, green, marigold and purple carnival glass, porcelain and pottery, watches and clocks, pipes, jewelry, beadwork and embroidery (a Victorian footstool embroidered with glass-bead flowers costs $15), and some miniature pictures and engravings of American interest—General Goffe repulsing the Indians at Hadley costs $1.80, Thomas Jefferson only $1.50.

Thomas Humphrey Ltd., 24 Old Brompton Road, London S.W.7, England

Thomas Humphrey specializes in unusual antique objects and decorative oddities. A photograph of one of the rooms shows an appealing conglomeration of cherubs asleep on rose-garlanded cushions, naked women riding lions, galloping fairground horses, shining brass pots, and lots of smaller things that might be Elizabethan shoehorns, fairground scales, blacksmith's signs, ships' models, scientific instruments or almost anything else. The manager, Mark Rimmell, has written an article for *Antique Finder* about the unusual beauty to be found in functional objects which previously only seemed to have historic or sociological interest, and clients interested in such things write to him. If a client is looking for something not in stock, Thomas Humphrey immediately circulates an appeal to their buyers asking them to watch out for it. But costs are not negligible; a Sheraton mousetrap will cost $109, and an eighteenth-century spinning wheel $156.

FINE ARTS

Christie, Manson and Woods (U.S.A.), 867 Madison Avenue, New York, N.Y. 10021
Catalogue subscription list, free. Prices in $.

Sotheby and Co., P.O. Box 2AA, 34—35 New Bond Street, London W1A 2AA, England
Catalogue subscription list, free. Prices in $.

These grand English auction houses almost daily auction off "the things most worth living with," as one of them put it, frequently achieving world-record prices (I read recently in the *New York Times* that Christie's got a world-record price for an undrinkable old bottle of wine; the next week that Sotheby's got one for a Stradivarius). Comes the revolution, all this will be done away with, but meanwhile, in spite of the phenomenal record sales that get international publicity, there are plenty of things that people who are merely moderately well off can afford. You can subscribe to semi-illustrated catalogues throughout the season, more or less the academic year, for prices between $7 for something like musical instruments, and $72 for English and Continental antique furniture, ormolu, carpets, tapestries and textiles. Auctions are held of furniture, clocks, works of art, ceramics and glass, silver, jewelry, coins and medals, arms and armor, Art Nouveau, art deco posters. In fact, many people receive catalogues not to bid, but to keep up with market trends.

You receive catalogues about two weeks before auctions, and if you want to bid you can write the house for an estimate of what the bids will be, and then send in your own. At the actual auction a member of the staff will bid for you. If you win, you are notified within two weeks and must inform the house where you want your prize shipped or stored. You can also subscribe to price lists that will arrive later telling you what each item finally went for, and who got them.

I asked a man who worked for Parke-Bernet, which is owned by Sotheby's, what the difference is between the two houses. He said that Christie's has a larger turnover, but no "better" than Sotheby's, and that Christie's has a "better record" on silver, while Sotheby's has a "better record" on French impressionists.

Phillips Son and Neale, Blenstock House, 7 Blenheim Street, New Bond Street, London W1Y OAS, England
Subscription list, free.

Puffing and blowing along behind the giants comes another auction house, 175-year-old Phillips Son and Neale. Indignant that the others get more publicity, they have made a movie about themselves showing behind the scenes at an auction house—they lend the movie free to interested groups (antique collectors and bankers mostly). All year there are daily auctions of furniture, paintings, porcelain, silver and art objects in their Bond Street auction rooms, with goods coming to them from all over the world and often going back to equally distant countries. But although you can attend these auctions when in London, the catalogues are never ready in time for mail order.

On the other hand, there are special-sales catalogues that overseas collectors can subscribe to and receive in time to bid:

Two toy-soldier catalogues, $2.50.

Six pot-lid catalogues, $6 (last year Phillips Son and Neale got a world-record pot-lid price for "Washington Crossing the Delaware"). In the nineteenth century, English manufacturers often decorated the lids of pottery jars in which foods and cosmetics were sold, with full color transfers of famous people, events, humorous scenes or animals. These round lids, rarely larger than 5″ across have become collector's items and are often framed for display.

Four stevenograph catalogues, $5. In the middle of the nineteenth century Thomas Stevens, an English textile manufacturer, invented a way of weaving multicolored pictures in silk. These pictures of royalty, historical scenes, famous buildings, etc., are also collected.

Four Art Nouveau catalogues, $3.50 (glass, pottery and objects).

Six private-house catalogues, $6. The private-house sales usually consist of entire contents of private homes, or, to quote the catalogue for Old Plaw House, Sussex, "the valuable old English and reproduction contents of the residence."

None of the catalogues are illustrated.

Spink and Son Ltd.; 5—7 King Street, St. James's, London S.W.1, England

The omnipresent Spink's main enterprises are the fine arts sections, which contain only the most rare and important pieces. They send their old customers *Octagon*, a quarterly journal with articles and illustrations of new acquisitions (without prices). If you are serious and wealthy enough to want to become an old customer, write and inquire about your interests. Their Oriental Art is perhaps their best-known department, but they also have English silver and English paintings, and now a small gallery of early English furniture.

FURNITURE AND GENERAL

Crowther of Syon Lodge Ltd., Busch Corner, Isleworth, Middlesex, England
Occasional catalogues. Photographs on request.

Crowther of Syon Lodge, a family firm with one of the largest antique businesses in England, specializes in statues and garden furniture, mantelpieces and grates, wrought iron and period-paneled rooms, mainly eighteenth- and early-nineteenth-century. As you can imagine, their clients are

3

3
Edward Golemberski An early-nineteenth-century
stoneware tobacco jar, decorated in white with lions
and Prince of Wales feathers; chipped rim. $10.60.

4
Thomas Humphrey Ltd Rare Oriental processional
figure in dry lacquer, late seventeenth century, possibly
from Kansu province.

4

5
Thomas Humphrey Ltd 3'-high ivory-veneered cabinet
from East India (circa 1750). Recently on exhibition at
the Victoria and Albert Museum, London. $1,650.

6
Thomas Humphrey Ltd Eighteenth-century Italian
carved wooden figure with original polychrome
decoration 48" high. $900.

7
Spink and Son Ltd A rare George II mahogany
commode chair (commode fitment removed), English
(circa 1730). Recently sold.
photo Raymond Fortt Studio

8
Phillips Son and Neal Set on rare Bow "Seasons of the
Year," each figure brilliantly decorated in polychrome
enamels and gilded. The set of four was recently sold
for $2,168.

9
Crowther of Syon Lodge Ltd Stone groups of children
with animals mounted on baroque pedestals; one of a
pair of carved stone lions; one of a pair of terra-cotta
jardiniers decorated with lion masks and swags of oak
leaves.

10
Christopher Sykes A corner of the shop: Queen Anne
padfoot oak side table (circa 1690), $250; stick
barometer by P. Cossa $224; 1750 pewter chocolate
urn, $100.

11
Christopher Sykes Rare 1790 Staffordshire figure, $75;
small Staffordshire horse in yellow and brown, $23; red-
coated Staffordshire huntsman holding fox. Firing crack
on back, otherwise perfect, $36.

12
Eric Vejerslev Antique Russian candlesticks, over 100
years old 21¾" high. The original glass shades have
clear blue or red rims. About $110 a pair, including
postage.

5

6

7

10

8

9

11

12

dealers, decorators or very wealthy people. If you happen to fit into one of these categories and are looking for something grand, you will probably find it at Syon Lodge. Most of the stock is not available in America, and Crowther's says that American dealers sell what they acquire from Crowther's for five times their purchase price.

In the catalogue that I looked at there was a room of Georgian paneling in perfect condition. If the customer's room size is slightly off, Syon experts can adjust the proportions of the paneling. (No price given!) Apparently there are usually about forty rooms waiting to be renovated, which is done by stripping off the layers of paint and stain, and finally wax-polishing the original pine. Then, for a fireplace, a simple Directoire mantel with Doric columns supporting a plain frieze might cost $545, while a sober French Empire *gris-perle* marble mantelpiece with small ormolu mountings of Greek gods costs $1,176. Simpler to install are the antique grates: a mid-eighteenth-century andiron made of nickel with elaborate details costs $336, and a Louis XVI steel-basket grate with brass mounts costs $168. There is also sumptuous antique furniture: a pair of Sheraton-period blackwood armchairs paneled with pastoral scenes, $1,064; a Carlton House writing desk with a mail slot to a locked cupboard, $1,932; or a Regency chaise longue with tasseled cushions upholstered in turquoise and willow-green silk, $350.

The garden statuary is mainly eighteenth-century lead or marble and very decorative: sundials, birdbaths and urns; lions, sphinxes, griffins and classical figures. A slim and graceful Apollo and Narcissus, a marble pair from the collection of Lord Leverhulme, cost $2,520.

Photographs of stock can be sent to you by return mail, and shipping costs can be given within two hours (presumably cabled or telephoned). Anything not in stock can be found.

Margery Dean Antiques, The Galleries, Wivenhoe, Colchester, England
List, free; 40 cents air mail.

Margery Dean, author of *English Antique Furniture* has, for twenty-three years, been selling reasonably priced English period furniture. She puts out a neat list giving rough prices for over thirty kinds of seventeenth- and eighteenth-century furniture that she usually has in stock, but as she says, prices vary according to age, condition, patina and extent of repairs. Besides the 1600–1838 furniture listed, there are separate showrooms for Victorian furniture and "economical" country furniture, so this is a very well organized firm for anyone who wants antiques that are not too expensive. Seventeenth-century gate-leg tables cost from $130 to $530, depending on size; eighteenth-century bureaus from $185 to $1,000, depending on whether they are made of oak, mahogany or walnut. Oak and fruitwood side tables are from $36 to $55. Polaroid photographs can be sent on request.

Fountain House Antiques, East Bergholt, Suffolk, England
Fountain House Antiques has dealt mainly with American dealers, but they will be very happy to answer inquiries from ordinary citizens as well. If you write and ask about their nineteenth-century decorative pieces—pottery, glass, silver and jewelry—they will tell you what they have, and if you place an order, mail it themselves. If you ask about rarer and more expensive things, such as eighteenth-century pottery and porcelain (English and Continental), English silver and rare glass, photographs can be sent with complete description and approximate date of manufacture. Expensive and fragile pieces are sent via London packers.

Abelardo Linares, Carrera San Jeronimo 48, Madrid 14, Spain

Probably now Spain's largest antique shop, Abelardo Linares is a four-generation family firm with a branch on Majorca. They have no catalogue of their antiques, but they do answer serious inquiries for paintings by old masters, sculptures, Spanish furniture, tapestries, paperweights, porcelains. However, be specific about whether you want an antique or a reproduction, as they have both.

Moubray House Antiques, 51 High Street, Edinburgh, Scotland
Moubray House Antiques says that in the twenty years since their foundation, they have never had a complaint. They will answer inquiries about Georgian furniture, their specialty, and also about silver and silver plate, of which they have a little.

Christopher Sykes, 11 Market Place, Woburn, Bletchley, Buckinghamshire, England
Photographs, $2, returnable at first purchase.

Christopher Sykes has three antique shops, one of which is an old converted parsonage filled to the cellar with seventeenth- and eighteenth-century English furniture. He is wonderfully well organized to sell by mail, and since more than half his sales go to America, this is probably the best antique shop for you. Send $2 and inquire about specific interests, e.g., snuffboxes, and he will send photographs of what he has. Lots of small things can be mailed very easily: glass, porcelain, early lighting fixtures, barometers, scientific instruments. Larger pieces are shipped professionally: military chests, secretaire-bookcases, chests of drawers, tea tables and dining tables, chairs. To give you an idea of prices: a mahogany chest of drawers, c. 1790, Sheraton period, with original brass handles and escutcheons, $300; a George III mahogany bureau with original brass handles, fitted interior and six secret drawers, $650; six country Chippendale chairs, $575.

Alan Tillman Antiques Ltd., 9 Halkin Arcade, Motcomb Street, London S.W.1, England
Stock list of paperweights, free.

Alan Tillman sells fine and expensive seventeenth-, eighteenth- and nineteenth-century English and Continental glass, and French glass paperweights, mainly mid-nineteenth-century. He also runs an art and antique packing and shipping service called *Fine Art Packers Ltd.*

Erik Vejerslev, Hyskenstraede 7, Copenhagen K, Denmark
Photographs on request

Mr. Vejerslev sells old pewter, porcelain, lamps, mirrors, and pretty things for the house. However, *please* write only if you are seriously looking for something, because his letters are written out in longhand, in cautious English, and I can see that if he gets too many complicated inquiries, he'll have to shut the shop in order to answer them all. He does get a lot of American tourists, and says that Russian samovars and Russian brass candlesticks are a "big success" with them and usually available.

JEWELRY

N. Bloom and Son Ltd., 40 Albemarle Street, Piccadilly, London W.1, England
Monthly leaflets, free; a catalogue before Christmas, free. Prices in $.

A winged cherub on a Georgian heart-shaped brooch, a gold and turquoise bracelet "in the gothick taste," a Victorian "dearest" ring—N. Bloom sells unusual antique jewelry that ranges from the slightly odd, (an Egyptian-style, Victorian

13
Keith Harding Antiques Completely overhauled music box by Nicoles Frères, with drum bells and castanets, sold for $550.
photo Harvey Johns

14
Denise Poole 1793 cruet by Peter and Anne Bateman. The three larger bottles are original; the two smaller, Sheffield 1819. Mint condition, $230.

15
Denise Poole Hester Bateman teapot, London 1787, crested on one side, $750. Hester Bateman sugar basket, London 1786. Mint condition, $245.

gold brooch with a scarab, $180), to the magnificent (a ruby-and-pearl watch with bow fob, obviously ex-royal property, $840). In between, there are some gorgeous pieces of antique and Victorian jewelry for a person looking for something more interesting than any modern jewelry. Prices start at $125 and go up to $8,000. Some of the Victorian pieces are the least expensive: a rich-blue enamel brooch with pearl flowers and gold decorations costs $350; an Etruscan-style bangle in gold and diamonds, $550; and an engraved gold-and-turquoise flexible bracelet, $310.

N. Bloom sends out a page each month illustrating about fifteen items from their stock, which, besides jewelry, includes English and some Continental silver, snuffboxes and nineteenth-century *animalier* bronzes and enamel.

MUSIC BOXES

Keith Harding Antiques, 93 Hornsey Road, London N7 6DJ, England
Lists of cylinder and disk music boxes, list of spare parts for antique boxes, list of modern music boxes, list of books on music boxes, all free. Prices in $.

The last lines on the Keith Harding music-box price list are: "You might think we go to a great deal of trouble to give you exactly what you want. We do." And this does look like a place where music boxes and music-box lovers will be equally cared for and cosseted. There are eight craftsmen working and four floors of showrooms, museum, workshop and storage, plus a main workshop in another building. Modern boxes are made there, and antique boxes are overhauled before they are sold, with a guarantee that they leave the shop in the best possible condition. Hymns, operatic selections, waltzes, popular airs, and even "the British Army Quadrille" in five turns. Inlaid rosewood or painted boxes by Nicole Frères and other makers, from $280 to $600. Photographs and recorded tapes are available.

Customers' own music boxes are repaired and cylinders repinned at $5.50 per inch.

SILVER

Denise Poole, South Thoresby, Alford, Lincolnshire, England
54-page catalogue, free. Prices in $.

Denise Poole sells choice eighteenth- and nineteenth-century English silver almost exclusively by mail and she is well set up for it. Mugs, jugs, spoons, salt dishes, wine labels, sugar baskets, teapots, trays and more are photographed and described in detail in the catalogue, and she has a mailing list to keep customers up to date on recent acquisitions. Prices are not low, but include insurance and air-mail postage; they run from $13 for 1838 sugar tongs to $1,400 for a "most noble large sized six bottle cruet, London 1810" in mint condition and clearly marked. Returns are accepted and full refunds given. Also illustrated are some seascapes and landscapes.

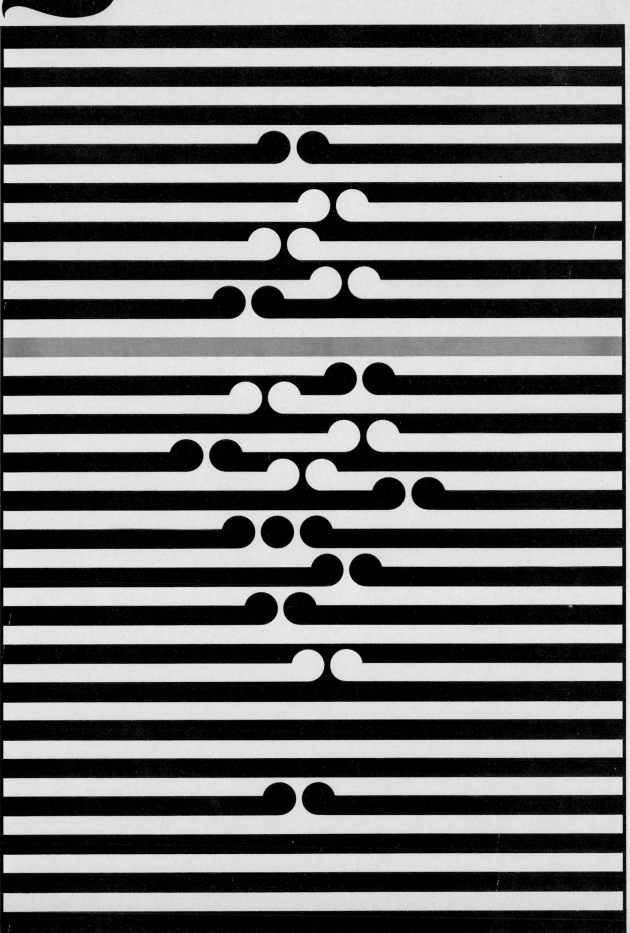

Some galleries publish catalogues for people who aren't able to get to certain exhibitions, others specialize in selling by mail. One way or another, the shops, galleries and museums in this section broaden the choice available for everyone, because even people living in art centers like New York can't buy locally some of the works listed here.

Oil paintings are obviously the hardest to choose by mail, but collectors do it, and there are firms willing to supply anyone who wants to try. Reproductions are the easiest, and there are great bargains in those areas: see the famous Italian Alinari reproductions, for instance.

There is a section called Graphics, which lists shops that sell original prints made from a block, plate or stone on which the artist himself worked, and from which a high-quality small edition has been produced. In another section, Maps and Prints, original prints are listed which are made from a block, plate or stone and on which an artist or engraver has worked, but some of these prints have been produced in large editions for magazines and other mass media.

There is no duty on art.

DRAWINGS

John Baskett Ltd., 173 New Bond Street, London W.1, England
Occasional catalogues, free.

A magnificent but expensive selection of old-master drawings and prints. Serious collectors should write with specific requests.

Martyn Gregory, Gregory and Kruml, 9 Lancashire Court, New Bond Street, London W1 9AD, England
12-page catalogue, free.

Lower-priced English and Continental drawings and watercolors. Drawings that cost under $50 are listed and described, drawings and paintings that cost more—mostly between $50 and $300—are illustrated in black-and-white. In the catalogue I looked at there were quite a few portraits and landscapes, and also some less expected works by well-known English artists: figure drawings by George Romney; end papers by the children's-book illustrator Walter Crane; watercolors by George Cruickshank, including a jolly set called *The English Spa;* and a sepia study of a woman by George Frederick Watts, the once famous and fashionable Victorian historical painter who was married to Ellen Terry.

GRAPHICS

Ganymed Original Editions Ltd., 11 Great Turnstile, London W.C.1, England
Mailing list for occasional illustrated prospectuses.

Ganymed publishes limited editions of graphic works by modern artists, usually between fifty and seventy-five copies. Publications have included suites of lithographs by Kokoschka, Sidney Nolan and L. S. Lowry, and etchings by Ben Nicholson and Arthur Boyd, all on handmade paper, carefully boxed and presented. Prices vary from $60 for a single lithograph by Nolan to $4,000 for forty-four lithographs by Kokoschka. Ask to be put on the mailing list and you will be sent prospectuses as they become available.

Kegan Paul, Trench, Trubner and Co., 43 Great Russell Street, London, W.C.1, England
Occasional catalogues and lists, free.

One of the best dealers in the world in Japanese and Chinese prints, Kegan Paul issues lists and catalogues throughout the year on all aspects of Africa and the Orient, especially art. I have seen two illustrated catalogues, one of them from an exhibition of sixty Japanese drawings of artists known and unknown in the West from the first half of the nineteenth-century. The prices started at $36 for a fan painting of a pair of cranes by Toyo, and several other items at that price, including a few humorous drawings by Naohiki, a pupil of Shigehiko. A bird and tree trunk with a slight red wash and *sumi* by Nanrei cost $72; a Hokusai-school sketch of a girl by a lantern, $240; and the most expensive of all, a magnificent dragon by Hokusai, was $1,320. The other catalogue of Japanese prints had an exact description of the condition of each print, with prices starting at $180 for an eighteenth-century print—a picture by Torji Kiyomasu II of a nobleman inscribing a letter before a princess—though a more typical price was $300 for a print by Choskai of three girls under a flowering cherry.

Richard Kruml, 9 Lancashire Court, New Bond Street, London W1 9AD, England
Occasional catalogues, free. Prices in $.

Richard Kruml deals in "fine Japanese color prints" and once or twice a year sends a catalogue to the people on his mailing list. The catalogue I looked at was of Hiroshige landscapes and gave information on the quality of the impressions, the state of the prints, and the types of seal. About two thirds of the listed prints were illustrated, and prices were mainly around $300—though they went as low as $72 and as high as $700.

Lumley Cazalet Ltd., 24 Davies Street, London W.1, England
Mailing list for forthcoming exhibition catalogues, free. Exhibition catalogues, $2 each. Price list for artists usually in stock, free.

Lumley Cazalet sells twentieth-century original prints by English and European masters. They hold exhibitions six or seven times a year and will put you on their mailing list to receive notice of all forthcoming exhibitions. You can then ask to have any exhibition catalogue air-mailed to you for $2.

Apart from the special exhibitions, Lumley Cazalet always has other graphics in stock, and have a standard list giving names of artists whose work is usually available, as well as approximate prices. To give you an idea (alphabetically): Bonnards start at $90; Braques at $200; Calders at $20; Chagalls at $12. These starting prices are for large, unsigned editions. The prints can be seen in standard catalogues on the artist, or if you can't get hold of one, Lumley Cazalet will send photographs. This gallery also receives many requests for rare prints which, if not in stock, are tracked down.

William Weston Gallery Ltd., 10 Albemarle Street, London W.1, England
A year's subscription to at least twelve brochures, $8. Prices in $.

Perfectly set up for mail order, the William Weston Gallery issues monthly black-and-white brochures of recent acquisitions. They stock original etchings, engravings, lithographs, etc., by nineteenth- and twentieth-century masters and hold occasional special exhibitions for which they also send out brochures. I was sent a current brochure and one from a recent exhibition. The monthly brochure illustrated seventeen works by artists such as Albers, Feininger, Manet, Munch, Palmer, Roualt, Vuillard, and a few others not so well known. Prices started at about $47 for an etching, "L'Intérieure au Canapé" by Vuillard, initialed on the plate, and went as high as $1,240 for an initialed color aquatint, "Clown Assis" by Roualt. The brochure for an exhibition of color lithographs

16

17

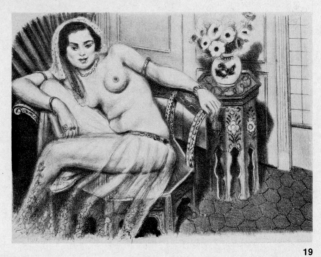

18

19

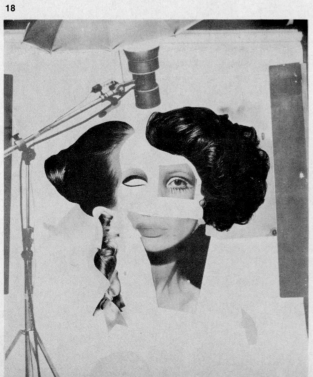

16
Richard Kruml Utamaro, a recently sold print.

17
Richard Kruml Hiroshige "Station 37 Miyanokoshi." A fine impression in very good condition. Sold for $660.

18
Lumley Cazalet Ltd Paul Helleu "Looking at the Watteau Drawings in the Louvre." 11¾" × 15¾", Signed drypoint (circa 1895). $910.

19
Lumley Cazalet Ltd Henri Matisse "Hindou, Jupe de Voile." 11" × 14¾". Signed lithograph (1929). $9,500.

20
Lumley Cazalet Ltd Richard Hamilton "Fashion Plate 1969/70." Signed color silk screen. Sold.

20

21
Louise King James Gillray "Uncorking Old Sherry."
Hand-colored etching. $23.70.

22
Louise King Johannes de Bischop (Dutch, 1646–1686)
"Young Man Turning Around." Etching. $10.60.

23
Louise King "Two Men Burning a Bishop." 1472
woodcut, heightened with color. Printed at Augsburg.
$21.20.

and etchings by impressionists and post-impressionists had
some illustrations in color, and the prints were more
expensive, starting at $240 for "Aux Champs-Elysées" by
Henri Edmond Cross, apparently one of the few pointillist
lithographs, and going up to $2,450 for a signed linocut,
"Picador et Taureau," from an edition of fifty by Picasso.

**The Yoseido Gallery, 5–15 Ginza 5 Chome, Chuo-Ku,
Tokyo, Japan**
*100-page catalogue with some color, free; air mail $2.
Prices in $.*

A first-rate catalogue of limited-edition, signed wood-block
prints by modern Japanese artists. As the wood block is still
highly valued and much used in Japan, and as the Yoseido
Gallery handles the works of all the best-known Japanese
artists using this medium, the catalogue shows a huge and
varied collection that should please all but the choosiest of
customers. Most modern styles are represented, and many
pictures show overwhelmingly Western influences—some look
like Klees, others like Calders, there is even a blue-purple
"Chicago—Night View" by Fumio Kitaoka. Prices are
generally between $10 and $50, and there are also about
fifteen unlimited, signed prints at $7.50 each.

MAPS AND PRINTS

**Collectors Treasures Ltd., 91 High Street, Amersham,
Buckinghamshire, England**
List of maps, free.
List of books about collecting antiques, free.

This is a list with only brief descriptions of some of the types
of maps available, so you have to know what you want.
Decorative maps by Tallis (c. 1850) of most of the world cost
between $15 and $30 and are adorned with views of notable
buildings, local costumes, etc. Another decorative series, by
Thomas Moule (c. 1836–43), shows the counties of England
with vignettes, heraldry, sometimes first railways. Each map
costs around $15.

   There is also a book list that includes books on maps and
prints, silver, gold, furniture, porcelain, pottery and glass,
clocks and watches, carpets, weapons and military items,
wine labels and coins.

**Louise King, 36 Gloucester Circus, Greenwich, London
S.E.10, England**
*100-page catalogue, 65 cents surface mail, $2 air mail. Free
to regular clients.*

Mrs. Louise King sells original and inexpensive prints and
engravings by mail, and publishes two riveting catalogues a
year listing about a thousand items from her very varied
stock. She gives fairly detailed background information and
an illustration or two for each type of print; otherwise, prints
are just listed and described. There is an approval service for
old customers, and new customers may return anything they
don't like.
   The catalogue I looked at had all sorts of tempting things.
For $3 to $5: etchings after drawings by Millais (some
illustrating lines from Tennyson such as "She drew out the
poison with her balmy breath"); proofs of Thomas Bewick's
woodcuts for *Aesops Fables*; seventeenth-century etchings
after Raphael's Bible paintings; "Horsemanship," a series of
comic riding disasters by an eighteenth-century caricaturist
called Bunbury; and some very pre-Spock, delightfully
emphatic moral comics, printed in Paris for the Humoristic
Publishing Co., Kansas City, Missouri., *Cecilia the Babbler,
Charles the Disobedient Boy, Proud Matilda,* and the amazing
story of the little rich boy who wanted to be poor.
   At various, higher prices there were fifteenth-century

woodcuts from the Nuremberg chronicles; nineteenth-century French fashion plates; obscene political caricatures by James Gillray; early and rare reproductions of drawings by Edward Burne Jones; etchings, woodcuts and engravings by William Blake; and prints from the four lost plates of Goya's "Los Proverbios."

And anyone who gets carried away and wants to start collecting prints seriously can buy books here on the history and identification of prints.

Paul Prouté, S.A., 74 Rue De Seine, Paris VI, France
Catalogue, $5.

Paul Prouté is well known for its immense stock of half a million prints, which are sold to private individuals and American dealers. Stock ranges from the fifteenth-century to contemporary artists, and includes old-master prints, views of cities, portraits, old maps.

P. J. Radford, Denmead, Portsmouth, Hampshire, PO7 6TT, England
50-page map catalogue: Americana, free.
50-page map catalogue: British Isles, free.
50-page prints catalogue, free.
General catalogue, free.

P. J. Radford, author of *Antique Maps*, published in England, has a magnificent stock of prints and rare maps, especially Americana, described and displayed in his temptingly well designed catalogues. Even nonmap collectors might be seduced by some of these; indigenous inhabitants, ships in full sail, sea monsters, mythological figures, the seasons and the elements crowd the maps with decorative activity. Prices for rare maps start at about $70 and seem to depend partly on how much demand there is for the country. A map of Bohemia, for instance, in spite of marvelous pictures of cities and costumes of all the social classes, tends to be less expensive than, say, of America. Near the top of the price scale, at $425, comes something like "Novissima Totius Terrarum Orbis Tabula," by Nicolao Visscher (c. 1685), with full original coloring. The world is shown in two hemispheres (with California as an island), and the whole is surrounded by a profusion of allegorical figures representing the elements and the signs of the zodiac.

If you want to pay much less, ask for the prints catalogue and look at the nineteenth-century prints of Europe and America, about $10 each. Taken from engravings, they were often used as tourists' mementos, and show a blissfully unspoiled, pastoral world.

Uchida Art Co. Ltd., Kyoto Handicraft Center, Kumanojinja-Higashi, Sakyo-Ku, Kyoto, Japan
Color leaflet, free. Prices in $.

This firm sells the kind of modern Japanese wood-block prints you often see on Christmas cards and calendars. Here the prints are larger, for framing, and subjects are mostly birds, flowers, horses, Japanese landscapes, and figures in Japanese costumes. Each one costs about $6.

PAINTINGS

Christie, Manson and Woods (U.S.A.) Ltd., 867 Madison Avenue, New York, N.Y. 10021
Catalogue subscription list, free. Prices in $.

Sotheby and Co., P.O. Box 2AA, 34–35 New Bond Street, London W1A 2AA, England
Catalogue subscription list, free. Prices in $.

The subscription lists give information on the price of subscriptions to catalogues for sales in each field.

Christie's and Sotheby's, England's two leading auction houses, have art auctions throughout the season (September to June) in which Monets are sold to the Metropolitan, Géricaults back to the French, and Rembrandts to collectors from Los Angeles, all for thousands of dollars and so much publicity that closed-circuit television has been installed to accommodate all the would-be buyers. Anyone who can't be there, may bid by mail. Subscribe to a season's worth of catalogues for any favorite category, and the partly illustrated catalogues will arrive about two weeks before the sales. Then, if anything catches your fancy, you can ask the house for an estimate of the bids and send in your own. At the appropriate time a staff member will bid for you. You can also subscribe to price lists that arrive later and tell you who bought each item and what they paid.

Both houses sell old-master and modern paintings, drawings and prints in various combinations. At Christie's this year there were twelve art categories: a subscription to catalogues for old-master and modern prints cost $7; impressionist, modern paintings, drawings and sculptures, altogether $20; old-master paintings up to 1900, $40. At Sotheby's there were nine categories: catalogues for eighteenth- and nineteenth-century drawings and watercolors cost $7; old-master drawings, $16; and impressionist and modern paintings, drawings and sculptures, $41.

In looking at a Christie's after-sale price list of old-master-drawings, I found that about a quarter of the drawings had gone for under $100. One of the most expensive by far, a chalk drawing by Boucher of "Cupid Fondling a Dove" had gone for $1,386. The impressionists, modern paintings, drawings and sculpture, which I also looked at, were naturally far more expensive, the prices of most pictures falling between $600 and $5,000.

The Giles Gallery, 11 Hind Street, London W.1, England
Price list, free. Prices in $.

If you are looking for an old English seascape, landscape, rustic scene or portrait, or for a certain subject rather than a certain painter, try the Giles Gallery, which has a stock of nineteenth-century paintings by unknown or little-known artists. Paintings throbbing with long-despised sentiment are now becoming fashionable again: poignantly wistful dogs, children and rustics look out at the world with reproachful eyes, tiny fishing vessels battle with gargantuan waves and winds, lonely mountains are enveloped by night mists. It's an emotion-laden world, usually going for $140–$500. Typical titles and prices: "Fishing Vessels off the Coast," signed B. B. Henry, $288; "Children in a Garden," eighteenth-century French school; "An English Beauty," Abbey Alstone, $300. The least expensive item on the list I looked at was a 10″ by 14″ painting called "Romantic Harbour Scene," $120; and the costliest, 39″ by 32″, was "Stolen Glances," signed John Calcott Horsley, 1873, costing $1,080.

The gallery answers specific inquiries by supplying colored photographs of picture and frame, all known details of artist and date of painting, and a quotation on what it would cost to send the picture by air freight to the customer's nearest airport.

Jensen Arts, Ewalds Alle 81, DK 6700 Esbjerg, Denmark.
Price list, free, Prices in $.

Since 1955 Jensen Arts has been supplying dealers around the globe with "contemporary *oils individually hand-painted and signed.*" They will also supply private citizens—but after choosing your size and your scene, the actual picture is a complete gamble as Jensen Arts doesn't bother with illustrations. They point out that dealers buy in large batches and assume that a picture one person doesn't want hanging

24

25

26

27

28

29

24
P.J. Radford A map of Virginia by Henry Hondius
(1636). $300.

25
The Giles Gallery Alfred Pollentine, exhibiting 1861 –
1880 "Santa Maria de la Salute, Venice." 20″ × 30″.
Sold for $396.
photo Jack Kilby

26
Peter McLeavey Gallery M. D. Smithers "Dinner Time."
30″ × 48″. Oil on board. $330.

27
Peter McLeavey Gallery Gordon Walter "Maihi."
48″ × 36″. Oil on canvas. $440.

30   31

32

above his bed, someone else will. Subjects include fishing and harbor scenes, seascapes, forests in summer and winter, landscapes of Danish, Greenland and Scandinavian views, as well as southern lands, flowers, still lifes. Prices go by size, with a reduction for quantity; as I write, the smallest size (9″ by 12″) costs $4, including postage, and the largest (24″ by 48″), $16.50. For immediate delivery, choose sizes 20″ by 24″ or 24″ by 36″.

Peter McLeavey Gallery, 147 Cuba Street, Wellington, New Zealand
If you feel adventurous enough to look at modern paintings not usually seen in America, write to this gallery. They will send slides of their paintings by leading contemporary New Zealand painters. Prices from $200 to $1,000.

Old Hall Gallery Ltd., Iden, Rye, Sussex, England
48-page catalogue, $1. Prices in $.

The Old Hall Gallery is a small family firm that sells seventeenth-, eighteenth-, and nineteenth-century paintings, but specializes in the "rising field" (though all the art fields seem to be "rising fields") of Victoriana. They supply museums and galleries; in England they have supplied institutions such as the Victoria and Albert, London, and the Ashmolean, Oxford, and in America, the Capitol Museum, Washington State, the Princeton Museum, and others. Everything is efficiently organized: catalogues with black-and-white photographs of framed paintings are published several times a year, prices include air freight to America, and there is an explanation of terms of attribution generally used in the London Art World (their capitals). "Signed," for instance, means a signature of the artist, whereas "signature" means a signature which *may* be by the artist. After seeing the catalogue, ask for color slides of any picture you are interested in.

Subjects are much the same as the Giles Gallery's, but almost all the painters were successful enough in their lifetimes to exhibit in London, and prices are correspondingly higher—mostly between $400 and $1,000, though there are several above and below those prices.

POSTERS

Lecuyer, 107 Avenue Louise, Brussels 5, Belgium
Lecuyer has a fantastic collection of original American depression posters, '30's artwork and ironically Pollyanna-ish sentiments make them fascinating comments on the time: "WHO SAID CAN'T?" "SOMEONE IS ALWAYS DOING SOMETHING SOMEONE ELSE SAID WAS IMPOSSIBLE. TRY TRYING." "STRUT YOUR STUFF. YOU'VE GOT THE GOOD'S— STEP OUT AND SHOW'EM." "ARGUING WASTES TIME— SPOILS TEMPERS—KILLS TEAMWORK—STALLS PROGRESS. LET'S AGREE TO AGREE." "PLUCK MAKES LUCK." "ONLY HITS WIN." "MEAN IT AND YOU'LL MAKE IT." There are fifty different posters at about $12 each, including post and packing. Lecuyer also has original Art Nouveau and art deco posters, including old ads and old theater posters, of varying prices.

The Lords Gallery Ltd., 26 Wellington Road, St. John's Wood, London N.W.8, England
Catalogues available at the time of writing, $1 each. Prices in $.

"100 Years of Posters" (166 illustrations)
"Patriotic Posters: World War I" (149 illustrations)
"English Posters 1919–1931" (134 illustrations)
"Gay '90's" (43 illustrations)
"Chéret Posters" (94 illustrations)

28
Old Hall Gallery Ltd Henry Howard R.A. exhibiting 1794–1804 "Caroline Carey" oil painting in the original frame. This picture comes with a letter describing its history. $1,400, including delivery to the customer's nearest airport.

29
Old Hall Gallery Ltd George Morland (1763–1804) "Bargaining for Fish" 27″ × 35″. This oil painting has been exhibited at the Victoria and Albert Museum, London, and comes with two books on George Morland in which the picture is mentioned. $1,750, including delivery to the customer's nearest airport.

30
Lecuyer Original American Depression poster. $12, including postage.

31
Lecuyer Original American Depression poster. $12, including postage.

32
The Lords Gallery Ltd Poster by Greifenhagen in red, white and black. $38.

The Lords Gallery specializes in rare, old, original posters, many designed by famous artists and unobtainable elsewhere. Lautrec, Bonnard and Beardsley are here, and styles range from marvelously intricate *fin de siècle* theater posters and book jackets to bathetic advertisements for Eno's Fruit Salts.

There are heavily tressed women, windswept Edwardian couples, period exhortations, and an extraordinarily gloomy poster of St. Paul's and London silhouetted against the night sky with the legend, IT IS FAR BETTER TO FACE THE BULLETS THAN TO BE KILLED AT HOME BY A BOMB. GOD SAVE THE KING.

Prices start at $25, but most of the really attractive posters cost over $50, and the Lautrecs are in the $1,000's.

Old Motor Magazine Ltd., 17 Air Street, London W.1, England
Leaflets, free. Prices in $.

Hard-to-find, old photographs of various means of transportation for fans, schools or decorators reproduced 30″ by 20″ in nostalgic sepia at just over $2.00 each, including air postage (Old Motor say they have to use air because customers who wait for over four weeks assume Old Motor has absconded with their cash).

For experts there are named old trolleys, buses, ships, trains, old planes, and two mysterious machines, one called an *early Burrell engine*, and the other called *Princess Mary*. And, of more general interest, a picture of Laurel and Hardy sitting hopelessly on top of a pile of a collapsed car between two trams; also marching guards and taxis outside Buckingham Palace; Regent Street full of hansom cabs; and a beautiful photograph of Piccadilly Circus in the summer of 1919.

In color there are some very period transportation posters. One, a particularly nice ad for the spanking new Underground, shows an old-fashioned but unpleasantly familiar traffic jam, and below it a glamorized space-age subway station.

Posters by Post, 43 Camden Passage, London N.1, England
Leaflet Zodiac/Penthouse Nudes, free.
Children's Posters/Educational Charts, free.
Vogue/Aubrey Beardsley Posters, free.
Student posters free; air mail for one or more, 60 cents.

Lots of useful charts to decorate children's walls or give to adult hobbyists: "Yacht Rules," "Sails thro' Centuries," "Golf," "History of Aviation," "Music," "Animals," "Birds," and "Nature." Also the usual catholic selection of Pop posters: Beethoven, Brahms, Bach, Byron, Beardsley, Bernhardt, and Bardot, Karl Marx, Mao, Ho Chi Minh and Mike Jagger. Also slim, aristocratic nudes.

The posters cost under $3 apiece, and some are in color, others are not.

The Poster Shop, 7 New College Parade, London N.W.3, England
12-page brochure, free; 50 cents air mail.

Posters for the younger generation—some sexy, some psychedelic, and some even sentimental (Colorado at sunset). Steve McQueen with short hair or long, and Allen Ginsberg wearing a Stars and Stripes top hat, about $2 each.

REPRODUCTIONS

Adachi Institute of Woodcut Prints, CPO Box 362, Tokyo, Japan
Catalogue, including surface postage, $6. Prices in $.

A few of these very fine reproductions of Japanese woodblock prints are on sale in American museums, but this is the only place where you can get the whole range. Reproductions of the works of Moronobu, Hiroshige, Sharaku, and other masters of ukiyo-e, are carefully done. The originals are perfect specimens in the Tokyo National Museum, the materials used are specially prepared and similar to those of the originals, and only the most skillful engravers and printers work on them. Prices range from $7 to $28 per print, including surface postage and insurance.

Fratelli Alinari, Lungarno Corsini 24 R, Florence 50123, Italy
44-page catalogue with some color free. Prices in $.

The magnificent Alinari reproductions are widely exported and can be found wherever good reproductions are sold, but they can be bought for a fraction of the price directly from the makers. Color reproductions of paintings cost only just over $2 each, while beautiful and unusual reproductions of drawings cost half that. Both can be mounted on wood with gold-leaf borders so that they don't need frames and still only cost $4.50 and $5.50. Most of the painters are Italian—Giotto, Fra Angelico, Botticelli, Piero della Francesca, Da Vinci, Michelangelo, Raphael, et al.—and there are some interesting Etruscan frescoes and Pompeian mosaics, and some painters from other countries, including the French impressionists. Religious paintings and drawings mounted on triptychs and diptychs finished in gold leaf cost $14 and $17.

Pictures also decorate a stunning collection of objects for the house: trays, boxes in various shapes and sizes, book ends, and lamps with reproductions on the shades and hand-carved bases finished in gold or silver leaf, at $33.

Information Center, Greater London Council, The County Hall, London S.E.1, England
Price list, free.

The Greater London Council sells fine-line black-and-white lithographic reproductions from the collection in the Council's library at very low prices. There are sixteenth-, seventeenth-, and eighteenth-century maps of London in black-and-white for $1.30 each, and various old views of London: the Tower, Westminster and Whitehall, the Dockyard at Deptford (a view of the Royal Dockyard with its ships), and various London scenes by Hogarth—all of these for about $1 each. Also of interest is "Buck's Long View," a set of five panoramic views of the Thames published in 1749 by the brothers Buck. These can be bought as a set or singly for $1.30 each. Postage will be quoted by the Council when you tell them what you want.

The Israel Museum, Jerusalem, Israel
Price list, free. Prices in $.

Lists of exhibition catalogues, archaeological slides, reproductions, posters and lithographs. Unfortunately nothing is illustrated or described. The posters cost $1.50 each and represent "Far Eastern Art," "Miró," "Jerusalem" (to take the first three on the list). The reproductions cost $1 each and are of works by Israeli painters. Eight lithographs, also by Israeli painters, are signed and numbered. They include two abstracts and two etchings, one of which is a portrait of Ben Gurion. These cost $5 to $100 each. Add 50 cents for postage, however many you order.

Misrachi, Avenida Juárez 4, Mexico 1, DF, Mexico
Color brochure, free. Prices in $.

Color reproductions of paintings by modern Mexican artists—mostly Rivera and Siqueiros, but also some big-eyed, soulful children by Gustavo Montoya, all $4.80 each. For $6 each

33
Adachi Institute of Woodcut Prints Cover of catalogue showing five hundred reproductions of Japanese woodcut prints. Price of catalogue $6, including surface postage.

34
Mary Potter Designs Knight and lady from medieval church brasses reproduced as two wall hangings 7″ × 20″. Black design on white cotton, about $2 each. Black design on orange or mustard, about $2.50 each. Air mail 50 cents for one, 75 cents for two.

35
Mary Potter Designs A scene from the Bayeux tapestry reproduced on a wall hanging. $9 and up.

there are two books of plates for framing of Mexican birds and flowers with the text in English; and for $10 each, delightful old views (1628) of Mexico City, Acapulco and Veracruz.

The National Gallery, Publications Department, Trafalgar Square, London WC2N 5DN, England
32-page color brochure, 60 cents.

A good brochure of small reproductions with a separate price list. The National Gallery is intelligently pessimistic about rising prices and advises customers to ask for a new price list if the brochure has been around for more than six months.

The actual reproductions are of 138 famous and favorite European masterpieces from Fra Angelico's "The Rape of Helen by Paris" to Monet's "Pond with Water Lilies," both about 10 square inches and both 65 cents. Prices go by sizes, and range from 25 cents for pictures around 6 square inches to $6.50 for pictures 2′ by 3′. But there is very little choice in the largest sizes. Postcards also available.

Mary Potter Designs, Hunters Wood, Laughton, Lewes, Sussex, England
Leaflet, 25 cents.

Facsimiles of knights and ladies on medieval church brasses have been made into wall hangings by Mary Potter. Silk-screened in black on white, red, orange or gold cotton. Prices from $3 to $13, including air-mail postage. There are also hangings based on the *Bayeux tapestry* — stylized little pictures of William's ship and Harold riding to Bosham — which cost about $1 each, while a 6-foot-long frieze of the Battle of Hastings on orange or red cloth costs $11, including postage.

The Tate Gallery, Publications Department, Millbank, London S.W.1, England
Publications catalogue, free.
Color-slides catalogue, free.

Another of England's national museums sells reproductions, here mainly of English and modern French paintings. The publications catalogue rather annoyingly has pictures of the books listed (37 books, mainly about the Tate Gallery and English artists), but not of their 82 reproductions, which are only named. Prices for reproductions of Blake, Gainsborough, Turner, Dali, Klee, Dufy, et al., range from $1.25 for drawings to about $6 for largish paintings. Available and illustrated in the catalogue is an unusual three-dimensional reproduction of Ben Nicholson's "White Relief, 1935" in a chrome frame (about $40, including postage). Also something intriguingly called *The Kiss Box*, which turns out to be four views of Rodin's statue "The Kiss" reproduced on a small paper box (about $1.60).

The Victoria and Albert Museum, P.O. Box 569, London S.W.7, England
Price list of general reproductions, sectional list no. 55, free.
Price list of brass-rubbing reproductions, free.

London's largest museum of fine arts has a few small, interesting and very inexpensive reproductions showing some of their exhibits. In color, 9″-by-12″ pictures of seventeenth-century English embroidery of flowers and insects, 30 cents; a sixteenth-century majolica plate of the Three Graces, 20 cents; an Italian terra-cotta statue of the Virgin with laughing Child, 30 cents; and several reproductions of Indian paintings and oil paintings. Slightly larger, but in monochrome, there are pictures of a Bavarian porcelain group, a Spanish luster dish, an embroidered Elizabethan cushion cover, etc., for about 10 cents each. These come with descriptive captions and are, the catalogue says, particularly suitable for classroom use.

For the phenomenally low price of 45 cents, including surface postage, the Victoria and Albert sells reproductions of brass rubbings in the museum. Mostly pictures of medieval knights or their wives, each reproduction is roughly 12″ wide, and 24″ high.

Books have traditionally been sold by mail, and a system of catalogues and mailing lists has been developed to a very impressive extent. There are dealers for practically every kind of book and it is possible to do all one's buying by mail. This is, in fact, the way most university libraries now build up their collections, and their budgets explain in part why mail-order bookselling has continued to prosper as it has. As you leaf through an exceptionally elaborate catalogue—in itself an impressive example of the bibliographers' craft—you may reflect that this is due to the lavishness of some of our own state university systems. The Texas taxpayer may well be the unwitting patron of your ability to buy just about any book by mail.

For Americans, the most efficient bookselling comes from England. While each country has its own network of antiquarian book dealers, the English are the most proficient when it comes to selling current books by mail. It would be hopeless to try to list the hundreds of Continental specialists in old books, so I have limited this section to a few such dealers, besides listing some of the major British ones. Before describing these, a few words on *what* it makes sense to buy from abroad and *why*.

CURRENT BOOKS

Several of the English booksellers listed below can supply you with any new British book, and for many an American book lover it is worth buying from abroad just to get the marvelously complete catalogues issued by these firms. The English dealer will still service customers in ways that few American stores bother with, and in many cases, this alone makes it worth buying by mail. Out-of-the-way books, out-of-stock titles, and of course, out-of-print titles, can be bought in this way with no trouble at all. However, you should note that the time when British books were automatically cheaper than American ones are now past. Specialized titles in nonfiction now tend to be about the same price; the English edition may even be more expensive, and the physical product—paper, binding, etc.—may well be better in the American edition. Certainly American bindings are better suited to the overdry and overheated atmosphere of most American homes. On the other hand, novels and some children's books are still considerably cheaper in England. There is also the fact that a considerable number of books, particularly those for children, are available in inexpensive or paperback editions from England. It's practically impossible to buy paperbacks by mail from an American bookseller, and in this respect British stores offer exceptional service. The children's-book dealers listed below have no American equivalents.

BOOKS IN SPECIAL FIELDS

Because so many British booksellers deal with universities, in addition to the far-flung alumni of the British universities they are able to supply you with lists of titles that simply cannot be found in the United States. Certain catalogues, such as those of Hammersmith Books, are works of exemplary scholarship in themselves and offer readers a service that goes far beyond the mere provision of books. The major university booksellers all offer specialized catalogues, and if you are interested in keeping up not just with new titles, but with bibliographic research in certain fields, then you should get on these mailing lists.

ANTIQUE BOOKS

This is, like prints or works of art of all kinds, a field all its own. Prices vary enormously and collectors will want to compare them on an international scale. Bargains are possible, of course, but chances are that the dealers involved will know more than you do, and your chances of finding an unnoticed first edition are probably better if you browse

through the stalls on lower Fourth Avenue in New York City. On the other hand, the catalogues that are available will keep you up to date with both prices and what is available on the market. Since so many old books include illustrative material, this is also a useful way of looking for prints and related material.

ESOTERICA AND EXOTICA

The days when, as in Ogden Nash's poem, lovers of such books needed the service of Railway Express to avoid the frowns of the post office, are now past. Pornography is widely available domestically and the need to look through old French masters to find a bit of erotica is now past. Today, such material is sold openly at Parke-Bernet; but the lure of books to enter forbidden fields is still there. For some reason, the unknown is still thought to be contained in these mysterious old tomes, and a large number of stores still specialize in the mystical, the magical and the supernatural. One such store is listed below, again largely English, though as in other categories foreign works are usually available through British dealers devoted to the supernatural.

At the end of this section you will find shops specializing in *Children's Books* and listings of *Booksellers on the Continent, Bookplates, Maps* and *Useful Paperback Guides.*

CURRENT BOOKS

THE BIG FOUR

Most Americans who have gone to England to study, along with a vast number of other colonials, usually leave their name with one of the major university booksellers they have patronized; keeping an account at, say, Blackwell's is a way of keeping in touch with old memories. These stores are quite used to dealing with Americans; their letters to me all charmingly assured me that they are more than accustomed to mail-order selling—a bit like the family butler assuring the uncertain guest that he is indeed in professional hands.

W. Heffer and Sons Ltd., 20 Trinity Street, Cambridge CB2 3NG, England,
is the major bookseller in that town but also a leading international supplier. It has just moved from its rambling thirties quarters to a very handsome new building facing Trinity College, and like the galling zip code at the end of its address, symbolizes the modernization of English bookselling. Like the other stores in this section, Heffer's can supply you with any new British book (along with a number of American ones).

Heffer's issues a large list of specialized catalogues, covering just about any field, such as archaeology, management, chemistry, linguistics, etc. Chances are that your particular interests will be served. Their recent 114-page catalogue on Oriental and African studies, for instance, deals with close to two thousand items, covering every aspect of these fields.

Heffer's also issues a special listing of remainders, an area of definite interest for bargain hunters, since titles remaindered in England are not at all the same as those remaindered here, and, in fact, are often books that have never been published here at all. There is also a very intriguing list of antique and rare books, starting with a 1562 edition of Aquinas, at $120, and ending with various first editions of Yeats. You can pay Heffer's in just about any manner you want, and they have an account with American Express in New York. Heffer's also have an exceptional children's-book shop, about which more below.

Blackwell's, Broad Street, Oxford Ox1 3BQ, England,

is the Oxford equivalent of Heffer's, and has also recently moved to ultramodern and rather soulless quarters, where on endless underground floors you are likely to find any book in print and a great many that aren't. Their stock allows them to fill almost any orders on receipt; if not, the book is ordered from the publisher or the order is kept until the title shows up. Blackwell's specifies that they will bill you upon receipt of order, and the charge for postage, insurance, etc., tends to run about 7 percent of the cost of a book. Again, specialized catalogues are available in many fields.

Dillon's University Bookshop Ltd., Malet Street, London WC1E 7JB, England,

is the London equivalent of these university stores. Because of its location in the heart of London, near Russell Square, it is the one bookstore that most visitors may have happened to come across. There is a sense of excitement for any book lover in discovering Dillon's and finding that what looked like one store goes on and on, to cover several buildings, each housing departments that are complete stores in themselves. Here, as in the others mentioned above, one finds not just a complete stock of books but pamphlets, little magazines, teaching aids, etc. Dillon's stocks 75,000 new titles, besides maintaining a substantial second-hand department, and they too cover most academic fields with special strength in areas such as psychology, languages, education, and history. Their recent catalogues include theology, archaeology and industrial history. They will quote prices in dollars, and like their competitors, will open an account for any serious customer. Finally, they have a special department handling old and rare manuscripts, but the export of these, they warn, requires a special license from the British government.

These three stores will probably cover most of your needs, though it should be stressed that a number of others, such as Bowes and Bowes, 1–2 Trinity Street, Cambridge, offers a similar range of services.

Hatchard's, 187 Piccadilly, London W1V 9DA, England ♛♛♛

For those with less academic interests, Hatchard's is probably as good a store as any to keep in touch with British general publishing. Located on Piccadilly next to Fortnum and Mason, they cater to the carriage trade and are very much the literary equivalents of these splendid purveyors of gastronomic self-indulgence. They call themselves The World's Finest Bookshop and I suppose "fine" must be read in the context "of social quality." Certainly their stock cannot compare with the above-named stores, but if you want the latest British novel, mystery or gift book, they are most likely to have the book you want in stock. Their letter to me refers to hundreds of parcels that go to America each week, and their catalogue (illustrated) gives you a fair sample of the new and popular, which, as I said, is also most likely to be less expensive. The latest, albeit short, Mary Stewart is listed at under $2, and a number of gift items are less expensive than they would be in America. Hatchard's also has an out-of-print department and a special stock of leather bindings. A unique aspect of their service is that you can order any book to be bound in full or half leather.

BOOKS IN SPECIAL FIELDS

Hammersmith Books, Barnes High Street, London S.W.13, England

Judging purely from catalogues, Hammersmith Books must be an extraordinary place to visit. Their catalogue tells you how to get to the outlying part of London in which their vast stock is located, and it must be worth the trip to meet the kind of people who compile their catalogues. Their letterhead simply

36
Hatchards Hatchards Bookshop, 187 Piccadilly, London. Established in 1797.

says, "Scarce literature on social economic movements, Afro-Asian-Soviet Affairs, War, Revolution and Peace," and their catalogues live up to that comprehensive heading. Their latest, on the Middle East, includes a wider range of material than one would have thought possible to collect, all meticulously annotated, and it is reasonably priced. These are obviously the people to get in touch with if you are interested in contemporary politics and international affairs, or in the history of the modern left.

Collett's, 39 Museum Street, London W.C.1, England,
has a number of books in English published in Russia and the other East European countries, as well as a large stock of Russian-language material and English-language books on Russia. Catalogues are available.

Francis Edwards Ltd., 83 Marylebone High Street, London W1M 4AL, England,
offers a number of very satisfactory specialized catalogues in a number of classic fields of interest in which England has always excelled, such as military books, economics, industry, technology and transport, family history and heraldry, etc. The economics catalogue, for instance, includes sections on agriculture, brewing and wool. Mostly older books, and including such items as autograph letters, etc.

ANTIQUE BOOKS, MANUSCRIPTS, ETC.

Since this is a category that could include literally hundreds of names, the following is but a sampling. Starting your own bookstore is the ambition of a vast number of people, and England is obviously the ideal place to deal in antique books. Lists of such bookstores are available and journals such as the *Times Literary Supplement* will carry ads for a great many of these. Here are a few:

Henry Sotheran Ltd., 2 Sackville Street, Piccadilly W1X 2DP, England
One of London's oldest booksellers (est. 1815), this shop specializes in early printed works and color-plate works, especially in natural history. They also stock old bindings of standard authors, letters, maps and old views of British scenery.

Charles W. Traylen, Castle House, 49–50 Quarry Street, Guilford, England
This store specializes in its own reprints of old prints, maps and scholarly works (such as Ackerman prints) reissued at very reasonable prices, as well as having an extensive stock of out-of-print titles, particularly of the classic English interests in sport, travel, natural history, naval and military history, and theology.

Covent Garden Bookshop, 80 Long Acre, London W.C.2, England
This very attractive, airy store in the midst of the theater and operatic district specializes in modern first editions, of which they claim to have the largest stock in England. They also have a number of British first editions of American authors such as Pound and Hemingway, and their attractive 150-page catalogue is filled with the fascinating footnotes of modern literary history, from a first edition of Virginia Woolf's *A Room of One's Own*, signed, one of 492 copies, for $100, to the carbon copy, also signed, of Henry Miller's "apparently unpublished" preface to an early Parker Tyler book ($88).

Bernard Quaritch, 5–8 Lower John Street, Golden Square, London W1V 6AB, England
This shop specializes in the publications of various learned

societies and is an excellent source for the reports of everyone from the British Museum to the Royal Horticultural Society. Some of these items are reprints, others cover the original output of such diverse groups as the Egypt Exploration Society or the Librairie du Liban. It is, obviously, for specialists.

They also have a very extensive collection of materials on English literature, including private letters and manuscripts, which, as always, offers intriguing insights into the lives of people whose letters are worth keeping and selling, and sometimes give you the feeling should have remained unread by outsiders, e.g., T. S. Eliot, letters and telegrams "describing the mental and physical collapse of his wife and his own unhappiness and illness" ($960.00), or somewhat less moving, Norman Mailer's three letters to Alexander Trocchi, complaining about what Hollywood does to your novels: "It came out as if they'd run a garbage truck over the pages of the book . . ." ($432).

Bertram Rota Ltd., 4–6 Savile Row, London W.1, England
A leading dealer in modern first editions, letters and manuscripts, who has dealt with special needs of customers in all sorts of areas, ranging from first folios and whole libraries of scholarly books. As with many dealers, if you are looking for a specific rare book, you can write and see what is available at what price.

ESOTERICA

Watkins Bookshop, 19–21 Cecil Court, Charing Cross Road, London WC2N 4HB, England
Entering Watkins Bookshop is like stumbling into a tea party given by Alistair Crowley, the self-styled English magician and eccentric. Located just off the major theatrical and second-hand-book area in London, Watkins represents a vast enclave of esoteric and fascinating expertise. Here is that unique English blend of magic and religion, of psychology and alchemy, of the erudite and the exotic. The shop has expanded into two buildings, accommodating youth's vast new interest in magic, alchemy and related subjects. The selection is a serious and professional one; the mysterious can be sold efficiently, and the store and its catalogue command both respect and attention. The latest catalogue includes a variety of titles in various religions, serious works in psychology, as well as a selection of their vast stock of books on alchemy, cabala, tarot, occultism, diet and health, and "astrology, palmistry, graphology, numerology and allied subjects."

CHILDREN'S BOOKS

Children's Book Centre Ltd., 140 Kensington Church Street, London W.8., England
There is unfortunately no American equivalent of the Children's Book Centre, and anyone who has ever taken a child into this marvelous place will know what a loss that is both to parents and children. Every city should have its own version of this splendid institution, even though they might not be expected to stock the five thousand titles that are on display in the Centre. The Centre will sell you all its books by mail and will supply you with its four reading lists at 50 cents each: one for two-to-five year-olds, one for six-to-eights, one for nine-to-elevens, one for twelves and up. Each one is an excellent 40-page annotated brochure containing 28 pages of descriptive material, so that it is possible to buy by mail with ease. A great many English children's books are not available in the United States, and also, a great many titles are available as inexpensive paperbacks. The first-rate Puffin list

37
Bertram Rota Ltd A typical selection of first editions:
Saul Kain (pseudonym for Siegfried Sassoon), $66;
Edith Sitwell, $132; Beatrix Potter, $198; Marianne
Moore, $66.

38
Branners Bibliofile Antikvariat First edition of "Rabanus
Maurus" (1503) in red and black with Roman letters,
two large woodcuts and "figure poems." One of the first
printings from Pforzheim.
photo John U. Duurloo

published by Penguin Books offers an enormous selection for
young readers. English children's records also on sale here.

Heffer's Children's Bookshop, 27 Trinity Street, Cambridge, CB2 1tb, England

While much smaller, the Heffer's store is an excellent model
of what a college bookstore of any size should be able to
offer to its community. Heffer's will supply you with some of
the publishers' brochures and has a good stock of most
popular titles.

The Folio Society Ltd., 6 Stratford Place, London W1N OBH, England

This is in a separate category, but should be listed here as
another way of buying books from England. Like the American
Heritage Club, the Folio Society publishes its own illustrated
and deluxe editions of books, but it puts out a large number
of titles itself. The society says it has a growing number of
American subscribers and offers an American catalogue of its
books, which cover a wide variety of areas and are very
reasonably priced. For example, *Homage to Catalonia*, by
George Orwell, illustrated with contemporary photos, sells at
$4.75, less than an ordinary American edition of the book
would sell for. Most of the titles are of more classic genres
but are certainly good bargains for those seeking the kind of
book that used to be available, for instance, in the illustrated
Modern Library.

BOOKSELLERS ON THE CONTINENT

Each country has its own leading bookstore and each country
its own network of second-hand bookdealers. A list of stores
as long as the one for England could be compiled for the rest
of the world, but that would lead to a separate book. I am
therefore confining myself to just a handful of stores; if you're
looking for a more complete list, you can write to the New
York commercial attaché of the country in which you're
interested, or simply look at the ads in the literary journals
published in each language. Books are always easy to order
and there is little room for confusion, even if you're ordering
in English. Anyway, here are a few additional names.

DENMARK

Branners Bibliofile Antikvariat, Bredgade 1o, 1260, Copenhagen K.

Copenhagen is one of the world's great book cities; it has
more good English bookstores than many an American town,
as well as a host of second-hand stores. Looking for a rare
old book can be as international a process as looking for an
old print, and it is worth keeping stores like Branners in mind
when one is searching. Branners deals with many American
individuals and libraries, and is typical of the kind of store,
outside of England, where books in English can be found.

FRANCE

Brentano's, 37 Avenue de l'Opéra, Paris II,

is probably the most famous bookstore as far as Americans are
concerned and their English-speaking staff should be able to
supply you with any current French title, whether book or
periodical. They have an excellent stock of gift books, and
carry the specialized French fashion and decorating
magazines.

La Joie de Lire

is known in France and among visitors to Paris as the best
serious bookstore in that book-filled capital. Just about any

book in the social sciences, literature or the arts can be found there, including rare university-press books in French. This is not the store for fancy non-books, but you should be able to get any current French-language title in the above fields, as well as books on the film, paperbacks, a very wide selection of political journals and all books on Marxism and left-wing political thought. The store has now established a special mail-order address, 44 rue Vieille du Temple, Paris IV, and an idea of its range can be had from the following list of catalogues, available at this writing: Marx and Engels, Lenin, Flaubert, The Commune, Contemporary Greece, Czechoslovakia, Children's Books and Periodicals.

GERMANY

Marga Schoeller Bücherstube, Kurfürstendamm 30, 1 Berlin 15,
is a bookstore which over the years has come to supply customers all over the world. While not specializing in mail order, as does Van Stockum, they do periodically mail their customers lists of new titles in such fields as literary criticism, history, education, sociology, psychology, etc.

HOLLAND

W. P. Van Stockum, N.V. 36 Buitenhof, The Hague, Holland, ⌣
is a specialized bookseller similar to Dillon's or Blackwell's in England, as well as serving by appointment to the Queen of the Netherlands. They are one of the leading general and scientific bookshops in Holland, a country noted for the quality of its bookstores, and are equally strong in the sciences and in the humanities. They can be paid through their account with Chase Manhattan Bank in New York.

HUNGARY

Kultura, P.O.B. 149, Budapest 62,
is the agency in Hungary specializing in the export of all books and periodicals published in that country. Other East European countries have similar organizations, but Kultura is of particular interest because it has made a point of publishing specialized material in English, particularly in the sciences. Of course, it is to them that you should address orders for anything published in Hungarian, but you may wish to see their English-language catalogue of foreign-language materials, which includes an impressive list of medical literature, e.g., *Critical and Theoretical Pictures of Some Renal Diseases*, 313 pages with many illustrations, $10. Kultura also distributes the English-language Corvina publications, books for the most part on art and literature, which may include many Hungarian literary works, as well as an extensive list of picture books on Hungarian paintings, crafts, music, cooking, etc. Probably the most extensive literature in English of any of the East European countries.

BOOKPLATES

Book-Care, 110 Horseferry Road, London S.W.1, England
Book-Care sells six decorative plates which cost, including surface postage: $8 for a hundred, $10 for two hundred, $15 for five hundred. All the plates come plain (without inscription), or printed with either of two type styles at no extra cost. When ordering, remember to give the quantity that you want, the number of the plate, the letter of the type style, and in clear capital letters the inscription you want, e.g.,

"JOHN BLOGGS," "EX LIBRIS JOHN BLOGGS," or "EX LIBRIS."

MAPS

Edward Standford Ltd., 12—14 Long Acre, London W.C.2, England
List of recommended maps for any one area in the world, free.
Complete lists of recommended maps for the whole world, in two loose-leaf binders, $37.50.

The largest and best-known map retailers in the world can solve any map problem put to them. Modern maps of every kind: road maps for tourists, town plans, geological and thematic maps, maps for sales and educational purposes, and maps printed to order. Also magnetic maps, maps mounted on board or cloth to order, maps dissected for the pocket, atlases, globes, and guide books.

USEFUL PAPERBACK GUIDES

INTERIOR DESIGN
The Council of Industrial Design, 28 Haymarket, London S.W.1, England
Publication list, free.

The government-sponsored Council of Industrial Design sells various magazines and books of interest to designers, or anyone interested in design, and have a collection of books published by the Design Centre that should be useful to anyone building, remodeling or furnishing a house. Although the books recommend specific English products, some of which are available by mail, they are mainly helpful because they give the kind of unbiased, factual information that amateur interior decorators need on subjects such as children's rooms, kitchens, storage space, lighting. The book on kitchens, for instance, compares the advantages and disadvantages of different kinds of flooring materials, wall coverings, work surfaces; tells you the most convenient heights for different appliances and where they should be in relation to each other and storage; how much of a splashback you need in each area, etc. The books cost about $1.30 each, plus postage.

VACATION
Farm Holiday Guides Ltd., 18 High Street, Paisley, Scotland
Farm Holiday Guide
Britain's Best Holidays
Furnished Holidays in Britain
Scotland's Best Holidays
Holidays in Wales
Each guide costs $1.50 including postage, and is available from January to May.

Bearing in mind that British food and summers are both likely to be watery, people with young children might think about a fairly inexpensive vacation in the English countryside. The 600-page *Farm Holiday Guide* lists farms and country houses all over Britain which take guests. These places pay for inclusion in the guide, but have filled out questionnaires both about their own facilities and about local sports available, such as fishing or pony trekking. Prices start at $27 a week per person for bed, breakfast and supper (lower for children).

There is a special section on riding holidays with thirty-three residential riding schools in England, Scotland and Wales listed.

Furnished Holidays in Britain gives details of places for rent, but most, though not all, of these are on caravan sites (trailer courts) or seaside resorts, so you'd be surrounded by other holidaymakers. Trailers start at $27 per week, and houses at $55.

* * *

Incidentally, no one should take a holiday in England without first arming themselves with the *Good Food Guide*, which contains reports on the best value-for-the-money places to eat all over the country recommended by local food lovers. It is on sale in most bookshops in England, and in a few of the larger ones in New York.

Another book of interest to anyone planning to tour the British countryside is *Visitor's Guide to Country Workshops*, which lists craftsmen and craft shops all over England, Wales, Scotland and Northern Ireland. It is available, free, from the Council of Small Industries in Rural Areas, 35 Camp Road, Wimbledon Common, London S.W.19, England.

National Institute of Adult Education, 35 Queen Anne Street, London WIM OBL, England
Residential short courses, 80 cents. Spring.

If you are already planning to go to England and would like to add a touch of intellectual stimulation, try a weekend of antiques, archaeology, architecture, dancing, drama, flower arranging, music, needlework, photography, pottery, writing or discussion. Each year the National Institute of Adult Education compiles a list of two- to seven-day courses held from April through August. Many of the courses are held in universities or big country houses, and besides, hopefully, being interesting in themselves, are a good way to meet the English. I see in last year's brochure, for instance: "Sense and Nonsense in Christianity"—seven days at Sidney Sussex College, Cambridge, for $53, which includes tuition and board, or "Dressmaking with Ann Landbury"—three days in Epping for $15, including tuition and board, according to the brochure. There are lots of places and all sorts of odd subjects to choose from, some specially for entire families, and others mainly for people aged over sixty.

The National Institute of Adult Education would like to be paid for their brochure not in cash, but with an international money order or check. If you pay by check, remember to add 50 cents for bank charges.

Starfish Books Ltd., Starfish House, Brook Farm Road, Cobham, Surrey, England
A Lazy Man's Guide to Holidays Afloat.
Farm and Country Holidays.
Devon and Cornwall.
Holidays Flats.
Self Catering Holidays.
Bed, Breakfast and Evening Meal.
January; $1.75 each, including surface postage.

Starfish Books also sells a guide to farm and country holidays. Theirs is much smaller than *Farm Holiday Guide* (above), but it is very good on background information. Each paid entry tells you whether the farm is a working farm (most are), what animals there are, how many people the farm has room for, and a bit about the nearest town or village, population, atmosphere, buildings worth looking at, etc.

Starfish's *Lazy Man's Guide to Holidays Afloat* lists boats that can be hired on English, Welsh and Irish canals, sailing boats and motor cruisers for hire on the coasts, and sailing schools that can be attended in Britain. Non-sailors can go on leisurely horse-drawn, skippered trips down canals from $40 per week, all-inclusive, while people with more experience, or confidence, can hire yachts and self-drive cruisers for from about $50 per week for a two-berth boat. There is also a small section listing a few boats for hire in Scandinavia, Holland, France, Germany, Spain, the Caribbean and North America.

39

40

41

42

43

44

45

39
Book-Care Bookplate no. 21, gray-green on white, type style B.

40
Book-Care Bookplate no. 22, mauve on white.

41
Book-Care Bookplate no. 23, dark brown on white, type style B.

42
Book-Care Bookplate no. 24, gray on white, type style A.

43
Book-Care Bookplate no. 25, light brown on white, type style A.

44
Book-Care Bookplate no. 26, green on white.

45
Misrachi (see Art section) A portfolio of twelve pictures of Mexican flowers suitable for framing with text in Spanish and English. About $6.

Cars and Motorbikes

46
Halfway Garages Ltd 1936 Hispano Suiza V.12 convertible. When available, this car sells for around $25,000.

47
Halfway Garages Ltd 1935 Mercedes Benz, type 500 K cabriolet. When available, this car now sells for around $20,000.

48
Vintage Autos Ltd 1923 Rolls Royce Silver Ghost open tourer with coachwork by Barker, custom-built for an Indian prince. In mint condition a car like this sells for $20,000 or more.

New cars can't easily be bought by mail, but you can save money by buying new foreign cars when abroad, especially on the more expensive models. There is, for instance, about $4,000 difference between a Maserati you buy in America and one you buy in Italy. By the time you pay for shipping (roughly $400 to the East Coast and $450 to the West) and duty, you should save about $2,000. Arrange it through an American dealer.

It is possible, however, to send for a vintage car from abroad, and there are at least two English firms that sell regularly by mail to America.

VINTAGE CARS

Halfway Garages Ltd., Bath Road, near Reading, Berkshire, England
Three or four lists a year; year's subscription $3.

Halfway Garages has specialized in restored vintage cars for twenty-five years. The periodic lists they mail are the same as the ones they have in their showroom (no markup for foreign buyers, they point out). Besides the inventory of cars, the lists contain mention of vintage spare parts which they send all over the world. The prospective buyer should write for a complete description, photograph, and price in dollars of any listed car he is interested in. The list I saw had twenty cars on it including: a Rolls Royce, a Rolls Bentley, a Daimler, a Vernon Darby, an H.E., a Horstmann, a Ferrari, Austins, a Mini, a Borgward, a Morris, a Sunbeam Talbot, and a Fiat. The cheapest was a 1935 Austin Ten, two-seater tourer, for $450. The most expensive was a Horstmann, also a two-seater tourer, believed 1914, at $4,900.

Vintage Autos Ltd., 20 Brook Mews North, Lancaster Gate, London, W.2, England

A firm with an excellent reputation which has been sending restored vintage and classic cars to all parts of the world for the last twenty-five years. They specialize in Rollses and Bentleys, and say that since these cars are getting scarce and restoration takes a long time, there are never more than fifteen in stock. Clients specify what they want, and when the managing director, Jack Bond, finds a car he thinks would be of interest, he sends details. Mr. Bond says that his cars are very much in demand in America where the cost is higher than in England. I'm not surprised that they are in demand after seeing photographs of two stunningly elegant cars recently sent to America: a 1935 Rolls Royce limousine by Thrupp and Moberley, $5,200, and a 1923 Rolls Royce Silver Ghost, an open tourer originally custom-built for an Indian prince, $17,000.

MOTOR-RACING EQUIPMENT

Les Leston Products, 315 Finchley Road, London NW3 6EH, England
Catalogue, free.

Specialists in motor-racing equipment. They have gadgets for the car and clothes for the driver: helmets and flameproof gloves, suits and shoes; also ties, cuff links and lighters with car badges on them, and umbrellas decorated with international racing flag signals. The Les Leston people say that although their products are sold in America, you save about 50 percent by buying direct from them.

MOTORBIKES

Paul Dunstall, 156 Well Hall Road, London S.E.9, England
Brochure, free. Prices in $.

Top-quality touring motorbikes. There are three basic models, and each one has features that can be varied to suit individual customers. Prices start at about $1,500. Brochure quotes ecstatic press reviews and lists races Dunstall Norton motorbikes have won.

MOTORBIKE CLOTHES

D. Lewis Ltd., 124 Great Portland Street, London W1A 2DL, England
64-page catalogue, free. Prices in $.

D. Lewis claims to have the largest stock of scooter and motorbike clothing in the world. They also have inexpensive "casual" leather clothes that can be worn by noncyclists— leather jackets from $39.30, including postage. An excellent mail-order catalogue displays racing suits, coats, jackets, jeans, trousers, gloves, boots, scrambles kits, goggles and "sundries" (suit-repair kits, stars and bars to decorate leather jackets with, rabbit's-foot pulls to add to zippers, etc.), and even construction kits of model motorbikes. Full instructions for people buying from abroad, including size conversion charts.

Christmas and Other Celebrations

Even though people grumble about Christmas having become commercialized, it is still possible to find some lovely handmade traditional decorations in small shops abroad. And shopping by mail is particularly agreeable for Christmas, when instead of tramping endlessly around crowded stores full of jostling, pushing people in search of inspired gifts, you can sit comfortably at home and with a flick of the wrist look through catalogues with tempting offerings of stores all over the world. You must do this no later than October, though, since unless you want to pay for air-mail postage, orders should be in by the very beginning of November.

DECORATIONS

Akios Industries, P.O. Box 219, Quitó, Ecuador
75-page catalogue, $1. Prices in $.

Akios sells Ecuadorian handicrafts made locally or in its own workshops, and has some beautiful Christmas decorations: a bread-dough Nativity set, very decorative and very inedible, as the figures have been painted, varnished, "sanitized" and preserved against mold. This technique must be quite widespread, for I have seen bread-dough figures from Czechoslovakia too, but the South American versions are the most colorful. Twenty-two pieces cost $13.12. Also small straw Nativity scenes for $4, and pretty straw Christmas-tree decorations: birds, fish, pigs, bells, dolls, flowers, angels for only $1.50 a dozen, plain or colored.

Akios also sells Christmas cards for $16 the hundred, hand-painted or embroidered with Indian figures and local scenes, but *everything* takes a minimum of eight weeks to arrive, so you should order way in advance.

Fortnum and Mason, Piccadilly, London W1A 1ER, England
40-page Christmas catalogue in color, free. August.
18-page wine and food list, free. Around February.

In their abundant Christmas food and gifts catalogue, Fortnum's has a page of very fancy snappers (an essential part of English Christmas). Dazzling gold or silver froths of net and flowers contain hats, headdresses and novelties for adults, $18 for a box of six. Dark-green snappers hidden by an overgrowth of holly and berries contain headdresses and novelties for the whole family, $16 for twelve. Then there are snappers just for ladies, snappers just for gentlemen, snappers containing only jewelry; and snappers just for children, decorated with toy animals on the outside, are $8 for twelve. The least expensive snappers for the whole family are also $8 a dozen. And for any time of the year, a children's-party centerpiece; in 1970 it was a white elephant filled with twelve hats, twelve balloons and twelve toys, about $9.

Hamleys of Regent Street, 200–202 Regent Street, London W.1, England ☺ ☺
39-page color catalogue, free.

The catalogue of London's largest toy shop has a couple of pages of party and Christmas things for children. Surprise snowballs and snappers, each containing a hat, a novelty and an indoor fireworks, cost $3.75 for twelve; a fairy for the top of the Christmas tree, $5; also shatterproof tree decorations; Christmas stockings (empty or full); party favors, party novelties, party jokes and party games (a pack with ten games for children aged three to ten, $2); masks and dress-up clothes; a pink rabbit for children up to the age of six, $4.75; an elaborate guardsman's uniform complete with brass buttons and furry hat, $16.

Klods Hans, 34 Hans Jensensstraede, DK-5000 Odense, Denmark
14-page brochure, free. Prices in $.

A neat and appealing little brochure showing handmade decorations at about one half of their New York prices. For Christmas: star, elf and angel tree decorations; choirboy candlesticks, musical angels, pottery elves and snowy cottages; mobiles, wall hangings, and calendars (one cotton calendar has twenty-four little girls with pockets in their aprons for small gifts, $3.50). An artless Nativity scene in hand-painted wood, $14.

For Easter there are hand-painted wooden eggs, chicks, rabbits and candlesticks, and wooden mobiles; and for any other time lots of little things that are bound to please children: face egg cups with hat cozies, people pencil holders, tiny ceramic animals, pinafores with appliquéd dolls in cradles—and a wall hanging with a dollhouse or farmyard on it and a removable doll, $4. For adults: brass candlesticks and oil lamps, and Royal Copenhagen figurines.

Tiroler Heimatwerk, Meraner Strasse 2, Innsbruck, Tyrol, Austria
16-page catalogue with some color, free.

Tiroler Heimatwerk sells fine hand-carved Nativity scenes in various sizes, plain wood or colored. The catalogue shows one that costs $31. Figures and stables can also be bought separately.

For Christmas-cookie molds, see Handicrafts: Holland; for Christmas embroideries, Hobbies: Eva Rosenstrand; for commemorative Christmas plates, Glass and China: Axel Brandt.

CARDS

Fratelli Allnari, Lungarno Corsini 24 R, Florence 50123, Italy
44-page catalogue with some color, free. Prices in $.

This firm, famous for its reproductions, issues twelve cards a year, each one a color reproduction of an Italian painting on handmade paper. Some of the cards have religious subjects—Raphael's "Madonna of the Chair," Fra Angelico's "Group of Angels," etc.—but not all of them are religious, and as cards are available with or without Christmas greetings, they can be used for other occasions as well. 27 cents each.

British Museum Publications, London W.C.1, England
Christmas card list, free.
Colored postcard list, free.
Black-and-white postcard list, free.
Transparencies list, free.

An unillustrated list of the museum's Christmas cards (13 cents each), which are decorated with scenes taken from illustrated manuscripts, woodcuts in fifteenth-century books, pictures of medieval and Oriental antiquities, or prints and drawings such as Rowlandson's "Skating on the Serpentine" and Copley Fielding's "Buckingham House from St. James's Park in the Snow." Also on sale: "Christmas folders" (6 cents) into which you slip an ordinary postcard to make it a Christmas card.

Konn's Fine Arts, Mail Order Department, The Hong Kong Hilton Hotel, Hong Kong
Samples, free. Prices in $.

Hong Kong's leading mail-order card firm produces Americanized Chinese-style cards with your name and address and any message you choose printed inside. $11 per

49
Klods Hans Red, white and blue hand-painted wooden elves with handknitted caps. About $1.13 each.

50   **51**
Klods Hans White paper angel mobile on brass wires. About $1.56.

51
Klods Hans Straw Christmas-tree star. About 22 cents.
photos Gunnar Larsen

52
Treasures of Italy Christmas Card "Choir Angels" by Guarnacci, from a box of twelve assorted cards. About $1.25 per box, including air-mail postage.

hundred (including postage) for birds, flowers or landscapes hand-painted on silk, or $14.50 per hundred for portraits of children, junks and harbor scenes reproduced from oil paintings. For $1 more, all the envelopes can be printed with your name and address too. These prices include postage.

Treasures of Italy, P.O. Box 1513, Florence, Italy
32-page color brochure, free. Prices in $.
Christmas card leaflet, free. Prices in $.
Silver leaflet, free. Prices in $.

Christmas cards, notes and stationery. The cards ($1.25 per box of twelve, including postage) are illustrated with scenes of the Nativity, the Adoration, the Annunciation by Botticelli, Raphael, Da Vinci and other famous Italian painters. The pictures are bordered by a classic Florentine scroll in gold, red and cobalt copied from Renaissance manuscripts. The scroll motif is repeated on the inside of the envelopes and on stationery. There are also cards for other occasions.

Cigars and Pipes

Astley's Ltd., 109 Jermyn Street, London S.W.1, England
18-page catalogue, free. Prices in $.

"You shall avoid all evil company, and all occasions which may tend to draw you to the same; and make speedy return when you shall be sent on your master's or mistress's errand," apprentice pipe makers were instructed in the seventeenth century. Astley's pipe shop displays the original document along with famous and not-famous antique pipes, some of which are for sale. However, their catalogue shows just their well-known new briar pipes and explains the distinctive characteristics of each one. Prices, including postage, vary between $9 for their Crusty and Atlantic briars and $44 for Super Straight grained briars. Lots of shapes are shown, and there is a pageful of unusual designs with a pipe made out of briar *root*. Also available are meerschaum pipes, special tobacco blends, pipe cases, tobacco pouches, smokers' knives and a repair service by mail for pipes of any make.

Davidoff et Cie, 2 Rue de Rive, 1200 Geneva, Switzerland
List of Cuban cigars, in French, free.

Davidoff et Cie is best known for its Cuban cigars. In fact, one line of Cuban cigars is named after the owner: Davidoffs Nos. 1 and 2, about $26.50 for twenty-five 6" cigars. Owing to U.S. government restrictions, Cuban cigars aren't allowed into the country, so if they are found being imported, they are confiscated. However, Canadians can buy them without fear, and Americans can either send them to friends in other countries or console themselves with cigars, cigarillos, cigarettes and pipes from any other country in the world, as Davidoff stocks them all (the cigars in special controlled-temperature cellars). He also counts as a free port when the cigars are sent out of Switzerland and they are exempt from the original Swiss import taxes.

Hayim Pinhas, P.O.B. 5000, Istanbul, Turkey
36-page brochure. Prices in $.

Meerschaum is a mineral found only in Turkey. It makes excellent lightweight, porous pipes which smoke turns dark-brown in time. Here you can get hand-carved pipes direct from Turkey and much cheaper than anywhere else. You can buy a sober "English style" or plain with straight or curved stem for $4.50. But if you would like to be more flamboyant, there are carved creatures—a busty "sea-girl" with hair flowing back over the pipe bowl, $9; Cleopatra; Abraham Lincoln; Shakespeare; Bacchus; a priest; a fisherman; an Indian; a Viking; and for $22, a hunting dog with prey in its mouth. Carved cigarette holders cost $1.25. Air-mail postage for each pipe is $1, but the minimum order is two pipes.

Pipe Dan, Vestergade 13, DK-1456 Copenhagen, Denmark
20-page leaflet, free.

Sixty-four pipes are photographed in this clear leaflet. Many of them are of unusual shapes, and they are divided into types: big bowls, verticles, chimneys, light-weight shapes, etc. Prices start at about $4 for a standard mini, and for the handmade pipes vary between $16 and $40. You can buy Danish pipe tobacco here, and pipes made by other Danish manufacturers if you give the number or sketch the shape of the one you want. And there are several unusual services: you can have a name or initials stamped on the pipe for free; you can have a pipe of your own design made up from your own sketch; or Dan will send you the raw materials and you can make your own pipe.

53
Davidoff et Cie Mr. Davidoff in his Geneva cigar shop.

54
Hayim Pinhas Hand-carved meerschaum pipe "D'Artagnan." $8.80.

55
Pipe Dan "The Tulip." Both machine-made and hand-carved pipes are on sale here.

Shannon Airport (see General section) stocks Kapp and Peterson pipes.

Clothes and Accessories

Although it seems so tricky to buy clothes by mail, they are in fact popular mail-order buys, both with people who know they can slip easily into standard sizes and, at the other extreme, with people who like clothes made to measure. If you like classic clothes you can do really well by mail. There is a wide and impressive choice of good tweed skirts, silk shirts (from Thailand), and lamb's wool and cashmere sweaters—often at marvelously low prices.

Great Britain, which has long had a worldwide reputation for good workmanship and excellent tailoring, has really latched on to the idea. Selling Scottish knitwear by mail is a booming business; posh Savile Row tailors and Jermyn Street shirtmakers send representatives over to measure their customers each year; and the rest of the country seems to be busily sending out brochures, self-measuring charts and swatches.

Hong Kong is another main source for clothes by mail. The tailors there are well known for their capacity to copy old suits—there are jokes about new suits coming back with carefully reproduced cigarette burns. However, although their workmanship is generally praised, the fabric swatches for men's suiting I was sent looked rather flimsy to me. But if anyone feels like trying these tailors (all listed in reputable American shopping guides), write and tell them what weight suit you want, and they will send you fabric swatches and self-measurement forms. Or if you prefer, send them an old suit to copy. The shoe shops, too, will copy any shoes you have grown fond of, and they will also copy purses, either your own or from photographs cut out of magazines.

The women's and children's clothes from Hong Kong look like great bargains—for one thing, they are made of fabrics such as silk which China has specialized in. The styles are all-American, the colors mainly pastel for children and strong for women—turquoise, hot pink, kelly-green, yellow.

Clothing sizes differ from country to country (see charts at the back of the book), so I think it best, while you ask for a certain size, always to enclose a drawing with your measurements. But never take your own measurements, and if you are having something made to measure, either send something that fits well to be copied, or have a tailor measure you.

FOR MEN AND WOMEN

Army and Navy Stores Ltd., 105 Victoria Street, London, S.W.1, England ♛♛
20-page women's fashion catalogues, free. Spring, fall. 90-page Christmas gift catalogue with some color, free. October. ♛♛

The Christmas-gift catalogue of this London department store has a few pages of with-it men's clothes—splendid mauve, orange, petrel-blue, gold, black or modern paisley, slim-cut Viyella (cotton and wool) shirts for $12, and $2 plain ties in exactly the same colors; pajamas in the same colors, and a nightshirt and "shahjamas" by Hardy Amies, the famous English designer. The "shahjamas" consist of a gold-and-red paisley Mao-collared top and black trousers, and cost $11.

But Army and Navy ladies must look very drab next to their men. The women's clothes (illustrated in the fashion catalogues) are much more conventional. Shirtwaists start at $9, lots of checks, paisley, pink, blue, yellow and turquoise. Winter dresses are more expensive, starting at $31 for a printed Viyella dress, but some Jaeger-brand skirts, slacks and sweaters cost around $16 each, much less than here.

W. Bill Ltd., Mail Order Dept., 40 South Molton Lane, London W1Y 1AT, England
General color brochure, free. Prices in $. Pringle and Barrie knitwear brochures, free. Prices in $.

This firm, which is well known to American visitors in London, runs a big mail-order business in clothes and fabrics, and puts out a brochure showing a little of everything. For women there are knit dresses and sweaters with skirts to match; for men, sweaters and tweed jackets from W. Bill's own exclusive tweeds. A Shetland sports jacket, illustrated in the current brochure, comes ready-made or made-to-measure for $70, postage and insurance $2 extra.

Cambrian Factory Ltd., Llanwrtyd Wells, Breconshire, Wales
Color leaflet and self-measuring chart, free, Prices in $.

At this factory, tweeds are made from Welsh wool by disabled people, and the entire process of wool sorting, dyeing, spinning, etc., can be watched by visitors. The tweeds are of high quality, and colors are fairly earthy: beige, mustards, gray, greens, in herringbone or checks. The tweeds are sold by the yard: the 8/10 oz. tweeds in 29″ widths cost $4 a yard, including postage. There is also a made-to-measure service: women's skirts cost $13 to $19; men's sports jackets, $37; two-piece suits, $58—all these prices include postage.

J. C. Cording and Co. Ltd., 19 Piccadilly, London W1V OPE, England
32-page catalogue, free.

Top English clothes for the sporty country life; hunting, shooting and fishing, or just walking; both ready-made and made-to-measure (self-measurement charts enclosed). The catalogue explains in admirable detail the various features of each of its classic models: the Yeo coat, "the original waterproof riding coat, often copied but never equalled," $46; "Grenfell" golfwear, cut from the cloth originally made for Sir Wilfred Grenfell, "heroic doctor/explorer," to wear in the arctic wastes of Labrador; the "Barlows" Norfolk jacket, based on the original Norfolk jacket, $66; the classic Ascot coat made out of Gannex for scientific weather protection, $55; "Idstone" handmade waterproof shoes, $47. (A pair standing in a pan of water has been on show in Cordings' Piccadilly showroom for several years—dry inside, of course.)

Creation Boutique, Duke Street, Dublin 2, Ireland
24-page brochure, free. Prices in $.

The director of this shop, who was formerly with Marshall Field, Chicago, has put together a neat little brochure with just a few choice items: two Irish handloomed dresses in off-white for about $27; two sheepskin coats, $120 for women and $135 for men; and four Donald Davies shirtwaist dresses for $36 each. Donald Davies dresses are made in featherweight tweed in the most magnificent colors: various shades of everything bright—blues, mauves, reds and yellows, either solid or checks or stripes. These dresses are sold in New York for $60 and up.

Irish Cottage Industries Ltd., 18 Dawson Street, Dublin 2, Ireland
30-page brochure, free. Prices in $.

This shop puts out a nice amateurish brochure, with all the people from next door modeling clothes and looking as though they are trying not to laugh. Clothes include several shapes and designs of the colorful, woven crios belt; the traditional, heavy, off-white Aran sweaters; gossamer-weight tweed dressing gowns ($24–$27), lumber jackets; hand-knitted socks for men; string gloves; and stoles, scarves and ties made out of gossamer-weight tweed in so many shades that they can't be listed.

Tweed is sold by the yard, and samples are sent on request for specific colors and weights.

56   57

W. Bill Ltd Shetland-wool roll-collar dress, made to measure, in dark aqua, green mist, barn red, camel, blue haze, green lovat, olive green and misty blue, or almost any other color.
photo Dudley Harris

57
Creation Boutique "Paddy Sprung," a Donald Davies handwoven featherweight tweed dress, available in checks, stripes, plaids or solid colors, in sizes 8 to 16. About $36.50.
photo Photographic Services

58
Lodenbaur "Fulpmes" jacket in gray loden, $39; in green or gray tweed, $36.

S. and M. Jacobs Ltd. Exports, 20 Dawson Street, Dublin 2, Ireland
16-page brochure and fabric swatches, free. Prices in $.

A huge mail-order business in made-to-measure suits and coats for men and women. Styles are good, classic, but not dowdy. The fabrics are 100 percent wool, Irish handwoven tweed in rich colors: reds, blues, purples, and the prices are quite low: about $18 for a fully lined skirt; about $53 for a ladies' suit, coat or cape; and $62 for a gent's coat. Jacobs says that no size or figure problem is too difficult for them. They also sell tweeds by the yard.

Ferner Jacobsen AS, Stortingsgaten 14, Oslo 1, Norway
14-page catalogue with some color, free.

Jacobsen's says theirs is a "high quality" store selling everything for men, and sports and casual clothes for women. Their neat and clear catalogue shows mainly sportswear: ski suits in all sorts of colors from $30, and marvelous wool vams (colorful decorated after-ski tunics) for men and women from $24; floating jackets for sailing for $38; Norwegian sweaters for well under their American prices.

Lodenbaur, Brixner Strasse 4, A-6021 Innsbruck, Austria
22-page brochure in German, free.

Loden cloth is woven in the Tyrol from the wool of the Himalayan goat, and the natural oil of the wool is kept so that the cloth is naturally showerproof. Loden is hard to find outside Austria and Germany, and is quite expensive. There are several shops that specialize in lodenwear and the Austrian Look—dirndl and lederhosen. Lodenbaur has a good selection of coats, capes and suits for men, women and children, both in classic shapes and in crisp new ones. Ask about prices; they are not listed in the brochure.

Loden-Frey, Maffeistrasse 7–9, 8 Munich 1, Germany
24-page color catalogue in German, free.

This German lodenwear is more international, more fashionable and more expensive than the Austrian. A man's classic coat costs about $90. A woman's straight-cut scarlet coat trimmed with braid, $51; a maxi-coat, $90; and a stunning embroidered dark-brown (antelope) suede suit, $280.

There are all sorts of variations on the dirndl theme, including some unorthodoxly low-cut ones, and one mauve-and-pink maxi-dirndl that looks fashionably peasanty and costs about $40.

Children's coats shown here are $19 and up; and dirndls for girls, $14.50 and up.

Loden-Plankl, Michaelerplatz 6, 1010 Vienna, Austria
12-page color brochure, free.

If you can't speak German, this is the loden catalogue for you. It shows traditional hunting clothes and also international styles. A man's modern raglan-sleeved coat with silk lining costs $56, and is always available in light or dark gray, camel or forest green; a classic hunting cape which comes in a choice of three different fabric weights, about $40. A woman's hunting costume (which looks like a perfectly ordinary classic suit to me), about $67; a splendid purple coach cape with (or without) black velvet collar and coin buttons, about $45.

Loden-Plankl also sells dirndls (about $23 each), knitted jackets, boiled cardigans, shirts, blouses, stockings, and cotton fabrics by the yard.

The Scotch House, Knightsbridge, London, S.W.1, England
36-page color catalogue, free. Prices in $.

The largest and most glamorous of the shops dealing in

Scottish goods. The Scotch House sells all sorts of sophisticated variations on the Scottish theme that will appeal to people without a trace of Scottish blood in their veins. Full-length evening kilts, $35; tartan blazers, about $52; a tartan dinner jacket with a black satin shawl collar, $60; wool tartan capes for little girls, $25. And a Viyella dressing gown for $21.50 that looks identical to one I have seen in New York for $46.

This is also a very good place for well-made and fairly expensive clothes in Scottish wools and tweeds. For men: jackets, trousers, suede vests and deerstalker hats. For women: classic coats, skirts and sweaters. For children: smart little coats, $26–$44.

Swan and Edgar Ltd., Piccadilly Circus, London W1A 2AY, England

Swan and Edgar's front doors on Piccadilly are a favorite meeting place for Londoners, partly because they are opposite an enormous clock, and tourists seem to magically discover the doors, too. The shop is a large fashion store which sells most good, medium-priced English clothes, many of them known to Americans as they are sold in the United States: Rodex, Aquascutum, Dannimac and Quelrayn Coats; Ricci Michael dresses; Braemar, Pringle and Morely knitwear. And there are three departments dealing exclusively with Jaeger, Berketex and Windsmoor clothes. Jaeger's are perhaps the most popular of all in England: excellent medium-priced classic tweeds and knitwear for men and women; coats, suits, sports jackets, trousers, skirts— everything. All these clothes are much less expensive in England, and although Swan and Edgar has no catalogue, they answer individual questions and try to send manufacturers' brochures when they are available.

59
The Scotch House Kilt skirt in any tartan, about $41; velvet vest, about $25; blouse, about $30.

GLOVES AND LEATHER

Anticoli Gloves, Via del Tritone 143, Rome 00187, Italy
30-page brochure with some color, free. Prices in $.

A good, illustrated selection of gloves at very low prices. Short, plain kid gloves for women are $2.25; silk-lined, $4.25; wool-lined, $4; and fur-lined, $4.50. Men's hand-stitched kid gloves are $4.50, and $6.25 fur-lined. Besides golf gloves, driving gloves, crocheted gloves and lots of plain gloves, there are women's gloves with cutouts and embroidery in various lengths. Children's white kid gloves with colored rosebuds cost $2.75, and children's fur-lined kid gloves in black, brown, navy-blue or red cost $3.75. Postage costs an extra dollar for two pairs. Leather billfolds, wallets and belts for men cost up to $7.50. Kid-skin purses and billfolds combined in all colors for women cost $3.75 and up. Pure-silk ties in traditional designs cost around $5.

60
Leather School Leather purse in bone, natural tan, medium or dark brown, red, navy blue, black or white. $32 plain, $32.80 with Florentine gilding.
photo Style

Catello D'Auria, Via Due Macelli 55, 00187 Rome, Italy
12-page leaflet, free. Prices in $.

A smaller and slightly more expensive selection than Anticoli's but in a wider variety of leathers. Here there are gloves in pigskin, sheepskin and doeskin as well as kid. Wrist-length kid gloves cost just over $4 for women and so do doeskin.

Denise Francelle, 244 Rue de Rivoli, Paris I, France.
Price list, free. Prices in $.

Finest Roger Fare and Kislav gloves that are hard to find in America start at $9.25. Also doeskin, suede, velvet and calf gloves, each kind in four lengths, and bags, scarves and umbrellas. For children, gloves and purses that match, but are unillustrated.

Kristine Leather Goods Workshop, 18—20 Fulham High Street, London S.W.6, England
6-page catalogue with crocodile-skin samples, free. Prices in $.

Classic crocodile handbags ranging in price from $176 to $200; also crocodile wallets, $41; billfolds, $23; key cases and glass cases. Postage and insurance included in prices.

Leather School, Piazza Santa Croce 16, Florence, Italy
32-page color catalogue. free, Prices in $.

The Leather School in the cloister of the Santa Croce Church was founded by monks to produce a complete line of Florentine leather goods and to technically prepare young boys who wish to specialize in this type of work in a morally sound atmosphere. (The atmosphere isn't so morally sound, however, as to prevent whoever wrapped my parcel from writing "*Niella valore*" on the customs form.)

There is a very wide range of wallets in calf, crocodile, lizard and tortoise skin (starting at about $5.75), and cigarette cases, glass cases, photograph albums, photograph frames, etc., in the gold-tooling-on-colored-leather that is typical of Florence. In cut velvet there are jewelry boxes, wastepaper baskets, picture frames, handbags. And in calfskin there are belts for men and attaché cases at about $75, and a wide range of handbags both tooled in gold (for about $35) and plain, including some chunky, casual, sport, and shoulder bags ranging in price from $22 to $60. A seven-piece desk set, gilded or plain, costs $55 and comes in all colors.

Loewe, Barquillo 13, Madrid 4, Spain
Occasional color leaflet, free. Prices in $.

Spain's poshest leather shop sells only exclusive designs made in its own workshops. There is a branch in London but none in America yet, so they can sell by mail. Prices seem high unless you compare them with similar top shops in other countries. A wallet with a coin purse costs about $14, and an attaché case about $65. Some styles are decorated with embroidered ribbons or contrasting leathers, others achieve noble simplicity. Besides the usual colors, there are lovely, unusual ranges of browns—grayish browns, toasted beiges, tobaccos, and burgundys.

Unicorn Leather Company Ltd., Woodhill Works, Bury, Lancashire, England
20-page catalogue, free. Prices in $.

This company has a shop in the Burlington Arcade in London, near Piccadilly Circus, and is known for its plain, strong leather goods in hand-grained morocco, velvet calf, pigskin and coach hide. There are handbags for around $30, wallets for around $10, and an excellent selection of folio cases, document cases, briefcases and attaché cases. Note special features such as alphabetical-index sections, keyless locks and push-button code locks that can be fitted when the cases are being made. Standard briefcases cost around $55.

HATS

Herbert Johnson Ltd., 38 New Bond Street, London, W.1, England ♡
18-page catalogue for men, leaflet for women, free.

Herbert Johnson opened his hat shop in the '90's at the suggestion of Edward the Prince of Wales, and now the shop justifiably prides itself in combining the best of old and new. There are hats to convince the most adamant hat haters. Besides every sort of classic hat for men they carry all-purpose felt, town and formal wear, tweed and leather hats and caps, sporting headwear, seasonal hats "for warmer times or cold comfort." They have a smashing collection of "character hats," including "the poet," "the artist," and the "38," originally sold by Herbert Johnson in the '20's. ("The fact that this style is immediately associated with the gangster just means the wearer can never be disregarded.") Felt hats cost between $13 and $33, and tweed caps are about $8.

The English *Vogue* uses lots of Herbert Johnson's hats for women in basic shapes and fashionably, completely undecorated styles. Prices are from $11 to $15.

Carlo Lambardi, Via Novembre 157 B, Rome, Italy
10-page brochure, free. Prices in $.

Instead of answering any of my letters, Carlo Lambardi has simply sent neat little brochures giving instructions on how to buy his Borsalino hats by mail. So I assume that he does have a mail-order business but that whoever answers the mail doesn't understand English. The impeccable brochure shows sixteen classic Borsalino models for men and women, lists, colors and American sizes available, and contains a handy order form. Men's hats are around $17 and women's around $14, both including postage and insurance.

KIMONOS

Hayashi Kimono, Tokyo Hilton Hotel Arcade, 2—10—3 Nagata-Cho Chiyoda-Ku, Tokyo, Japan
20-page brochure with some color, free. Prices in $.

A top Tokyo shop for antique kimonos which has a mail-order service for Westernized Japanese clothes, marvelous for exotic wear around the house. Full-length, flower-embroidered silk kimonos in almost any color cost between $22 and $36. Happi coats, which are less spectacular but more practical, since they are knee-length and have narrower sleeves, cost $16 to $20 in silk, $12 in rayon, and $6 in cotton. The cotton ones cost about $4 for children. Happi coats also come with trousers as lounging pajamas for men and women. Prices for men's clothes are mysteriously lower than for women, and are embroidered in gold with dragons or Japanese characters. Westerners have been impressed with the beauty of the black cotton coats Japanese firemen wear, and these are on sale for $11 with wide gold bands around the waist, and the name of the firehouse on the back, in a Japanese character. All the above prices include surface postage; air postage is given and is around $2 extra.

KNITWEAR

Copenhagen Handknit, Nikolaj Plads 27, Copenhagen K, Denmark
8-page color brochure, free.

This shop sells Juul Christensen hand-knitted sweaters and dresses in very beautiful, subtle color combinations and traditional Scandinavian designs. They also make skirts and stovepipe pants in fabric to match. Sweaters cost around $33 for men and women, and from $11 to $20 for children. Copenhagen Handknit claims that these same sweaters sell in the United States for from $47 to $65.

Heather Valley Ltd., Brunstane Road, Edinburgh EH15 2QL, Scotland
12-page color brochure and swatches, free.

Heather Valley's own made-to-measure lamb's-wool and Shetland sweaters with tweed skirts to match. The designs are all classic, the colors unusual. There are pinks, mauves and dusty blues that the internationally famous manufacturers don't make—you might prefer these. Sweaters cost around $11 each, skirts cost from $16 to $22.

61

62

63

64

65

66

61
Hayashi Kimono Cotton apron in any color. $4.67, including surface postage.

62
Hayashi Kimono Silk kimono in any color. $22.50, including surface postage.

63
Copenhagen Handknit Hand-knitted sweater for men and women, "Jesper" by Juul Christensen. Design in greens, browns, or dark blues on white. $34, including postage.

64
Wilson of Hawick Lyle and Scott's most classic sweaters available in merino wool, lamb's wool or cashmere, and thirty different colors. Prices from about $13.

65
The Scottish Merchant Authentic Fair Isle sweater knitted to order (takes six to eight weeks). Suggested color combination: mostly blue and red with some yellow on natural background. $58.

66
Burberrys Ltd Terylene and cotton gabardine in oyster, sand, black or navy. Styles change each season, but similar raincoats are usually on sale for around $65.

Hills Cashmere House Ltd., 6 Old Bond Street, London W.1, England
Barrie, Braemar, Pringle brochures, free.

Hunt and Winterbotham Ltd., 4 Old Bond Street, London W.1, England
Braemar and Pringle brochures and "color toned" fabrics, free.

W. S. Robertson Ltd., 13/15 High Street, Hawick, Scotland
Braemar, Drumlanrig, Lyle and Scott, Pringle brochures and wool samples, $2 a year. Prices in $.

Romanes and Patterson, 62 Princes Street, Edinburgh, Scotland
Barrie, Braemar, Pringle brochures and wool samples, free.

Wilson of Hawick, 30 Drumlanrig Square, Hawick, Scotland
Lyle and Scott brochure and wool samples, $1. Prices in $.

All the above shops sell knitwear by famous English and Scottish manufacturers by mail. Tell one of them which manufacturer you are interested in, and they will send the current brochure. Each manufacturer has two brochures going at once, one with sweaters for men and another with sweaters for women. The men's brochures show sweaters in merino, camel's hair, lamb's wool and cashmere, with prices from about $13 and up. The women's brochures have not only sweaters from about $13, but also skirts—either in exactly the same color, or else in tweeds to match, from $16.50. If you sew, you can buy skirt packs in matching fabric for about $11. You can save *roughly* one third of the price by buying from Great Britain and another advantage is the enormous range of styles and colors to choose from: each manufacturer has about twenty-four styles in around fifteen colors each.

Kløverhuset, Strandgaten 13, 5001 Bergen, Norway
12-page color catalogue, free. Prices in $.

This shop started as a small dry-goods store in 1852, but has gradually expanded to become Bergen's main fashion store, with a gift store that opens during the tourist season. The handy catalogue shows mainly traditional hand-knitted Norwegian sweaters and jackets in full glorious color. Children's sweaters and jackets cost $13–$22 according to size; sweaters for adults, $28; jackets, $30; caps and gloves, $6. On the back page there is a white, handloomed coat with pewter buttons and hand-embroidered ribbon in blue and red around the cuffs and pockets, $53.

Glen Lockhart Knitwear, Aberdour, Fife, Scotland
38-page brochure with some color, free.

Made-to-measure knitwear—sweaters, skirts and dresses, tartans and tweeds at low prices. In the brochure the fabrics are photographed in color, but swatches can also be sent if you ask for specific fabrics after seeing brochure. A pure-wool ribbed dress costs about $15, and a cashmere sweater and knitted skirt (lined) together are $55. A kilted mini-skirt is about $19, and a kilted evening skirt is about $30. Ponchos, capes and fabrics by the yard are also sold here.

Una O'Neill Designs, 30 Oakley Park, Blackrock, Co. Dublin, Ireland
Leaflet, free. Prices in $.

Una O'Neill sells hand-knitted, traditional, off-white Aran fisherman sweaters and jackets. The complicated symbolic stitches evolved centuries ago and are so distinctive that in case of accident a particular design of a sweater could identify the wearer's home village. Una O'Neill's prices are low: sweaters for children $7.50 to $12; for women from $19; and for men, from $20.

The Scottish Merchant, 16 New Row, London WC2N 4LA, England
Brochure, free. June.

Scottish Merchant specializes in very carefully authentic Scottish knitwear, often copied from antique Fair Isle knits now in museums. Apparently the Fair Isle patterns evolved when Scotland was under Norse rule, which is why the designs look somewhat Scandinavian. Patterns were modified as time went by, and when in the sixteenth century one of the Spanish Armada ships was driven ashore on Fair Isle, the local knitters copied the Spanish heraldic designs. Since then, true Fair Isle patterns have incorporated those symbols, including the Armada cross. Shetland sweaters with Fair Isle borders are on sale for $24, sweaters with Fair Isle overall patterns cost $64 and take four to eight weeks to make. Plain Shetland sweaters knitted on circular needles with no side seams cost $12 to $15. Lacy openwork sweaters, $24; Shetland shawls in natural-colored wool or rainbow stripes, $30; long zigzag scarves, $13; and zigzag hats, $5.50.

Le Tricoteur, 3 St. James' Street, St. Peter Port, Guernsey, Channel Islands
Leaflet and samples, free. Prices in $.

Loose, long casual sweaters in styles used originally by smugglers and sailors, and knitted on the island of Guernsey, traditionally a great knitting island. Guernsey men have been exporting their hand-knitted stockings since Queen Elizabeth's day. Mary Queen of Scots wore them. The sweaters are made from partly oiled worsted wool and are still good for sailing, fishing and smuggling. They come in plain colors: red, blue, navy, beige, white, and are priced according to size from $4.50 for a 22" chest to $15 for a 48" chest. Surface postage, $1.90 each.

RAINCOATS

Burberry's Ltd., Haymarket, London S.W.1, England 🐾🐾
12-page brochure, free.

Twenty-four of Burberry's famous coats and raincoats for men and women are shown in the brochure. Prices range from $50 for "ladies' walking Burberry" to about $230 for "Frome," a pure-cashmere coat for men. For about $23 there is a detachable fleece lining that fits into all the weatherproofs. Styles change each season.

SHEEPSKINS

Lakeland's Sheepskin Centre, Lake Road, Keswick, Cumberland, England
12-page catalogue, free.

This shop in England's Lake District is much visited by Americans in the summer, most of whom buy sheepskin and suede clothes too bulky to take home by plane. The Lakeland Sheepskin Centre has become experts in mailing their goods.

The policy of the shop is to buy a few lines in quantity so that prices can be kept down and quality up. At the moment the catalogue shows one well-finished sheepskin coat for men, $127, and one for women, $120; both are fingertip-length in medium brown, leather-bound, and with leather buttons. A suede mini-skirt costs $13, and a suede cardigan dress, $27.

Smaller things are inexpensive, too: sheepskin hats from $7; gloves for adults from $9; children's mittens, $2.50 (unbeatable for snow); calfskin handbags from $13. And a

53

long-haired Icelandic sheepskin rug in white, yellow, red or turquoise, $19.

For more clothes, see Fabrics: Thailand, and the shops listed in the General (Lace, Linen & Embroidery) and Handicrafts and Special Local Products sections.

SHOES

Kow Hoo Shoe Co. Ltd., 19—21 Hennessy Road, Hong Kong
Style leaflet, self-measuring chart, free. Prices in $.

Men's shoes starting at $16.25 for cordovan leather, but also in Du Pont Corfam, lizard skin, lizardgator skin, sea-turtle skin, ostrich skin, and French baby-alligator skin. Women's shoes starting at $15.25; purses, $22.

Lee Kee Ltd., 65 Peking Road, Kowloon, Hong Kong
Style leaflet, leather samples, free. Prices in $.

Men's shoes in the same leathers as at Kow Hoo (above), starting at $14 for West German calfskin. Women's shoes starting at $11.50; purses at $18.

UMBRELLAS

Swaine Adeney Brigg and Sons Limited, 185 Piccadilly, London W1V OHA, England ♛♛
72-page general catalogue, free.
Saddlery and riding equipment catalogue, free.

This very prestigious old firm has been making whips for English monarchs since George III, and provides everything necessary for the civilized country life—whips, canes and drinking flasks.

After six pages of mean-looking whips come things of more general interest: elegant canes, including swagger canes, and a Swagger-Dagger cane with a hidden dagger. Discreetly sober umbrellas in best silk with Malacca handles and gold or silver bands, or in nylon with lizard-skin handles; many different seat sticks, seat umbrellas and golf umbrellas; hunting and shooting accessories including silver-plated sandwich boxes; picnic baskets and race hampers for two, four or six people; "sporting gifts"—spoons and cuff links with animals on them.

At the end of the catalogue there is an impressive leather section, showing fitted beauty cases, jewel cases, briefcases, gentlemen's fitted dressing cases, writing cases, passport cases and purses.

No prices available as they are in the process of being revised, but you can guess they are high.

SHIRTS

FOR MEN

Ascot Chang Ltd., 34 Kimberley Road, Kowloon, Hong Kong
Style sheet, self-measurement chart, fabric swatches, free. Prices in $.

Shirts only, from $7 to $9.

A. Garstang and Co. Ltd., 213 Preston New Road, Blackburn BB2 6BP, England
Measuring charts and swatches, $1 refundable on first order.

Shirt and pajama specialists. Various styles of shirts can be made in twelve types of material with spare collars and cuffs, either from charts sent to you or copied from an old shirt you send them. Delivery time is five weeks, and prices range from

about $8 for all-cotton to $16.25 for silk. The plentiful swatches are in conventional checks, stripes and plain colors.

Harvie and Hudson Ltd., 77 Jermyn Street, St. James's, London S.W.1, England
Fabric swatches, free.

Nowhere else in the world is there a street like Jermyn Street, crammed with astronomically expensive, ineffably elegant men's haberdashery stores. The mind boggles—who on earth buys himself $26 shirts? If you'd like it to be you, try Harvie and Hudson, a firm with many American customers which will send you swatches of current fabrics—stripes, checks and plain colors in cotton voiles, zephyrs, poplins, broadcloths and oxfords. Prices for ready-made shirts, $14—$16; for made-to-measure, $22—$24, with a minimum order of three shirts.

Liberty and Co. Ltd., Mail Order, Regent Street, London W1R 6AH, England
List of available fabrics and swatches, free.
Swatches of shirt fabrics, swatches of tie fabrics, free.

Liberty sends out swatches of all their famous fabrics, including Tana lawn for shirts, and flowery cottons for their fashionable ties. But order promptly and give second choices, as the goods move quickly. Prices are about $13 for shirts and $3.50 and up for ties.

Turnbull and Asser Ltd., 71—72 Jermyn Street, St. James's, London S.W.1, England
Fabric swatches, free.

Like the Savile Row tailors, Turnbull and Asser, another Jermyn Street shirtmaker, sends a representative to Philadelphia and New York each fall to measure customers and show them the latest "shirting materials." Once customers' measurements are taken, more shirts can be ordered by mail with the help of fabric swatches if necessary. Prices are, roughly: poplin, $20; voile, sea island cotton, $25; silk, $39 and up. Ready-made shirts are about $16.50—$20.

SHOES

John Lobb, 9 St. James's Street, London S.W.1, England ♛♛♛♛♛
Tour schedule, free. Prices in $.

John Lobb is far and away the most prestigious shoe makers in the world. They have made shoes for at least three English kings and one American president (President Johnson). Each spring and fall a representative tours America taking measurements of new customers, and showing their latest models to old customers. Once measurements have been taken and permanent lasts have been made, customers can order new shoes by mail, with the help of photographs if necessary. Handmade shoes in calf leather start at $145, rarer skins are more expensive.

Alan McAlfee, 38 Dover Street, Piccadilly, London W.1, England
Color brochure, 25 cents. Prices in $.

Very good English shoes of every sort for men. Prices mostly between $40 and $50, and insured postage is $3 for one pair, $4 for two.

TAILORS

Jimmy Chen and Co. Ltd., 208—211 Hong Kong Hotel, Shopping Center, P.O. Box 5757, Kowloon, Hong Kong
Self-measurement chart, swatches, free. Prices in $.

Two-piece suits, about $85; shirts, $7—$12.

Fenwick of Hong Kong Ltd., First Floor Arcade, Hong Kong Hilton Hotel, Hong Kong
Self-measurement chart, fabric swatches, free.

Two-piece suits in English worsted, $91–$103.

Hawkes, 1 Savile Row, London W1X 1AF, England
Hawkes, unlike the other tailors in this section, has a department of Immediate Wear, in which they have "everything necessary to clothe the private individual for the public occasion." Besides lounge suits by Chester Barrie starting at $110, they sell sports jackets, shirts, socks, ties, and "all accessories for a well-dressed man."

H. Huntsman and Sons, 11 Savile Row, London W1X 2PJ, England ♡♡♡♡♡♡♡
Tour schedule, free.

A Huntsman representative tours America and Canada each spring with samples of cloth and models of "all types of riding coats, waistcoats, breeches, suits and evening dress wear." He visits thirteen American cities and two Canadian, measuring customers for suits which they will later pick up in London or which will be mailed to them. The Huntsman people feel that considering the workmanship, their prices are very reasonable, and even after duty is paid, compare more than favorably with American prices. Prices for a two-piece suit start at $315, and for a three-piece suit at $335.

James S. Lee and Co. Ltd., 101 Nathan Road, Kowloon, Hong Kong
Style leaflet, self-measurement chart, swatches, free. Prices in $.

Two-piece suits cost $44–$105, depending on fabric.

Henry Poole and Co., 10–12 Cork Street, London W1X 1PD, England ♡
Tour schedule, free.

Henry Poole were originally the first tailors established in Savile Row. Each spring and fall a director of the firm tours America with a large selection of new fabric swatches and takes customers' measurements. The measurements are sent back to Cork Street to be made up, and usually the customer comes over to London for a fitting. But suits can be completed without a fitting, in which case any necessary small adjustments can be made by certain American tailors at the expense of Henry Poole. Prices start at $245 for a three-piece suit.

William Yu, Room 112, Peninsula Hotel, Kowloon, Hong Kong
Style sheet, self-measurement chart, fabric swatches, free. Prices in $.

Two-piece suits in English worsted, $73–$77.

DRESSES, SWEATERS, ETC.

FOR WOMEN

Cleo, 3 Molesworth Street, Dublin, Ireland
Color leaflet, 25 cents. Prices in $.

Cleo sells flamboyant clothes based on traditional Irish styles to boutiques in America and also by mail. Aran knitting appears in all sorts of colors and shapes—as ponchos, full-length hostess skirts, knickerbockers, trouser suits and even as bedspreads. Bright crochet patterns and handwoven fabrics are used for skirts, vests, capes, hats and bags. And for evening wear there are colorful new versions of tinker's

67
Cleo Munster cloak in navy blue, maroon, green, purple or black wool. $86.18.
photo Bill Doyle

shawls, and the full length sixteenth-century hooded Munster cloak which used to be worn in southern Ireland. Most of the prices are under $25.

Colette Modes Ltd., 66 South Great George's Street, Dublin 2, Ireland
20-page color catalogue, free. Prices in $.

Ready-made clothes, sizes 12 to 18, in Donegal handwoven tweeds. Specific fabric samples can be sent on request. Most of the clothes are classic coats at around $49, but there are also a few other things—some dashing capes, and a trouser suit for $50. By chance, I met a regular Colette customer the other day who was very enthusiastic. She said she had just received the trouser suit and it looked terrific.

Cora Line, 17 Rue Duphot, Paris I, France
16-page color catalogues, free. Spring, fall.

The well-known French Rodier jersey dresses are available here and are much cheaper than in America. Prices vary, and dresses are about $39; coats in the $60 range. The clothes are fashionable but severe. The latest catalogue, as I write, has mainly long, skinny midis and the colors are plums, purples, browns and blacks.

Doreen, P.O. Box 6405, Kowloon, Hong Kong
Leaflet, free. Prices in $.

Beaded sweaters, $10–$18 each.

Highland Home Industries, 94 George Street, Edinburgh, Scotland
10-page brochure, free. Prices in $.

A beautifully organized nonprofit organization that encourages Scottish crafts. Their well-designed little brochure shows just a few attractive pieces for women. Shetland and Fair Isle sweaters, about $14 each; heavy Hebridean hand-knitted sweaters, $26; fully lined made-to-measure tweed skirts, $14.10. A mohair coat-stole, poncho, mittens and hat.

Home Industries Center, P.O. Box 82275, Mombasa, Kenya
12-page brochure, $1. Prices in $.

This center was started in 1964 by the National Christian Council of Kenya to train and employ "destitute" women, and encourage local handicrafts. Handicrafts well worth encouraging—the clear brochure shows five gorgeous dresses based on traditional styles and made in local fabrics. A couple of boldly patterned sleeveless dresses could have come from any stylish boutique, but others with wide-flowing sleeves look distinctly African. There's a dramatic Zanzibari hostess gown with big puffed sleeves and a beautiful design of lines and circles around the hem and down the front. All dresses are loose-fitting and come in small, medium and large. Also sisal shopping bags, beaded necklaces and some handsome beaded sandals. It is well worth getting together with friends to order from this firm, as orders for over $72 go for fantastically low wholesale rates; dresses, some fully lined, cost only about $6 each.

Lowe's Wear, P.O. Box 5718, Hong Kong
Beaded sweaters, color brochure, free; air-mail $1. Prices in $.

Double-knit dresses, color brochure free; air mail $1. Prices in $.

Beaded sweaters $13–$60 in lamb's wool, angora, cashmere. Plain three-piece double-knit woolen suits, $35–$45 including postage.

68
Highland Home Industries Hand-knitted in the outer Hebrides from home-grown wool and hand-spun yarn, a Shetland sweater with a Fair Isle yoke. Available with background in black, white, dark brown, navy, traditional beige or other colors. $15.10 to $17.70, according to size.

69
Highland Home Industries Mohair coat stole in coral, ruby, orchid, pink, flax blue, jade, turquoise, ice blue, oyster, French navy, black or white. $35.40.

70
Nikos and Takis White handwoven silk dress and coat, hand-embroidered in gold and silver metallic thread. About $175.

May Fashion House, P.O. Box 6162, Kowloon, Hong Kong
Knitwear, 16-page color brochure, $1. Prices in $.
Silk dresses, 16-page color brochure, $1. Prices in $.

Brilliantly colored silk dresses in classic styles, around $27; an evening coat in silk and wool worsted, $47. Silks by the yard, $5; brocades, $8; beaded trim by the yard, $5–$7. Knit dresses with jackets and pants suits, $25–$35, sizes 8–22.

Nikos and Takis, 10 Lisiou Street, Plaka, Athens, Greece
Brochure, $2. May, July.

Nikos and Takis, "foremost designers of Greece" according to their letterhead, design and make women's clothes in handwoven silk or mohair. I haven't seen a brochure, just photographs of some of their rather smart models. A black mohair set—trousers, skirt, blouse and cape edged with hand embroidery in gold—is $200; white silk tunic dresses edged with gold or silver embroidery, $150 and $175. Modernish gilded silver necklaces are also on sale for prices between $8 and $15.

Peter Saunders, Easton Grey, Malmesbury, Wiltshire, England ♡
18-page catalogue and fabric swatches, $1.50.

Peter Saunders makes good, casual clothes for country dwellers who don't like coming into town to "be jostled and elbowed to bits" before they find anything they like. In fact, the catalogue for this "Boutique in a Book" contains a poem about all the ghastly things that can happen to you if you make the foolish mistake of deserting shopping by mail to battle with traffic jams, inclement weather, crowds, and finally clothes that are the wrong size.

The Peter Saunders clothes, both ready-made and made-to-measure, are simple and look well cut. The colors are restrained—blue-grays, chalky greens, lavenders and corals—and are carefully co-ordinated so that you can buy a tweed skirt, about $17, match it to a poplin shirt, about $14, and a lamb's-wool cardigan, about $17. Separates, summer and winter dresses, coats, shoes and accessories are sold, and the catalogue is well illustrated and convenient.

Elsie Tu Ltd., 121 Chatham Road, Kowloon, Hong Kong
50-page brochure with some color, free. Prices in $.

Beaded and hand-embroidered sweaters from $12 to $30. Coats hand embroidered all over with wool, $30–$40.

FURS

C. Brandt, Postboks 938, 5001 Bergen, Norway ♡
Brandt writes: "We are already getting quite a lot of retail mail orders from the United States, and we are very interested to increase these mail orders.

"To give you some details of our firm, our main line is furs. We always carry a large stock of fur coats, jackets, stoles, capes and scarves of very different kind of furs. We have our own workroom with very clever furriers, and any special style can be made to order. For abroad we then usually make a canvas pattern of the style the customer wants and mail it to her for fitting.

"Besides furs of all kinds we have a men's store specially dealing in men's hats, like Borsalino, and other good-quality hats. Fur caps, fur hats, ties, gloves, and so on.

"And to give you an idea of the reputation of our firm, we have been By Appointment to the Dutch Queen since 1927. Before the First World War, we were By Appointment to the German Emperor Kaiser Wilhelm. Our firm was founded in 1852, and has ever since been in the family."

Cornelius Furs, 72 Castlereagh Street, Sydney, Australia 2001
Color leaflet and kangaroo-fur samples, free. Prices in $.

Kangaroo, Australian lamb, Australian fox, sueded sheepskin in coats and jackets—you choose your own fur, color, length and style. A sleek tailored midi-length kangaroo fur coat with leather trimming and buttons costs about $270. A horizontally worked Australian fox costs about the same. Also fur hats and bags at about $22. These are not shown in the catalogue, but photographs are sent on request.

Pels Backer, Kongens Gate 31, Oslo, Norway
No catalogue.

I suppose it is easier to buy a fur cape by mail than a fur coat. Pels Backer has a natural Norwegian selected blue-fox cape (which they say is their best seller) at about $200–$230. Besides saga mink coats, they have broadtail, beaver, ocelot, otter and mole, and also fur-lined coats. They say that if customers tell them exactly what they want by letter, Pels Backer will make an offer. They write: "We have the largest and most beautiful stock in ready-made furs here in Norway and possess our own five-story building in the shopping center of Oslo . . . the firm was established in 1856 and is now owned by Mr. Lars Backer, the grandson of the founder . . . American customers tell us they have to pay at least 30 percent more for the same goods after having paid the duty of 18½ percent."

J. A. Sistovaris and Sons, 14 Voulis Street, Athens, Greece ♡
18-page brochure, free. Prices in $.

Greece has a thriving fur industry and specializes in making coats out of fur scraps at reasonable prices. J. A. Sistovaris, the leading manufacturer, has a very good reputation. The brochure I have seen shows various fancy styles: a coat from tourmaline mink paws for $795, a coat from Persian lamb paws for $195, and mink capes from $125 up.

MATERNITY CLOTHES

Elegance Maternelle, Mail Order Department, 101 Marylebone High Street, London W.1, England
24-page brochure, free.

Maternity dresses, trouser suits, swimsuits and underwear for pregnant women. I have only seen the spring/summer catalogue, in which most dresses vary between $15 and $28. There is an Empire-line dance gown in Liberty voile with long full sleeves and a multicolored flower design for about $85, and the same style is available as a short cocktail dress for about $45.

For more maternity clothes, see Mothercare Ltd., under Children's Clothes in this section.

SHOES

The Small and Tall Shoe Shop, 71 York Street, London W.1, England
10-page leaflet, free.

Ladies' walking and fashion shoes, casuals, boots, slippers and sandals. Also tights, all in extra small and large sizes, and stockings in extra large sizes. Twenty-seven kinds of shoes, four kinds of sandals and one pair of slippers for women who have trouble finding their size in shoe shops. Styles are standard rather than fashionable. Prices start at $11 for leather shoes, and $9 for shoes of man-made material. Tights start at about $1.

71

72

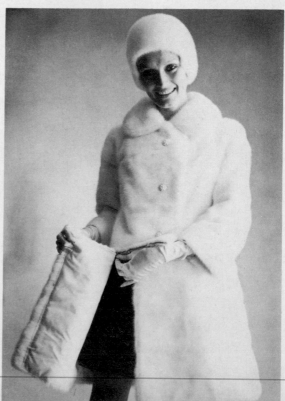

73

74

75

76

77

71
Cornelius Furs Australian fox coat. Maxi-length up to 54", $315 (length up to 40", $230).
photo Ian Morgan Pty Ltd

72
Pels Backer Natural Norwegian bluefox cap "Albatross." $200–$230.

73
Pels Backer Natural saga white mink coat, horizontally cut, "Piazza." $1,500–$1,700. Matching hat "Curia," $70–$80.

74
Clothkits Beach outfit in stretch toweling. The shorts double as swimming trunks, the elasticated sleeves stay above elbows for playing in the sand, and there is a hood for protection against the sun or wind. Styles change each season, but kits to make similar outfits are usually available for around $5 for ages up to eleven.
photo Alistair Creer

75
Clothkits A typical outfit. Kits to make similar clothes are usually available in gold on pink, turquoise on blue, purple on blue, or tan on natural needlecord.

76
Mothercare Ltd Machine-washable maternity dress, pink pattern on white background. Similar dresses are usually available for around $10.

77
Mothercare Ltd Bright red three-piece waterproof suit— dungarees, double-breasted raincoat and sou'wester, for children up to 40" tall. About $5.50.

59

78
Mothercare Ltd Blue and white suit to fit children up to
40″ tall. Similar outfits usually available for around $4.

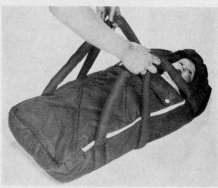

79
Mothercare Ltd Cocoon carrycot, fits into carriages so
that a baby can be moved from house to car or carriage
without being disturbed. About $12.

CHILDREN'S CLOTHES
Clothkits, 2 Mount Place, Lewes, Sussex, England
*12-page brochure with some color, 25 cents. March,
September.*

Clothkits was started by a housewife in her own home, and is
a great idea for people who want to keep their children
dressed in colorful and fashionable clothes without going
bankrupt. Clothes for children aged one to sixteen are screen-
printed directly onto the fabric and come ready to cut out and
sew up with all the necessary haberdashery and easy-to-
follow instructions.

No party clothes or Sunday best—everything is very casual—
denim for summer and needlecord for winter, but the styles
are the latest English eye-catchers and the colors are brilliant
mixtures of anything dazzling. In last winter's collection I
specially liked a flowery mini-skirt at $2.50; and a bush
jacket, $7, with trousers to match, $6—both in needlecord for
children up to the age of nine. In the 1971 summer collection
there were shirts, dresses, hot-pants with skirts, overalls and
bathing suits. All prices are within the $2–$12 range.

**Colts, 414 Richmond Road, East Twickenham, Middlesex,
England**
26-page catalogue, 50 cents. Spring, fall.

Trendy English and Continental clothes for boys aged five to
fifteen, possibly more popular with fashion-conscious boys
than with parents, as the prices are quite high. Shirts—scarlet,
brown or black French needlecord, $8–$10; tiny pink, yellow
or blue flowers on a white background, $6–$7; tie to match,
$1.75. Trousers—lightweight wool and polyester in pale olive,
brown or charcoal herringbone, $11.50; French flared jersey
trousers in petrel, coffee or black, $12–$16, flared Dutch
needlecord jeans in gold, navy, burgundy or black, $7.50–
$11. Also sweaters, very short shorts, suits and overcoats.

Incidentally, Colts deserves top marks for keeping
customers informed on basic aims and new plans. They even
send out questionnaires to find out what customers think of
the clothes *after* they have been worn.

**Gertrude Liechti, Storchengasse 13, 8001 Zurich,
Switzerland**
Gertrude Liechti stocks a whole range of children's clothes,
but says that the one with most appeal to American
customers is her Swiss dirndl. These dresses, in sizes for
ages one to ten, have white blouses and red skirts with
embroidered black velvet straps. Being 100 percent cotton,
they are machine-washable.

Mrs. Liechti has no catalogue, but here are the prices,
which include surface postage and insurance: ages one to
three, $15; four to six, $18; seven to ten, $20.

**Julie Loughnan, 18 Beauchamp Place, Knightsbridge,
London S.W.3, England**
Julie Loughnan makes the kind of classic English party
dresses that are almost unobtainable in America. Very pretty,
individually designed, hand-smocked dresses in Liberty lawn,
voile, etc., for children aged two to twelve cost from about $16
to $26. Enthusiastically recommended by a friend of mine.

**Mothercare Ltd., Cherry Tree Road, Watford WD25SH,
England**
180-page color catalogue, free. Spring, fall.

A terrific chain of over a hundred stores selling everything for
mothers, babies and children up to the age of five—at lowest
possible prices. I can't think of any other shop as efficiently

and thoroughly geared to mothers and babies. Anyone who is about to have a baby or who has just had one should look at this catalogue.

Starting with pregnancy, you can get attractive maternity dresses for $12. In the catalogue I looked at there was a sleeveless navy-blue nylon lace cocktail dress for $13, and a very smart midi-length red coat-dress for $18. Layette needs are listed, and besides everything else, Mothercare sells superabsorbent English terry-cloth diapers, $6.60 a dozen. There are wool blankets, and a sling for $2.20 for carrying babies from three months on. Baby dresses and shoes, and handsome clothes for slightly older children. Red-and-navy quilted snowsuits from $8. English Wellington boots for $1.50 and suede boots for $4.50. (There is a foot-measuring chart in the catalogue.)

Pollyanna by Post, 660 Fulham Road, London S.W.6, England
6-page color brochure, free. August and February.

A smallish English organization that designs, manufactures and sells "better designed, more amusing" children's clothes and likes to think they have done for this age group what Mary Quant and Carnaby Street did for adult clothes. In fact the clothes, though very "now," are not revolutionary. They *are* well designed and co-ordinated—colors match and tops look good with bottoms. A small collection of medium-priced dresses, skirts, trousers and shirts (no coats) is put out each spring and fall. Size is determined by the height of the child. In the August 1971 brochure, the peasant look is rampant for girls: a printed calico dress with cutaway armholes and flounced hem costs $6.50; "Pollygypsie," a Terylene (polyester and cotton) smocked blouse with a printed voile midi-skirt in chocolate and blue costs $10–$12 depending on size. For boys, slim-cut corduroy jeans with flared bottoms in dusty pink, dusty blue or beige cost $6.50 to $8 according to size. A "grandfather vest" T-shirt in yellow, pink or beige knitted cotton, $2.50. I bought my daughters some flared trousers here last year and they wore (and washed) beautifully.

Rowes of Bond Street, 120 New Bond Street, London W1Y 0BN, England ♡
Self-measurement chart, free.

I went to look at Rowes clothes at the Hotel Pierre in January and saw what must have been a typical Rowes customer—reed-thin and stunningly dressed, choosing some clothes for her children that their grandmother had forgotten in London (understandably, as the grandmother annually buys complete wardrobes for ten children). Rowes sells its classic English clothes and shoes to the international set, who pass them around between siblings and cousins. Dresses tend to be flowered or hand-smocked ($28 and up). Coats and boys' clothes are very traditional ($60 and up), perhaps the best known being the Rowes coat, or the coat now known as the John-John coat worn by John Kennedy, Jr., and widely copied by other manufacturers. Clothes can be bought in London or Paris, otherwise write to Rowes with your requirements, and they will reply with self-measurement forms drawing of models you might be interested in, fabric swatches and prices. If you prefer to look at the actual clothes, Mr. Kenneth Barnett comes to New York, Washington, Middleburg, Philadelphia, Boston and Chicago in January and June, takes measurements and orders. Summer clothes are ordered in January and winter clothes in June, and if you want to choose for a year or two ahead (styles barely change), orders can be taken and measurement charts sent at the appropriate time.

George Sim Mfg. Co., 9 Carnarvon Road, Kowloon, Hong Kong
12-page leaflet, free. Prices in $.

Little girls' embroidered polyester-and-cotton dresses about $4; women's embroidered polyester-and-cotton blouses, $5.

Strength and Co. Ltd., 40 Cameron Road, Kowloon, Hong Kong
30-page brochure, fabric samples, free. Prices in $.

Very inexpensive nylon rainwear for adults and children. Baby's snowsuit, $5; children's lined and cotton-filled jackets, $4. Colorful sleeping bags, around $11.

Yee Cheong and Co., 69 Granville Road, Kowloon, Hong Kong
32-page brochure, free. Prices in $.

Very inexpensive cotton-and-polyester hand-smocked and embroidered baby clothes and dresses for girls up to the age of ten shown in an extremely efficient brochure; prices are from $2 to $5. Five different dresses for teen-agers, $9 each. Postage is about $1.50 per dress for air mail; $2 for any quantity by surface mail.

CIGARETTE CARDS

London Cigarette Card Company Ltd., Cambridge House, 34 Wellesley Road, Chiswick, London W.4, England
Catalogue and handbook Part II dealing with all known cigarette cards issued in the United Kingdom between 1918 and 1940, numbered and autographed edition, $5.85.
Mini abridged catalogue, 25 cents.

Apparently cigarette cards originated in America (the earliest known card is in the Metropolitan Museum, New York). However, they were dropped here early in the century, while they grew more popular in England. Anyway, the London Cigarette Card Company says that it is the largest and most reputable dealer in cartophilic items in the world. Besides catalogues they put out a friendly magazine, *Cigarette Card News*, for $3 a year. The issue I looked at had, among other more serious articles, a piece describing kinds of cigarette-card collectors, including the swopper, the fanatic, the specialist (mortal enemy of No. 5, who is only interested in pretty pictures), the perfectionist, and Mr. Average Collector, whose "cards are not particularly immaculate—neither are they grubby," and who sorts his cards only when he feels like it. In the post-1940 list, prices range from about 25 cents to $1.20, and it covers a fascinating variety of subjects from Batman to Budgrigars.

COINS

Spink and Son Ltd., 5–7 King Street, St. James's, London S.W.1, England ♛♕
Numismatic Circular, twelve volumes, one year's subscription, $13.
Modern Coins and Banknotes, five journals a year, $6.50.

Spink's, a three-hundred-year-old family firm, is not only mentioned in *The Lost World*, by Sir Arthur Conan Doyle, but they were delighted and amused to find their name dropped by "M" in a James Bond novel: "As Spink and the British Museum agree . . ."

They send their two illustrated journals by air. *Numismatic Circular* has a catalogue of Greek, Roman, Byzantine, English and foreign coins, war medals and books offered for sale, and it also has articles, reviews, news and correspondence of interest to collectors.

Modern Coins and Banknotes is more of a catalogue of Spink's modern coins and bank notes of all periods—the issue that I saw also had three short articles.

MATCHBOX LABELS

H. S. Labels, 48 Enfield Road, Brentford, Middlesex, England
Price list, free.

H. S. Labels has old and modern matchbox labels from all over the world, and possess one of the two oldest labels known to exist. They sell mixed selections by nationality, as well as sets by subject matter: forty prehistoric animals from Czechoslovakia, about 50 cents; forty castles from Spain, about $1; twelve signs of the zodiac from Portugal, 20 cents; ten space travel from Yugoslavia, about 35 cents; and many others.

MODEL AIRPLANES

Aero Nautical Models, 39 Parkway, Camden Town, London N.W.1, England
A very wide range of the best aircraft- and boat-modeling goods from England and all over the world. Sweden, Italy, Japan, and especially Germany, Austria and France are main sources of supply for aircraft, boats and engines, every sort of kit and all the materials needed. They are official agents for most well-known brands with a knowledgeable staff, who, when asked, likes to give advice and solve problems. Their letterhead encouragingly says: "Phone, write, or call, the SERVICE is the same for ALL."

Henry J. Nicholls and Son Ltd., 308 Holloway Road, London N.7, England
Model aircraft—mainly ones that are radio controlled. They import from every European country and have had a mail-order department for over twenty years.

Spielzeug-Rasch, Gerhart-Hauptmann-Platz 1, Hamburg 1, Germany
Toy catalogues in German, free.
200-page model catalogue in German, $1.75.

Spielzeug-Rasch's illustrated special models catalogue is extremely imposing, and a must, I would think, for anyone interested in model planes or ships. Modern planes and famous old ships (the *Santa Maria*) are shown, as well as all sorts of engines and spare parts, in two-hundred professional-looking pages, but you do need a translator unless you are such an expert on models that you can deduce what the text says.

MODEL RAILROADS

Cherry's Ltd., 62 Sheen Road, Richmond, Surrey, England
Price list, 25 cents. Prices in $.

Cherry's, which has become known and thoroughly visited by American model railway buffs, specializes in very high-class, second-hand working steam engines of all types, most of them not obtainable in America. Their list gives a detailed description of each model, including marine models, traction engines, locomotives, steam plants, boilers, vertical engines, horizontal engines, miscellaneous combustion engines, Stuart Turner (used, completed models and also new products), useful accessories and pressure gauges. And "special items" which, in the catalogue I looked at, were a generating plant, $156; a nineteenth-century, six-pounder field gun, $84; and a working steam-driven replica of a 2-2-0 Birmingham Dribbler, $60.

Hamblings Ltd., 29 Cecil Court, Charing Cross Road, London W.C.2, England
132-page catalogue, 50 cents.

The largest and oldest established "oo" specialists, and probably the only firm in Great Britain that manufactures, wholesales and retails exclusively model railroad products, parts and accessories. They stock British prototypes which are almost impossible to buy in America; although, strangely enough, there is a demand. Anyway, any model railway lover should be deliriously happy here, for there are the most detailed and perfect kits and parts of every kind on which an infinite amount of care can be taken (how about a scale lattice girder section, "Just the thing for those who enjoy soldering"), though lazier enthusiasts can buy a completely painted train and track. There are scenic models and accessories for building, about 30 cents each card. Signal boxes, loco coaling stages and entire villages can be built, complete with half-timbered or Georgian houses, modern bungalows, blocks of flats, fire stations, schools, libraries and churches. In fact, these villages and their landscape backgrounds might inspire people who don't have model railways. Tools and books and magazines about model railroads are also listed.

80
Spink and Son Ltd Edward III gold noble (circa 1363–1369).

81
H. S. Labels *Reading from top to bottom:* Matchbox labels from Austria; England (issued 1934); Japan (issued 1914); Belgium; England; England (issued 1934).

82
Kendal Playing Card Sales "America" court cards show pre-Columbian art; "Comedia," a modern Swedish pack; pack designed for Simpson's of Piccadilly.
photo Kevin Kirby

MODEL SHIPS

Egon Wiedling, Theatinerstrasse 13, 8 Munich 2, Germany
Price list, free.

Toy-shop owner and collector of model ships himself, Egon Wiedling has a list of ships from many countries in 1:1250 and 1:1200 scale. He stocks Delphin, Hansa, Mercator, Atlantic, Mercury, Navis, Copy, Neptun, Star, Trident, Triang and Wiking.

See also Spielzeug-Rasch (above).

PLAYING CARDS

Kendal Playing Card Sales, 3 Oakbank House, Skelsmergh, Kendal, Westmorland, England
Regular list and Once Only list, free. Prices in $.

Two playing-card collectors sell by mail new playing cards from various countries. Some of the packs sound fascinating even for noncollectors. From Spain there is a double pack for about $3, *Discoverers and Explorers of the Americas,* with a named portrait on every card, Columbus' ships on the backs and an explanatory booklet. From France, *Versailles* ($2.65 for a single pack) shows the courts of kings, queens and statesmen associated with Versailles, and the aces show buildings in the Versailles gardens. Also from France, *Napoleon* ($8 for a double pack produced for the bicentenary of his birth) with members of the Bonaparte family on the court cards and the insignia of various orders on the aces. Or you can be put on waiting lists for cards from Iceland—some have figures from Icelandic mythology on every card, with mythological sea creatures on the back ($2.65); others have characters from the Icelandic sagas on the court cards. There are also magician's packs (seven extra cards), solitaire packs, and eleven different kinds of tarot cards including the *Ancien Tarot de Marseille,* the most famous of all. Books about cards, too.

STAMPS

Stanley Gibbons Ltd., 391 Strand, London W.C.2, England
Price list, free.

World-famous for their stamps and authoritative catalogues, they will send lists of albums, stamp catalogues, accessories, and books that are available. Catalogues vary in price from about $1.50 for *United States and Possessions* to about $5.50 for *British Commonwealth.*

TOY SOLDIERS

Joseph Kober, Graben 14–15, A 1010 Vienna, Austria
Price list in German, free.

Using turn-of-the-century molds, this toy shop in the middle of Vienna hand-makes the military units of the Austro-Hungarian Empire and civilians of the time. The figures are made out of tin and lead and are hand-painted. Although the list is in German, most of it consists of names, so it isn't too hard to figure out that a "*Trompeter*" in the "*Gardetruppe*" costs about $2.25 as do "*Husaren,*" "*Dragoner*" and "*Ulanen*" cavalry officers, and Kaiser Franz Josef I in "*Galauniform.*" A set of "*Infanterie im Marsch—Offizier, Fahne, Trompeter, Trommler und 10 Mann*" costs about $16—just over $1 each.

James E. Luck, 34 High Street, Southgate, London N.14, England
Military book catalogue planned.

They specialize in new military books, especially those about uniforms and toy soldiers. And they also have a large collection of the old type of model soldiers, toy soldiers and flats. Collectors should write and tell them what they would like.

65

Phillips Son and Neale, Blenstock House, 7 Blenheim Street, New Bond Street, London W1Y OAS, England
Two auction catalogues per year. $2.50 annual subscription.

This well-known London auction house holds two auctions a year of lead toy soldiers and say they have many American customers who bid by mail.

WEAPONS

Inter Antikva AB, Utställning, Renstiernasgatan 22, 116 31 Stockholm 4, Sweden
32-page catalogue in Swedish, $1. Prices in $.

Sweden's largest weapons shop sells antique and reproduction weapons by mail. The reproductions are imported from Germany, England, Italy and Spain, as the Swedes only go in for collecting, not manufacturing. A couple of gorgeous shields, sporting highly dramatic chariot battles ($40 each). Also decorative, oddly shaped Pakistani daggers, Spanish and Italian swords, pistols (for which import licenses are needed), handcuffs, night sticks and military uniforms— mainly Nazi and Japanese, for some reason.

WINE LABELS

Wyatt Druid, 5 St. James's Street, London S.W.1, England
Price list and photographs, free.

Apparently decanter labels were all the rage from 1730 until 1860, when they were replaced by paper labels on wine bottles. During that time the great silversmiths made beautiful labels, very hard to find and mostly already being tucked away in collections. Wyatt Druid has started reproducing some of these labels by famous Georgian silversmiths such as Hester Bateman, Paul Storr, Benjamin Smith and Edward Farrell. At the moment there are sixteen hallmarked sets, and prices for each individual label start at about $70 for sterling silver and $184 for 18-carat gold. Labels come packed in black leather presentation boxes lined with purple velvet, and so they should at those prices.

83
Joseph Kober Model of Franz Josef I. Just over $2.

ENGLAND

W. Bill Ltd., Mail Order Dept., 40 South Molton Lane, London W1Y 1AT, England
General catalogue, free; swatches, free. Prices in $.

W. Bill has a large mail-order service to America. They sell clothes, knitwear and also good fabrics for clothes. Harris tweed from $3.75 per yard; Shetland and Irish tweeds from $5; worsteds from $11; cashmeres from $23; and many others.

Hunt and Winterbotham Ltd., 4 Old Bond Street, London W.1, England
Swatches free. Prices in $.

Hunt and Winterbotham, not very modestly, claims to make the "world's finest cloth." Still, the company is very old (over five hundred years) and very well thought of, and stocks over six thousand wool patterns, including men's light and heavy suiting, Harris tweeds, Shetlands, gabardines, flannels, cashmere and vicuna. Also tweeds and woolens for ladies, and Pringle and Braemar sweaters.

Liberty and Co. Ltd., 210–220 Regent Street, London W1E 5LE, England
Swatches free, price lists (no illustrations). Spring and fall.

Liberty is one of London's most imaginatively stocked department stores, but it is best known for magnificent fabrics, especially their own dress-weight printed cotton lawns and silks. They have what they call an "extremely large and efficient" mail-order service in dress and upholstery fabrics and send out tiny swatch books on request. If customers want larger samples they are charged $1.30, which is refunded when the sample is returned. Fabrics $1.30–$8 per yard.

Redpath Campbell and Partners Ltd., Cheapside, Stroud, Gloucestershire, England
8-page leaflet and swatches, 25 cents surface mail, 65 cents air mail.

One of the very few firms that sells suede and leather in small-enough quantities for the home dressmaker, Redpath Campbell has a helpful leaflet/price list for people who have never sewn leather before (which must be most of their customers), describing the different leathers, what they are best used for, and clear hints on how to sew each type. They tell you how to adapt ordinary patterns for use with leather, and they also sell their own patterns for a skirt and a short or long waistcoat. Eighteen colors in leather and suede, sheepskin and chamois, a fashion material which hangs like wool and looks like suede. Enough leather for a mini-skirt costs about $8; a larger skirt up to midi-length, $16. You can also buy cut suede and leather patches to make the patchwork skirts and coats (or bags and cushions) that are so incredibly expensive ready-made.

The Scotch House, Knightsbridge, London S.W.1, England
Bute Tweed swatches, free.

Bute Tweeds is the trade name of tweeds made on the Isle of Bute, Scotland. The original mill was one of the oldest in Scotland, but new looms have been installed and the tweeds have been redesigned. They are now stunning high-fashion fabrics that have been used by Bonnie Cashin, Bill Blass, Balenciaga and Nina Ricci, and they are stocked in a few American stores. Write to the Scotch House and tell them what weight, pattern and color you are interested in, and they will send you four samples.

84
Central Cottage Industries Emporium Crewel-embroidered fabric from Kashmir, hook woolen embroidery on a cotton base, $5.10 a yard. Also available as drapes.

Coat-weight tweeds come in three main patterns: checks, herringbone, or a woven stripe using mohair. One color usually predominates, e.g., the fabric can be a blend of browns, blues, lilacs, purples or reds. To match the coat weights there are dress-weight fabrics in plain colors. There is also a medium-weight printed wool in a sort of Persian tapestry design that is popular for evening skirts. It comes in predominantly turquoise, dark red, bright red or gold. Prices mostly $2.50 to $7 per yard.

FRANCE

Rodin, 36 Champs-Elysées, Paris VIII, France
Swatches, free.

This very large fabric shop on the Champs-Elysées is well known to Americans and can sell *haute couture* silks and wools as well as upholstery fabrics by mail to America. However, their choice is so wide that you have to be very specific in describing what you want, and prices are quite high.

INDIA

Central Cottage Industries Emporium, Janpath, New Delhi 1, India
22-page color catalogue, $1.50; swatches, free.

The catalogue has some color photographs of the really unusual fabrics gathered from all over India at this government-sponsored handicrafts shop. For furniture: cottons, raw silks and crewel embroideries from $3 to $7 per meter. For dresses; hand-blocked cottons and silks costing up to $5 a meter, and Banaras silk with silver or gold motifs, $5 – $7.

IRELAND

Brown Thomas and Co. Ltd., Grafton Street, Dublin 2, Ireland
38-page general catalogue, 50 cents, prices in $.
Linen sample card, free. Prices in $.

Brown Thomas sells church, table, bed and dress linen by the yard in various widths and weights. The dress linen comes in shell green, primrose, eggshell, peach, pink, beige, gray, blue, tan, coral, lilac, apple green, red, brown, navy, charcoal, black, and white. A 36"-wide fabric is $2.50 per yard. Also Irish tweeds.

Kevin and Howlin Ltd., Nassau Street, Dublin 2, Ireland
Swatches, free.

Handwoven Donegal tweeds in 29" width cost only $4 a yard here. Designs are very sober and classic: misty blues and earthy browns in checks and herringbones and traditional Donegals.

SCOTLAND

Mairi Macintyre, Fort William, Inverness-Shire, Scotland
Color cards, $2; refundable at first purchase.

Mairi Macintyre produces its own beautiful tweeds by the yard in colors with names like "grouse" and "pheasant"; also knitwear and knitting yarns specially dyed to match.

THAILAND

The Thai Silk Company, GPO Box 906, Bangkok, Thailand
Price list and swatches, free. Prices in $.

Gorgeous Thai silks are some of the most astounding bargains I have seen. Iridescent, stylized flower designs, checks and solid colors are all magnificent; if you can find them in America, they cost several times as much. Upholstery-weight cotton, $1.50 a yard; silk, $4 – $8 a yard, depending on weight. Prices of the fabrics made up: men's ties in classic shape, $2.25; in last year's narrow shape with square ends, $2; in *this* year's superwide 5" shape, $3.25; cummerbund, $4.50, and matching bow tie, $5.50; sports shirt, $11; neck scarf, $1.50; 16" by 16" cushion cover, $5; eight cocktail napkins, $3, and a luncheon set of eight place mats and eight napkins, $20.

I should add that air mail from Thailand is expensive and parcels by sea take two months, so to save as much money as possible, order way ahead of time — in September for Christmas presents.

For more fabrics, see the stores in the General section.

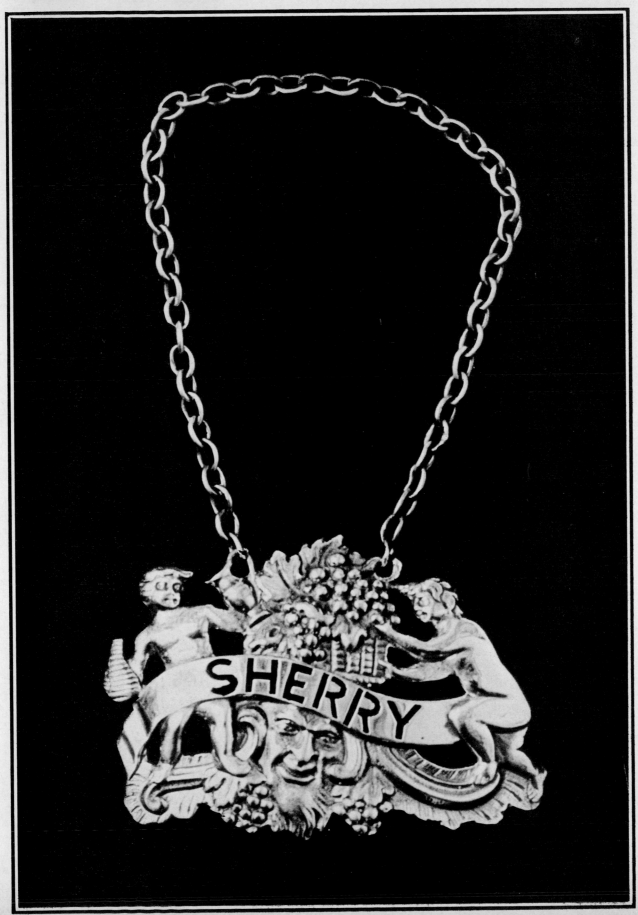

A. Abdullah and Sons, 2/3 Helmet Court, Wormwood Street, London E.C.2, England
Price list, free.

I couldn't find anyone in India organized to send spices to needy cooks, but here is a shop in London bursting with ajwan, kokum, tamarind, bhindi, dahls and poppadums. Not only that, but also cardamom, coriander, cumin, and spices used in other countries. All Abdullah and Sons asks is that you remember to say whether you want your spices ground or whole.

Mark Austin, 169 Kingston Road, Wimbledon, London S.W.19, England
Catalogue, free. Prices in $.

Mark Austin's is quite used to mailing parcels to America. An efficient catalogue gives complete descriptions of the superior teas and food this firm specializes in sending by mail. In lithographed tea caddies you can get pure Ceylon, Darjeeling, Assam, Keemum and Lapsang Souchong for about $3.95 a pound (all prices include postage) or even less if you buy in quantity. Jackson's teas are here (they were the first to blend Earl Grey), Floris' handmade chocolates and glacéed fruits, marzipan walnuts, peppermint creams and chocolate ginger, Peak and Frean cookies and Florentines, spekalews, almond petits fours lusciously described ("Honest pure almond macaroons, large size, made as they should be only from ground almond, sugar, and egg whites"). Christmas puddings with pretensions (not to be confused with mass-produced puddings) and rich fruit cakes.

Buderim Ginger Factory, Buderim 4556, Queensland, Australia
Hamper price list, free.

Australia's only ginger factory is visited by thousands of ginger-loving tourists a week, who shop at the ginger shop and eat at the ginger bar—ice cream with ginger topping, and hot scones with cream and ginger marmalade. Ginger connoisseurs in other countries can send for ginger in every shape and form, from one-pound presentation gifts of crystallized ginger for about $3.25, including postage, to large hampers that sound a bit excessive. One costs about $10, including postage, and contains crystallized ginger, young stem ginger, ginger marmalade, ginger topping, ginger date-nut spread, ginger in syrup, and rosella and strawberry preserves. It comes, like the other hampers, with a recipe booklet that tells you what to do with it all—"new ideas for *every* meal," the brochure hopefully announces.

Charbonnel et Walker, 31 Old Bond Street, London W.1, England ♥
18-page color brochure, free; 25 cents air mail. September.

A posh little shop in Old Bond Street selling chocolates in lacy, velvety, flowery boxes—most suitable for a romantic gesture. The brochure says these chocolates are a compliment to the discriminating taste of both sender and recipient. Besides the elaborate boxes (some of which are designed to be used afterward for tissues or cigarettes) there are two gratifying services: one is foil-covered chocolates with letters on top that can be used to spell out a message—the message can be as banal as "Thanks for a Lovely Weekend" or as interesting a quotation or private allusion as you can make—provided you can be brief. The other service is that centers are numbered so you can choose your own favorites (and avoid whatever you don't like). In my case, I think soft centers are too perfumed at Charbonnel et Walker and advise nuts, etc. Prices start at about $5 a pound. As well as chocolates, you can buy Marzipan Amandé in the Lubeck

85
Mark Austin These two caddies are part of a 3-lb. assortment which consists of ½ lb. each of Choice Assam, London Blend, Ceylon, Darjeeling, Indian and Keemum in six decorated caddies. $11.85, including postage.

86
Confiserie an der Pferdeschwemme Pistachio-marzipan, hazel-nougat chocolate-covered "Mozartkugeln." Packed in a box decorated with an old engraving of Salzburg.

tradition, Marzipan Gingembre, marzipan with assorted nuts, crystallized peppermint creams, crystallized ginger, glacéed pineapple, marron glacé, burnt or sugared almonds, etc.

Chocolaterie International, Damrack 65, Amsterdam, Holland
Price list, free. Prices in $.

This firm sends boxes of delicious Ringers full-strength liqueur chocolates in wooden export boxes (at the moment 200 grams, $5, including surface postage). It is illegal to import these into America (though a friend of mine did it for years until I told her she was breaking the law). They can, however, be sent to friends in other, luckier countries.

Confiserie an der Pferdeschwemme, Sigmundsplatz 11, 5020 Salzburg, Austria
Price list, free. Prices in $.

Salzburger Mozartkugeln are filled with pistachio marzipan and hazelnut nougat and coated with chocolate in the form of a ball. I can happily report, having received a free sample, that they are *very* rich and *very* delicious. Each one is wrapped in silver foil with a rather blurred picture of Mozart on it and packed in a box which shows an old engraving of Salzburg and is tied with a ribbon with the colors of the Austrian flag. They cost, including surface postage (it takes about three weeks), $4.55 for a mini package (15 pieces); $8.50 for maxi (32 pieces). A suitable present for a musical gourmet or a greedy music lover.

Christie, Manson and Woods (U.S.A.), 867 Madison Avenue, New York, N.Y. 10021
Catalogue subscription list, free. Prices in $.

Sotheby and Co., P.O. Box 2AA, 34—35 New Bond Street, London W1A 2AA, England
Catalogue subscription list, free. Prices in $.

Both these illustrious auction houses have sales of all kinds of fine wines usually unavailable in America, which you can bid for by mail. Subscribe to a season's worth of catalogues, roughly October to July, which will tell you what is being offered. When you receive each catalogue, you can ask the house what their estimate of the bids is, then send in your own bid. You can also subscribe to lists that arrive after the auctions which tell you what the wines actually fetched. Friends of mine who have bought wines from Christie's (they sell more than Sotheby's) tell me they used to make fairly low bids and were quite often lucky, but prices are going up and low bids aren't as rewarding any more. The lowest going price in a March 1971 price list for claret and white Bordeaux which I looked at was $24 for three dozen bottles of 1957 Château Trottevieille *premier grand cru*, Saint-Emilion. About the most expensive lot was a mixed one of a dozen bottles of 1955 Château Latour and 1959 Château Margaux that went for $120.

But check whether you are allowed to import your own wine into your state, as this is illegal in some states. There are no formalities in the others, just customs duty and state taxes to pay.

De Franse Kaasmakers, 192 Marnixstraat, Amsterdam, Holland

A good bottle of wine without cheese is like a rendezvous without a woman, says the De Franse Kassmakers letterhead. If these possibilities sound horribly unappetizing, you can at least send for a cheese. Four pounds of uncut Edam can be safely sent by boat (about five weeks) to the United States for $6; eight pounds of Farmer's Baby Gouda for about $11 at the time of writing, though prices will probably increase.

Fauchon, 26 Place de la Madeleine, Paris VIII, France
50-page general catalogue in French, free.
Export leaflet, free. Prices in $.

Fauchon is France's Fortnum's (see below) with the difference that when in 1970 Maoist students looted Fauchon and distributed their goodies to the poor, Fauchon refused to prosecute. When Emily Pankhurst and the suffragettes smashed Fortnum's windows, Fortnum's merely sent a hamper of delicacies to sustain them in prison.

The general catalogue austerely and simply lists the many foods that they import and export, some of which will be no great treat to Americans—"Rice Krispi" and "Coco Pops," for instance. However, everything is neatly divided into categories and countries (Congo, Malaisie, Mexique, Indonésie), so it easy to find things that one could hardly find anywhere else: Coffret Safari: (Tigre-Eléphant-Serpent) and Nopalitos Finos (Feuilles de Cactus en escabèche).

The little export leaflet is more useful, as it simply lists the goods most popular with American mail-order customers. Ten kinds of goose liver from $12 for 7 oz.; truffles from $1.70 for ½ oz.; glazed chestnuts, $5.15 for 14 oz.; currant preserves; French tuna fish; French sardines; biscuits; herbs (these eighteen times cheaper than in my local supermarket— though, presumably, that isn't the reason people buy them from France); white peaches; French asparagus; mustards; snails; dried mushrooms; cheeses (Munster, Camembert, Brie, each $1.20 for 8 oz.); and, of course, patés (hare, thrush, baby wild boar, deer, pheasant, partridge, blackbird, and lark), each $1.50 for 4½ oz.

R. W. Forsyth, Food Hall, 3 St. Andrew Square, Edinburgh EH2 2BG, Scotland
Christmas list, free.

Forsyth's, the Edinburgh department store, has lower-priced delectable local foods useful for small presents. Cheeses in earthenware jars, honeys and preserves in china pots, stem ginger (costing $3.30, half as much as at Fortnum's), rum-and-brandy-flavored mincemeat, Scottish shortbread, Bendick's mint crisps and bittermints, Christmas puddings, and completely iced and decorated Christmas cakes.

Fortnum and Mason, Piccadilly, London W1A 1ER, England ♔
40-page color Christmas catalogue, free. August.
Wine and food list, free. Around February.

Started in 1707 by Hugh Mason and William Fortnum (royal footman with excellent connections at the palace), Fortnum's have purveyed food to royalty and top people ever since. They are thoroughly experienced in mail order to Englishmen abroad, officers in the Napoleonic wars would rely on their hams, tongues, butter and cheese, and write desperately: "Candles are articles dreadfully in request and you have sent none"; "No news yet of your hams, which I must regret, for my housekeeping is now ruinous." In the Crimea, officers wrote and begged Fortnum's to stop stenciling their name on crates as it led to an "undue leakage of luxuries during the voyage." Queen Victoria sent Florence Nightingale crates of concentrated beef tea through Fortnum's; and Charles Dickens, describing a Derby day, wrote about their famous hampers: "If I were on the turf and had a horse to enter for the Derby, I would call that horse Fortnum and Mason, convinced that with that name he would beat the field. Public Opinion would bring him in somehow. Look where I will—in some connection with the carriages—made fast upon the top, or occupying the box, or peeping out of a window, I see Fortnum and Mason. And now, Heavens! all the hampers fly wide open and the green Downs burst into a blossom of lobster salad."

Now Fortnum's has expanded into a small department store, and the lavish, sybaritic Christmas catalogue has a little of the best of everything. The food pages are magnificent, with full-color photographs of caviar and paté, English and Scottish cheeses, salmon, nuts, desert fruits, and crystallized fruits prepared exclusively in France, ginger and honey, handmade chocolates, and of course, the hampers—famous as Christmas gifts complete with champagne and cigars.

And if you are looking for presents and have money to fling carelessly away, this is a place to buy even more things for those people who have everything, provided they have a taste for luxury. This is the place for silver—leaf-shaped ashtrays, fish-shaped peppermills, for old-fashioned rocking horses, black-velvet suits, and eighteenth-century cushions. But the Fortnum's label is costly and identical articles cost less in any other English shop. Probably the only bargain in this store is the super scale electric Blower Bentley car, which can be driven by child or parent. It costs around $700 here and $1,500 in a New York toy store.

The House of Floris, 39 Brewer Street, London W1R 4BE, England ♔♔
Price list, free.

This famous chocolate shop has a not very descriptive price list which seems to assume that you are an old customer responding like a Pavlovian dog to their call. However, if you are prepared to throw caution to the winds and send them $3.25 (plus postage) for one pound of "hard and nutty" or the same amount for "soft," I am sure you won't be disappointed. The chocolates are handmade from traditional recipes gathered throughout the Continent of Europe by a firm that likes to think it is one of the few who have "steadfastly ignored the march of so-called progress."

M. M. Poonjiaji and Co., 42 First Marine Street, Bombay 2, India
For $12, M. M. Poonjiaji will mail twelve bottles or cans of their Sweet Sliced Mango Chutney, Hot Mango Chutney, Major Grey's Mango Chutney, Sliced Mango Pickle, Lime Pickle, Combination Pickle, or Curry, in powder or paste—whichever you choose—by registered parcel post.

Ritchie Bros., 37 Watergate, Rothesay, Bute, Scotland
A family firm on the Isle of Bute that has been air-mailing their own bland, cured, smoked salmon to fastidious American gastronomes since a mention in the *New York Times*. Mr. Ritchie sent me a letter from a grateful lady in New York saying that the salmon is always of excellent quality and she keeps it refrigerated for three to four weeks with no problem at all. She also says that the speediest delivery took eight days after she wrote and the slowest took three and a half weeks (for a friend in Florida), but it was ordered in mid-December.

A two-pound side of salmon will probably cost $18, including postage, by the time this book appears, but if it costs less, Ritchie will send a little more salmon.

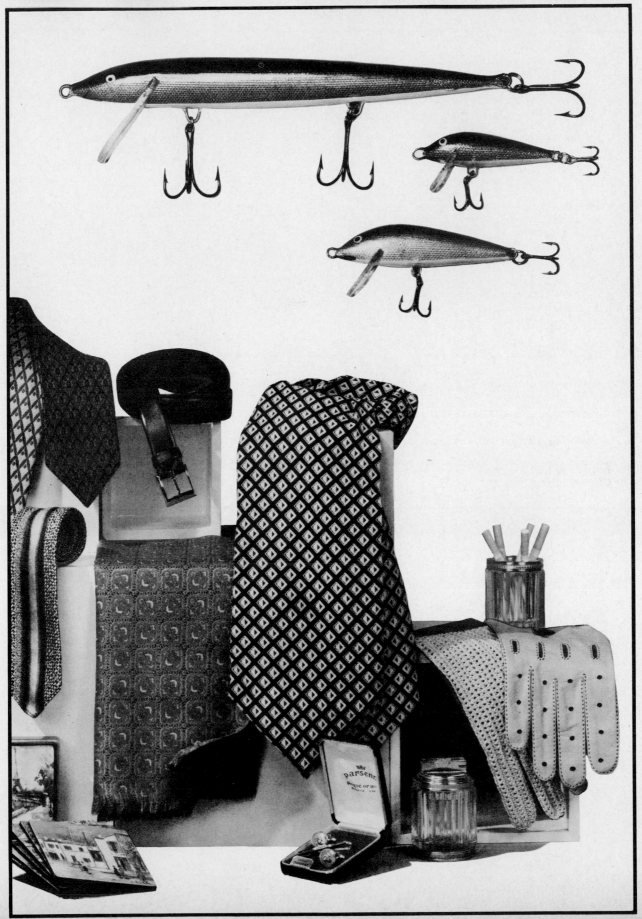

This is the section for real mail-order maniacs, the people who read the Sears, Roebuck catalogue in their bath, and send away for anything as long as it is new and out of the ordinary. People who aren't looking for anything special will have lots to mull over in the large catalogues from the big stores and mail-order firms in this section where almost everything looks just slightly different from the things you see in America.

But this is also a useful section for inexpensive basics, more clothes are illustrated in full color in these catalogues than anywhere else, more shoes, raincoats, fabrics, pots and pans, lamps. And if you are looking for something special from a certain country that isn't in any of the other sections, it might be here.

CZECHOSLOVAKIA

Tuzex, Export Department, Rytirska 13, Prague 1, Czechoslovakia
General catalogue, free. Prices in $.
Leaflets on Bohemian garnets and glass, free.

Czechoslovakia's Foreign Trade Corporation runs a series of twenty stores throughout Czechoslovakia, as well as an efficient twelve-year-old mail-order and export business selling tax- and duty-free goods, both domestic and other countries'. These shops cover a wider range than any other shop in this book—prefabricated weekend cottages, food, cigars, cars, electrical appliances, clothes, fabrics, etc,—but the general catalogue suffers from the ghastly defect of not being illustrated. So, tempting as low-priced clothes sound—silk and cashmere scarves, $1.25 and $2.30; Italian leather shoes, $5–$8; men's shirts, "fashionable collars and design," $2–$3,—most listings are useless for mail-order shoppers. However, you can send for illustrations of Czechoslovakia's most famous products: Bohemian garnets and glass. A brochure for hand-cut crystal tableware shows the three best and richest cuts, which are, indeed, astonishingly intricate in vases, bowls, plates and boxes. Prices include mailing charges: vases, $13–$50; ashtrays, $5 (for a 3") to $23 (for an 8"). (Twenty percent discount for diplomats!)

The garnet jewelry is set in gilded silver and is also very inexpensive; earrings are from $10 up. I bought myself two rings for $11 and $12 each, including postage (no customs duty was charged), and the service was first-rate, though in true Middle European style: all my communications with them have been stamped and signed by two people.

DENMARK

Havemanns Magasin A/S, Vesterbrogade 74–76, 1548 Copenhagen, Denmark
Color catalogues in Danish, free. Spring and fall.

Havemanns, a department store, shows only clothes and furniture in their catalogues, but the clothes are fairly snappy. For women, quite a few midis and trouser suits and a Miss H range of "younger" clothes, a page of gorgeous kints: pale-violet trouser suits about $50 each, and dresses for about $27. A "Young Shop" for men with patterned and purple trousers about $27 each, and some "London designed" suits in light gray or brilliant blue for about $115.

Quite a bit of the furniture is reproduction and dark wood, and there is a handsome, but not inexpensive, range of mahogany "campaign" furniture, including wall systems, beds, divan sofas, about $280, and chests starting at $80.

ENGLAND

Army and Navy Stores Ltd., 105 Victoria Street, London S.W.1, England ♛♛
20-page women's fashion catalogues, free. Spring, autumn. 90-page Christmas-gift catalogue with some color, free. October.

Founded in 1871 as an exclusive club to provide top-quality goods for the gentry at reduced prices, this is now a large and well-established department store with an enthusiastic export department. No longer selling rose water by the gallon for finger bowls, nor bras by the gross to Indian maharajas, the stores have a useful stock of good English things that I haven't seen illustrated elsewhere: Morely gloves, Moreland slippers, decorated Wolsey tights, woolen underwear, spencers and pantaloons. Also there's a good selection of standard gifts: Kent hairbrushes (much cheaper than in America), Reeves paints, Ronson and Colibri lighters, Dartington glass, Irish linen, leather books, food and cigars.

Freemans of London, 139 Clapham Road, London S.W.9, England
800-page color catalogue, $4. Spring and fall.

One of England's biggest mail-order firms, Freemans puts out two whopping catalogues a year of their own products and of other manufacturers'. The catalogues should give mail-order addicts many happy browsing hours. Glancing through them, I see a lot of things (such as furniture and appliances) not worth buying, but amusingly different from things you see in America.

The clothes are mostly rather ordinary (over thirty "larger" dresses starting at $10), but there are also various sections of more with-it clothes, maxis (a heavy wool maxi-coat, $38), shiny, "wet-look" raincoats, and jump suits (a multicolored print one, $16); a couple of things by the French designer Feraud—a charcoal-gray trouser suit, $49; and a scarlet belted midi-coat, $52. Gypsyish accessories: beads, belts, buckled bags (from $11) and brilliantly colored, long silk scarves, $11. Leather shoes by England's best-known firms: Brevitt, Clarks, Lotus, Norvic—start at $9 and come in all shapes from the most casual to clumpy modern.

For men there are blazers, corduroy jackets, tweed jackets, $22; Daks trousers, $20; suits made to measure for $90; heavy wool sweaters from $10; and leather shoes from $11.

For the house, various things look interesting such as wool blankets starting at $11. Drapes ready-made or by the yard; the prices are the same as American prices but the fabric patterns are different—more flower designs and brightly colored modern ones. Stainless-steel Oneida flatware at $13 for a twenty-four-piece set. A selection of stainless steel by Old Hall and Prestige, leading English manufacturers.

There is also a big toy section with Matchbox and Corgi cars (I see that Chitty Chitty Bang Bang, which costs $5 in New York, is $3 at Freemans').

Harrods Ltd., Knightsbridge, London S.W.1, England ♛♛♛
28-page color brochure, free. Prices in $.

London's most established, most establishment department store, so well known that it doesn't bother to give a street address, has a special export brochure for Americans showing famous British goods. The brochure concentrates on quality rather than economy, and the one I looked at had, among other things, Harrods' own silver reproductions, a copy of an eighteenth-century punch ladle, $54; a silver-plate melon tea set, copy of an 1830 set, $220; gold charm bracelets, $39; London charms from $12; Waterford glass; fine bone china; London-view place mats—a set of eighteen mats and coaster, $36; a set of rural-British-scene place mats, $35; a handmade, three-tiered leather case, $140; a double bottle holder in soft, padded nappy with four stainless-steel cups and an opener, $30; traditional English embroidery kits: a Jacobean pack with a Warwick design on fire screen, cushion, stool, $8.30; a rose or leaf on 18″ by 18″ canvas squares, $17, six of which can be joined to make a carpet; a Chippendale chair seat with the bird already worked, $38. Reproduction pewter tankards; hand-painted tablecloths; suit and coat fabric; sweaters ($14) for women; ties, shirts, dressing gowns, blankets and gloves.

Apart from the things in the brochure, Harrods is an outstandingly well-stocked department store, so you can write about anything else you are interested in. You can also open an account with them.

Oxendales Wholesale and Export Co. Ltd., Galleon House, P.O. Box 11, Stockport SK7 5DJ, Cheshire, England
150-page color catalogue, free.

Clothes for adults, linen, and a few gifts. The women's clothes in this large mail-order firm are, with a few exceptions, rather stodgy, but there are good buys for men. Wool sweaters start at $8.25, including postage; leather shoes; top coats at $25; Terylene worsted suits at $40; and fabric samples can be sent for made-to-measure suits "all sizes catered for."

Also Witney wool blankets, leather purses, tool kits, sewing sets, English and Russian watches, Ronson lighters, all at modest prices.

FINLAND

Stockmann, Export Service, 10 Aleksanterinkatu, Helsinki, Finland
Manufacturers brochures in Finnish, free.

Finnish design in some ways seems to be more with-it than Scandinavian design—brighter, bolder colors and shapes. Their children's furniture is particularly nice and is not too expensive if bought from Finland in quantity; ask to see the Muurame brochure. However, Helsinki's biggest department store, Stockmann, advertises a thriving export department but does not, alas, put out a catalogue. They seem to stock most of the famous Finnish furniture, rugs and fabrics that are exported, so if you already know what you want, write and ask.

FRANCE

Au Printemps, Relations Clientèle et Commandes, 64 Boulevard Haussmann, Paris IX, France

One of Paris' largest medium-priced department stores, Au Printemps is at your disposal to answer questions about any articles you are interested in. Unfortunately, like Finland's Stockmann, they don't produce a general catalogue. A great loss, because most of their departments stock goods with a typically French high level of design and color. But try them for any special French products you are looking for. French prices are generally high for Europe, but many exports get a 20 percent discount.

87
Tuzex Gilded silver and garnet jewelry. Earrings, about $37.

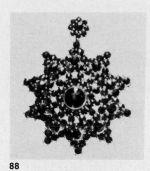

88
Tuzex Gilded silver and garnet jewelry. Pendant and pin, about $24.

89
Tuzex Gilded silver and garnet jewelry. Bracelet, about $32.

90
Stockmann Muurame painted beech bunkbed "Jetti,"
designed by Pirkko Stenros. Several color combinations
available. $88.

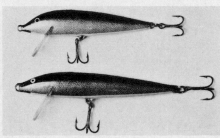

91
Stockmann Rapala plug baits for fishing salmon and
sea trout. The baits are made of balsa and covered with
plastic. $1.20–$1.90.

92
Stockmann Iittala glasses. A set of six costs about $10.

93
Stockmann Red tea cozy and table runner, design
"Forbidden Fruit." Tea cozy, about $9; runner, about
$11.25.
photos Kalevi Hujanen

GERMANY

**Mail Order House, Quelle Inc., 45 W. 45 Street, New York,
N.Y. 10036**
*750-page color catalogue, $3. ($2.40 refundable). Spring,
fall.*

I strongly recommend Quelle, Germany's largest mail-order
house, which is streets ahead of its competitors in standards
of design. Whatever the section, their goods are easier on the
eye than the goods in similar catalogues from other countries.

Quelle has an office in New York, advertises here, and
although the catalogue is in German, it comes with a
complete translation for the clothes and linen sections (the
most popular in America). Very clear instructions, including a
full table of exchange, so there is virtually no calculating
to do.

One of the reasons that their clothes are much more
attractive than clothes of American and English mail-order
houses is that the styles are new-looking yet pared down,
casual, and the colors, too, are subtler. Everyday summer
dresses cost from $12 to $17, with good selections for
pregnant women and larger figures. A more formal pale-
yellow dress with a matching jacket costs $30, and dressy but
simple Trevira dresses and matching coats in white, beige,
pale blue or green start at $45. Children's clothes start at
$3 for smaller sizes, and there are dirndl dresses for $3–$6.
Men's summer suits are about $35 to $65; regular suits, $35
to $80. Winter dresses for women cost $12 to $35; a jump suit
in dark Brazilian brown or black costs $13; while a ribbed
acrylic pullover and trousers in aubergine or juniper green
cost $17. There are lots of good coats, heavy sweaters, ski
clothes, hats and gloves for men, women and children.

Quelle's linens and fabrics also sell well in America; sheets
do look very different with frilly pillows, sateen, damask or red
roses on dark-blue cotton (these last start at $5.75 a single
sheet). And there are some *very* fetching curtain fabrics—
bright stylized flower designs in 48″ rayon, $2.25 a meter (=1
yard, 3″). I haven't seen as colorful, informal fabrics illustrated
anywhere else.

But the whole catalogue is full of things worth lingering
over: patterned umbrellas (there is one for children showing
Walt Disney's "101 Dalmatians," $1); clocks; some terrific
buys in jewelry—gold and semiprecious stones, Baroque
necklaces in rose-quartz, amethyst and garnet start at $16;
and a section called "hallo Teens und Twens" has little 14-
carat rings set with coral, amethyst and turquoise, for $7;
molded candles, starting at just over $1 each; toys; a twenty-
eight piece party kit for six with paper tablecloth, plates,
cups, napkins, name places and a table decoration for $1.50;
a roomful of children's red-and-white furniture—a bed, $27, a
desk, $19, and a wall unit with shelves and a cupboard, $40.
Lots of colorful enameled kitchenware, a German specialty, it
seems; saucepans from $4, kettles from $8.50. Minimum order
$18.50.

IRELAND

Mail Order Department, Shannon Free Airport, Ireland
*60-page catalogue with some color, free; 60 cents air mail.
Prices in $.*

Shannon Airport has a famous tax-free shop at which, the *New
York Times* says, our Secretary of State buys sweaters and
ambassadors do their Christmas shopping. The shop has a
vast and superbly organized mail-order business, with a very
efficient catalogue showing popular brand-name items at
greater savings than any other shop, and including an

estimate of the American duty you'll have to pay on each item.

The 1971 catalogue had mohair tams, $5.50; scarves, $3.80; ponchos, $19.50; and capes, $27, in glorious, faintly striped golds, blues and greens; sporty Connemara tartan fringed jackets and coats for women and children (a woman's fully lined coat, $28). Hand-crocheted coats, $33; hand-knitted heavy sweaters; Pringle sweaters (the Princess cashmere twin set, for instance, which sells for $62 in New York, is $44.60 *including* postage and customs); printed patterned sweaters for women, cashmeres for men at $20; and something called a Ryder Cup Shirt in merino wool, $10 (the catalogue says it was designed for golfing and approved by the PGA). Liberty of London silk head scarves; "ladies'" kilts; men's mohair, cashmere and wool sports jackets, $40; Viyella robes at $23; half their New York prices. Also Waterford and Galway glass, Wedgwood china, damask tablecloths at lower prices than other Irish shops, Kapp and Peterson pipes; Corgi toys; Peggy Nisbett historical dolls (Henry VIII, $8; Marie Antoinette, $6.50), and Anri painted-wood music boxes from the Italian Alps starting at $6.50.

SWEDEN

PUB (Paul U. Bergströms AB), Export Department, Box 40 140, Stockholm 40, Sweden
Rya rug kit catalogue, $1.50.
Kosta glass catalogue, $1.50.
Stainless-steel tableware price list, illustrated, $1.50.
Prices for all of these in $.

PUB is a large co-operative department store in Stockholm with a very efficient export service. They have no general catalogue, so you have to write and ask about any Swedish thing you are trying to track down. They mainly sell to America stainless-steel tableware and Swedish glass: Orrefors, Kosta and Skruv, but they also have manufacturers' brochures for Rya rug kits and a price list for painted-wood Dalecarlian horses (a symbol of Sweden to many Americans). I, and now my friends, have been buying PUB's Tiidstrand blankets by Viola Gråsten, which come in bright red, blue, green or orange with thin, darker stripes of the same color and cost about $15 from Sweden (but $30 in New York). One of the useful things about these blankets is that they make good bedspreads for children's beds.

SWITZERLAND

Jelmoli S. A., Mail Order Department, 8021 Zurich, Switzerland
200-page color catalogue in German or French, free. Spring and fall.

Switzerland's largest department store puts out two glossily abundant catalogues a year, full of good things in crisp, agreeable Continental shapes and colors. Of special interest: fondue sets, linens, kitchen gadgets and watches (from $10), but there is a $27 minimum for sales to America, and far more clothes are sold by mail to Americans than anything else. Not surprisingly, the clothes are attractively casual, come in good colors, and are well worth looking at, especially the children's clothes and clothes for the "not-so-slim" which are smarter than any other shop's. Admittedly that is not saying much, but the designs are extremely simple and the fabrics subtler than the ones usually destined for the plump. Women's dresses cost between $15 and $25, and like the rest of the general catalogues, Jelmoli has a section for teen-agers with the illustrated newest outfits, called "Spotlite."

There are good buys among the men's clothes too; styles are racy but not outrageously so. Most suits cost between $40 and $50, but there is a beige velvety suit for $35. A slim-cut cotton shirt with a wallpapery design of black flowers and stripes on white costs $7; a long, ribbed mohair sweater in coffee or red costs $9; a dark-green loden overcoat, $35; and a pale-beige midi-raincoat with big round collar and pockets, $40.

In the winter catalogue there are ski clothes, men's sweaters from $15, and children's parkas from $11. Also warm pajamas that look like track suits—navy blue with mustard piping, $4.50 for children and $10.50 for adults.

12 Handicrafts and Special Local Products

This section is a hodge-podge of shops that sell very traditional, handmade local crafts, and also shops that sell a whole range of products that their country happens to make especially well or inexpensively. So even if you detest anything ethnic, look through this section, as you might like the highly metropolitan perfumes and gloves in the French shops. For people who do like crafts, there are lots of marvelous and inexpensive things here.

AUSTRIA

Tiroler Heimatwerk, Meraner Strasse 2, Innsbruck, Tyrol, Austria
16-page brochure with some color, free. Prices in $.

Tiroler Heimatwerk, a showroom and shop created to encourage Tyrolean handicrafts, send hundreds of their otherwise unobtainable goods abroad, even their furniture with "rustical painting" on it. Mostly cheerfully decorated, peasanty household things—plenty of wood: carved and painted umbrella stands and tubs; "godparent" boxes of all sizes painted all over with bright flowers (from 35 cents); devil masks and carnival figures; baroque painted-and-gilded saints and angels, $27-up (one 18" angel with flying hair and golden wings conveniently holds a candlestick). There are traditional molded candles; rough-tin, copper and wrought-iron candlesticks; tumblers and kitchen implements (ladles, etc.). Oatmeal-colored Tyrolean tablecloths decorated with rust-colored woven braids in traditional eagle, deer or heart designs, from $4.30. And very pretty harvest garlands and flower posies made out of colored maize leaves, some of them mixed with "many spices exhaling fragrance."

CANADA

Canadian Art Products, 976 Granville Street, Vancouver 2, British Columbia, Canada
Leaflet, free.

This firm sells original arts and crafts made by Canadian North West Coast Indians. Their leaflet lists a *vast* and interesting assortment of ceremonial art, clothes, jewelry, prints and cards, but gives no details, no prices, no pictures, so only people who know exactly what they are looking for should write.

Iroqrafts Ltd., Box 3, Ohsweken, Six Nations Reserve, Ontario, Canada
Catalogue, 25 cents.
Collectors lists, 10 for $1.
Prices in $.

A serious firm that sells traditional and ceremonial Iroquois crafts to museums as well as shops and individuals. Many of the crafts are the highly decorative beaded and fringed things that have suddenly become popular: headbands, bracelets and necklaces, tasseled belts, flower-embroidered gloves, fringed and patterned bags, $3–$20; sheepskin slippers with white rabbit-fur cuffs and beaded toes, $6.25 children, $8.25 adults, and moose-hide jackets.

For the hundreds and thousands of children studying Indian at school there are instructive little models, totem poles, canoes, teepees, dolls in traditional costume; and a full-color wall map showing fifty Canadian tribal groups in typical surroundings, $2.50 including postage. For more serious collectors: hand-sculptured ceremonial false face masks "sold only on the understanding they will not be used pseudo Indian ceremonies or other sacrilegeous ways" and, on the collectors lists (irritatingly illegibly mimeographed), a whole lot of scarcer items: one-of-a-kind clothes, pillows, quilts, paintings, pottery, full-size canoes, etc.

ECUADOR

Akios Industries, P.O. Box 219, Quitó, Ecuador
75-page catalogue, $1. Prices in $.

A good catalogue for anyone who likes colorful South American handicrafts, Akios Industries is chock full of vividly decorated handicrafts. Magnificent woolen evening skirts with wide bands of hand embroidery, $22; jackets embroidered all over, $33; slacks with embroidery up the edges, made to order, $22. Handwoven, brightly patterned ponchos, $7; fringed vests, $4 for adults, $2.25 for children; belts, ties; and slippers. Over thirty bags of all sorts—calfskin or fabric—decorated with colorful handwoven ribbons, one for little girls is in the shape of a doll, $2. There are also embroidered cushions, $2.75; a receiving blanket with birds and flowers, $11; tablecloths and place mats. Sixty Inca-inspired carpets, similar to Folklore's, are light-fast, color-fast, and cost $40 a square yard—one, 6" by 8" costs under $200. Colored drawings can be sent.

And for decorating the house: carved and painted wooden dolls; shiny bread-dough figures; Inca wall masks, 90 cents and up; straw hats; mats; dolls; Indian musical instruments; onyx free-form ashtrays, $2.25 and up; chess sets with Inca figures, $13; oil paintings of local scenes and figures, $13.

Folklore, P.O. Box 64, Quitó, Ecuador
Rug color brochure, free. Prices in $.
Handicrafts list, free. Prices in $.

An unillustrated list of Ecuadorian handicrafts that seem very like the Akios stock and sound equally appetizing, but as there are no descriptions at all, you have to either know the name of what you want or enter into a complicated correspondence. Handwoven ponchos and shawls; hand-embroidered blouses, dresses, place mats, hand-knitted sweaters, hand-carved figures and boxes, dolls and copper sun wall plaques. Folklore also has things from the Amazon jungle: feather-and-seed necklaces, bow-and-arrow sets, $1.75; and tree-bark aprons, $6.75. And there is silver jewelry: cuff links, $1–$5; bracelets, $4–$8; necklaces about $10. Letter openers, about $2.50.

ENGLAND

Country Cousins, Gorse Croft, Ranmoor Lane, Hathersage, via Sheffield S30 1BW, England
Price list and fabric samples, 45 cents.

Mrs. Muriel Brown designs most of Country Cousin's toys, cushions, aprons and oven gloves, which are made up in gaily colored cottons by local people working at home. She says the cushions are by far the most popular with Americans and Canadians. First, the 17" square "Officers and Gentlemen" cushion with gold, scarlet, blue and black eighteenth-century soldiers printed on one side, and a solid color on the other, $4.50; then, patchwork cushions based on old English designs copied from museums: "Flower Garden" (top left) is a design used by Elizabeth Fry, who taught prisoners patchwork in Newgate Gaol before they were transported to Australia. The cushions, except for "Mosaic," which has a mixture of jolly colors, are made in predominantly brown, pink or turquoise-blue tones, but any other colors can be made, and customers' own fabrics used.

94
Canadian Art Products Grizzly bear and cub by Kwakiutl Indian artist Henry Hunt, carved from red cedar and painted black, red, green, 17½" high. $165.

95
Iroqrafts Ltd Scarce carved cedar Kwakiutl Indian sun mask. $220–$270, depending on size and carver.

96
Folklore Wall hangings woven by Salasacan Indians. The small ones are $1.20 each, the medium $2, the large $10 and up.

Patchwork quilts are made to order after a discussion of types and colors (single, $42), and old quilts can be restored.

After the cushions, the most popular things are the toys: a furry white mouse with removable shawl and apron; stuffed kittens; rabbits; rag dolls; a pink-and-red weighted doorstop; and a red or green patterned hobby horse on a red stick with a wool mane, bell and bridle, $8.25.

Douglas Hart, Aiblins, Cott Cross, Dartington, Totnes, Devonshire, England
Brochure, 25 cents. Prices in $.

Douglas Hart, an old friend of mine, is a professional woodturner and makes very simple, beautiful things out of ash, beech (light woods) and orangy brown teak. Waxed salad bowls from $8, polished bowls from $6, cheese board and knife from $3.50, a hanging salt box for $2.25, a bird house, $2.25. There are fifty-five items altogether, including lamp bases from $2.25 up, but these would need altering to fit American bulbs.

Taylor of London, Perfumery Shop, 166 Sloane Street, London S.W.1, England
Leaflet, free.

Taylor of London says they have been making *status* scents for royalty and the cream of English and Continental society for the past eighty years. Gardenia, lily of the valley, carnation and lilac are hand-distilled and made into soaps, bath essences, dusting powder, cologne and perfume, and during the summer, delivered in a horse-drawn brougham to customers in London's West End. Taylor also makes sachets to perfume drawers and potpourris of flowers to be emptied into bowls to perfume rooms for several months. But most popular of all are their Crown Staffordshire and Wedgwood pomanders filled with an Elizabethan essence, guaranteed to last for fifty years.

ETHIOPIA

The Olive Wood and African Curio Shop, P.O. Box 878, Asmara, Ethiopia
Color leaflet, 40 cents. Prices in $.

A highly designed and colorful leaflet announces an "accurate and prompt" mail-order service to any part of the world. The leaflet shows some decorated knives, barbed spears (the spears about 80 cents each), dolls, horn cups and birds, crocodile handbags and a leopard-skin hat and handbag. There is also the shop's specialty, olive wood, from naturally seasoned trees that have been standing dead for two to four hundred years. The olive wood has been carved into spoons, or turned (on a lathe, presumably) into smooth bowls, plates, candlesticks, pipe racks, sometimes decorated with inset bands of black and white porcupine quills. Almost all the olive wood items cost under $5, and most of them are about $2. Only the prices of the olive wood and spears are given, so ask about anything else when you write. Many other Ethiopian handicrafts are stocked but not illustrated: silver jewelry, paintings on skin, leatherwork, Coptic crosses, and unusual raw-wool rugs—bold designs of angular animals with human faces.

FRANCE

Freddy, 10 Rue Auber, Paris IX, France
24-page brochure, free. Prices in $.

There are several shops in Paris that specialize in tax-free

97
Country Cousins Patchwork cushions based on old English designs. *Reading left to right and starting at the top:* "Flower Garden," $9; "Autumn," $9; "Little Boxes," $9; "Morning Glory," $6 (these four made in mainly brown, pink or turquoise-blue tones). *Bottom:* Two "Mosaic" (in a mixture of colors), $6 each. Prices include surface postage, and cushions can be made in any color to order.

98
Country Cousins 17" square "Officers and Gentlemen" cushion, $4.50; 13" square "Train" (or "Ship" or "Rocking Horse") cushion in red and pink, $4.50; 6½" mouse with removable red cloak and blue apron, $3. Prices include surface postage.

99
Taylor of London Pomander in pale blue or green Jasper by Wedgwood, with a fragrance made from a sixteenth-century recipe claimed to last for fifty years. About $12.

gifts for tourists. They are expert at packing and shipping, and have well-established mail-order services for popular French goods at *around* half the price they are abroad.

The Freddy brochure has a perfume price list and also eight pages of gifts illustrated in colorful glory: mauve umbrellas lined with pink roses; purses embroidered with bouquets; gold-and-blue Limoges cigarette cases; famous-name silk scarves; Dior and Fath ties; and souvenir dolls in regional costumes.

Grillot, 10 Rue Cambon, Paris I, France
Price list, free. Prices in $.

Grillot has a price list with no illustrations, but besides perfumes, well-known French cosmetics are listed, and this is a good place to buy Lacoste (the clothes with the crocodile emblem): shirts, sweaters and dresses. The different styles are listed and measurement across the shoulders are given in inches. Prices for Lacoste seem to vary between half and a third off American prices.

Obéron, 73 Champs-Elysées, Paris VIII, France
20-page catalogue with some color, $1.50 (refundable). Perfume price list, free. Prices in $.

A good catalogue with excellent illustrations and an exhortation to ask for anything you don't see, as there are thousands of articles not shown. (Obéron says that they redo the catalogue each year "considering the requests of their customers.") A few pages of gifts "for him" and "for her," fancy gloves, petit-point handbags, designer scarves, and the rest of the space is given over to china and glass objects. Lalique and Baccarat figurines, table items, smokers' sets and ashtrays. In china there is palatial Limoges, countryish Porcelaine de Chantilly, and Fourmaintraux, very kitcheny hand-decorated earthenware.

Michel Swiss, 16 Rue de la Paix, Paris II, France
63-page brochure, free. Prices in $.

Michel Swiss, perhaps the best known of the tax-free shopping centers, has slightly lower prices than the others and is an outstanding place for highly civilized little gifts. The perfume list includes soaps, bath oils, colognes for men, and the brochure is crammed with (slightly blurred) pictures of clothing and accessories. For the house: all sorts of little boxes, bowls and plates in hand-cut crystal and bronze, or Limoges china with Fragonard scenes. For women: handmade gloves and purses, and leather, alligator, beaded or petit-point handbags, geometric silk scarves by Dior, Fath and St. Laurent, or flowery umbrellas with printed lining about $12 (an exclusive design by Lanvin costs $25). For men: Dior, St. Laurent ties, scarves and handkerchiefs (a Dior tie-and-handkerchief set costs $10.50), Lanvin shirts, cashmere sweaters, alligator belts and crocodile wallets. A decanter with four glasses hidden in a box disguised as four leatherbound books is $22. And for with-it (and rich) babies, Pierre Cardin clothes: a sleeveless dress in navy or red with a band around the waist costs $16.

GERMANY

R. Roeslen, Taunusstrasse 47, 6 Frankfurt/M, Germany
Color leaflets, free. Prices in $.

A thriving business in typical German souvenirs—music boxes and cuckoo clocks, of course. The music boxes are made of cherry wood; cigarette or jewelry boxes for $9 have reproductions of "ancient masters" on the lids (and new, there is one with "The Lovers" by Picasso) or chubby-children Hummel scenes. A wall music box that I have seen advertised in America for $10.95 in a choice of two Hummel scenes is shown in the Roeslen brochure for $5.50 with a choice of thirteen Hummel scenes. There are ten of the cuckoo-type clocks that children adore—the ones I would have loved are, in fact, called "swinging clocks," $7–$10, and have a little lady swinging underneath a tiny chalet with a bird flying around the balcony. The original Black Forest cuckoo clocks cost $14 and $21.

Also, ceramic regimental beer steins decorated with complicated "*Kavallerie*," "*Infanterie*," etc., scenes; German writing and molded lids, "gift-boxed" dolls in regional costumes; Bavarian leather shorts for boys and men; embroidered dirndl dresses, $11–$23 for girls, depending on size; Gobelins; dark Germanic tapestries showing gabled, cobbled villages and stormy landscapes.

GHANA

Ghana Export Co. Ltd., P.O. Box 2674, Accra, Ghana
16-page catalogue, free. Prices on request.

This company sells some of the ebony carvings that are now so plentifully produced for sale, but they also have a few other things less often seen. Bone carvings, for instance, of slim birds, glazed earthenware coffee sets, decorative bows and arrows, northern Ghanaian violins, one or two pleasingly round, fat straw baskets, and some extravagantly decorated hats.

GREECE

National Welfare Organization, Handicrafts Dept., 6 Ipatias Street, Athens 117, Greece
22-page crafts catalogue with some color, free.
48-page carpet catalogue with some color, free. Prices in $.

This fetching catalogue, showing the best Greek handicrafts, is put out by the official craft-encouraging National Welfare Organization under the title "Hellas." The big hitch is that prices are not given, and when you write to ask it turns out that half the things aren't available any more. However, I did buy a nice silver bracelet that only cost $12, including air-mail postage. (I wasn't charged customs duty.) Besides that bracelet (the rest of the silver jewelry and ashtrays are "off" at the moment), there are handsome, simple brass candlesticks along with copper jugs and coffeepots; some richly colored velvet slippers trimmed with gold; and a smart duffle coat, plain on the outside, but lined inside with a handwoven design. Most of the other things will probably only appeal to people who like distinctively local crafts: linen tablecloths with bird-and-flower regional embroidery; fish, mermaid and boat design needlepoint cushions, about $8 (these cost $25 and up in New York); embroidered purses; and multicolored square wool tagari bags.

Queen Corporation, Mail Order Dept., 39 Academias Street, Athens 135, Greece
Brochure, free. Prices in $.

This firm of exporters decided to start personal mail ordering when I wrote to them, and they quickly sent me the mock-up of a little brochure showing some of the Greek products they had been dealing with. Prices are *very* low, all the prices I quote include postage (but the minimum order accepted is $10). Some amazing buys in metal—silver-plated birds, for

example. A 12″ pheasant costs $5; and small fighting roosters, 5″ long, $10 the pair. I have seen similar (possibly better made?) birds that in England and America cost at least three times as much. Silver- or gold-plated "slave" bracelets, very curly, flexible bands that would look dashing on a suntanned arm, $2.80–$4. Tagari bags with the signs of the zodiac, only $2.50. There are also terra-cotta copies of Greek heads: Venus, Pericles, Democritus "Father of Atomic Theory," etc., prices up to $13. Reproductions of Greek vases are $1.50–$9.

HOLLAND

Holland Handicrafts, Dept. R, Pruimendijk 24, Rijsoord, Holland
8-page brochure, 25 cents. Prices in $.

Adrienne Trouw, an American living in Holland, sells, at Holland Handicrafts, a collection of Dutch products: a shiny old-fashioned brass iron you can put plants in, $14; sterling-silver Dutch charm bracelets from $5; pewter ashtrays in the shape of old brandy tasters, $6; small reproductions of old Dutch paintings in antiqued frames, $7 each. And, much the prettiest—hand-carved traditional Christmas-cookie molds. The molds are usually hung up as decorations, but they can also be used to cut patterned cookies—the recipe comes with them. Prices for molds start at $4, and all the above prices include postage.

HONG KONG

Swatow Weng Lee Co., P.O. Box 5972, Kowloon, Hong Kong
50-page brochure, free; air mail $1. Prices in $.

This fifty-year-old firm has just put out a new mail-order catalogue in which they say they will "strife further to elevate our strict standards of service and bring prolonged satisfaction like its been before to our clients always." The catalogue, which represents but a portion of their ability to delight, shows a fairly typical Hong Kong selection at typically Hong Kong low prices: rayon pajamas for men and women, $6; brocade robes and housecoats, around $10; Canton embroidered coats for $27. Also European-style needlepoint handbags at well below European prices (around $16); gold jewelry; ivory carvings; Chinese dolls; and other local gift-type things.

ICELAND

Icemart Mail Order Dept., P.O. Box 23, Keflavik International Airport, Iceland
48-page color brochure, free; 30 cents air mail. Prices in $.
Food price list, free. Prices in $.

This airy, modern shop in the free-port area of Iceland's international airport is owned and run by several of the country's leading manufacturers, and sells their products as well as local foods such as canned caviar, smoked salmon and cheeses.

The brochure for mail order is one of the most delectable I have looked at, with a stunning collection of expensive-looking clothes that use traditional Icelandic designs and materials together with modern shapes. This year there are gorgeous maxi- and midi-skirts, sweaters, vests, long tunics, ponchos and slacks, knitted or woven in white lamb's wool, edged with bands or designs in subtle mauves, browns or

100

100
Ghana Export Co. Ltd Black painted mahogany fertility dolls. 9″, $3; 12″, $3.50; 13″, $3.55.

101
Queen Corporation 12″ × 14″ tagari bags available in all the signs of the zodiac, and a wide variety of colors. $2.50 each, including air-mail postage. Minimum order, three.

101

102
Holland Handicrafts "St. Nicholaas" traditional hand-carved Christmas cookie mold, 13″ × 9″. $13, including surface postage.

103
Central Cottage Industries Emporium Inexpensive decorative toys: two string puppets from Rajasthan; on the right, string puppets from Andhra; rocking horse in red with Saurashtra mirror embroidery; Rajasthan doll carrying pitchers; satin elephant from Poona; snake charmer.

104
Central Cottage Industries Emporium Traditional Indian jewelry: silver Mina necklace with real stones on the left, $7 – $15; in the center, gold-plated necklace with synthetic red stones, $40; on the right, white metal folk necklace $16; Thapa mirror, $6; top, brass and copper Thapa pendant, $7 and up; Kundan ring, $2.10.

105
Treasures of Italy Seven small silverplated pieces, cocktail picks, butter spreaders, spoons, etc. A set of six of any one of these costs just over $2.50, including air-mail postage.

102

103

104

105

black. The ponchos and maxi-skirts cost about $24, the sweaters about $16. There are long, fluffy black or white knitted coats made of long-haired Icelandic lamb's wool and then teased, about $30 to $58; smart sheepskin coats (a white midi for men, $142), and lots of other sheepskin — hats, bags, boots and muffs, and some cushions that at around $11 are almost half the price of the ones I have seen in New York. In addition to the clothes, the brochure shows Icelandic wool blankets in natural colors, three medieval-style chairs, handmade lava ceramics, a few souvenirs, and some silver jewelry: charms, witchcraft symbols on pendants, reproductions of ancient ornaments, filigree and modern pieces.

INDIA

Central Cottage Industries Emporium, Janpath, New Delhi 1, India
22-page color catalogue, $1.50.

A gorgeous, tempting catalogue of handicrafts from all over the country (oddly entitled "Paradise Shopping in Instant India") is put out by this main government emporium. The large, air-conditioned building houses twenty-six departments, including a shipping department, and a vast assortment of beautifully chosen goods — an ideal shop for anyone looking for something new and interesting. (Unfortunately, the catalogue is a general review with only approximate prices, so every item will have to be inquired about individually. In fact, you can skip the catalogue if you know what you want.)

For the house there are all sorts of rare and wonderful decorations: ashtrays, cigarette boxes; and although some of the metalwork has been seen around a lot, there are still plenty of things that haven't: hand-painted papier-mâché, ivory, alabaster, filigree silver. A fretted copper bowl costs $7, and a silver filigree bowl, $15.50; a small silver box studded with moonstones, $26; and a square marble plate inlaid with a regular pattern of flowers in semiprecious stones, $31. There is a department for lamps, hand-painted, ceramic or metal, with silk or cotton shades made to order.

I have described the fabrics in the Fabrics section, but there are also table linens and bedspreads, a white cotton bedspread from Jaipur, hand-blocked with a delicate design of little olive-green and pink flowering shrubs, $5 single size; a silk bedspread with orange stripes on hot pink costs $26, single size.

For actual wear, there is what the catalogue calls a "flamboyant color riot" (in American sizes) for evenings or lounging around the house. A pink tunic with bell sleeves, handsomely printed in mauve and black, costs up to $6; a raw-silk cocktail dress embroidered around the bodice and hem, about $37. For children, tunics and trousers in cotton or silk (among other things), and for men, some dazzlingly colorful (some more sober) raw- or printed-silk ties; foulards; cotton bush shirts for $5, and silk shirts, $10. Cotton dressing gowns cost from $5, and silk dressing gowns start at $16, going up to $47 for a rare brocade.

IRELAND

Emerald Crafts, Slaney Place, Enniscorthy, Co. Wexford, Ireland
6-page brochure, only partly illustrated, free. Prices in $. Donegal tweed samples, free. Prices in $.

A cottage shop, with a small brochure of Irish crafts, which in spite of being visited by tourists has steered clear of souvenirs in favor of genuine local products: rushwork baskets, wooden bowls, crystal, marble and pottery. Shangarry jugs, black with brown rims and white inside, cost $1 to $5, and a pottery coffee set, freely hand-painted with flowers and fruit, costs $17.50.

Donegal tweeds, still woven by hill farmers, although centrally designed, cost about $4.50 a yard. Samples can be sent, but say which colors you are interested in. In addition to crocheted blouses, mohair stoles and cashmere sweaters ($18 to $23), there are heavy, creamy Aran sweaters for only $20 (in New York they cost $40) and unusual dark-brown sweaters in oiled, undyed wool from black sheep.

Mairtin Standun, Spiddal, Co. Galway, Ireland
Leaflets, free. Prices in $.

Maire Standun writes chatty letters saying that the Irish Tourist and Export Board will vouchsafe the excellence of her Aran sweaters. Apparently the knitters who purl and knit away by the fire through the long winter nights are not allowed to finish the sweaters—that is done by eight sewing experts, who put the pieces together and add the buttons. Besides sweaters, the shop stocks seven kinds of knitted Aran hats for adults and children from a funny leprechaun cap to a workman-like thatcher's hat in prices up to $3.50.

Other clothes not illustrated include featherweight wool blouses and dresses, kilts ($11), cashmere sweaters, ties, crocheted shawls and gloves. Various other handmade objects, such as tweed table mats and knitted tea cozies, are on sale, and there are Irish souvenirs as well as an illustrated leaflet of Foxford tartan travel rugs.

Sales Director, Switzers Department Store, 92 Grafton Street, Dublin 2, Ireland
20-page catalogue, free. Prices in $.

Switzers puts out a functional brochure showing a selection of Ireland's main exports. It is not as thorough nor as attractive as Brown Thomas' (see House: Lace-Linens), but it *is* free and it covers most of the same things: linen tablecloths and place mats, Celtic jewelry, Aran sweaters, Donald Davies dresses, Foxford travel rugs, glass and china (ask for special price list), and Carrickmacross lace. In addition, the brochure shows some Kapp and Peterson pipes and some Royal Irish handmade silver from the large silver department: A George II sterling tea set copied from one made in Dublin in 1728, and a modern sterling drinking goblet, the inside gilt with 24-carat gold.

ISRAEL

Hayadith Ltd., P.O. Box 45, Pardess Hanna, Israel
22-page brochure, free. Prices in $.

A collection made out of olive wood—light orangy in color with a dark marked grain. Besides the usual bowls, nutcrackers, salad servers and cheese plates, there is a fascinating, build-it-yourself model of Old Jerusalem, one hundred pieces of partly colored beech wood and a plan. The set, $6.20, is intended for children but looks engaging enough for any adult.

For pure decoration, simple jewelry made out of round wooden beads and small, vaguely modeled statues, just suggestive of family groups embracing, about $6–$20.

Export Division, Wizo Shops, Home Industries, 87 Allenby Road, Tel Aviv, Israel
Price list, free. Prices in $.

The Women's International Zionist Organization sells folkloric dolls and also very attractive hand-embroidered tablecloths, cushions, blouses and dresses for women and children. The cut of the clothes changes with the fashions, but the embroidery is based on very old Yemenite patterns and is done in cotton, silver or gold thread on cotton, crepe or velvet.

ITALY

Al Pellegrino Cattolico, Via di Porta Angelica 83, Rome, Italy

No catalogue, but this shop has lots of mail-order customers for religious articles, any of which can be blessed by the Pope. Rosaries of wood, crystal or mother-of-pearl set in metal cost from 25 cents to $4; set in silver they cost $4–$25. Rosaries with semiprecious stones: lapis lazuli, coral, amethyst, topaz, etc., set in silver, $30–$135; stones set in 18-carat gold, $120–$350. Also medals and chains in metal, silver, gold; crosses, pictures, statues and Papal Blessings.

Treasures of Italy, P.O. Box 1513, 50100 Florence, Italy
32-page color brochure, free. Prices in $.

A well-practiced hand at mail order, Treasures of Italy has a little brochure crammed with *very* inexpensive treasures, mostly under $5. Fully explicit directions about ordering are given, and orders are shipped the day they come in. A first-rate place for the Italian memento type of thing: branch-coral necklaces, $3.75; Venetian glass jewelry, silver filigree mosaic pins and tiny boxes, gold-tooled leather, baroque silver-plated ornaments (9" pheasants cost $9 a pair), gilt-tooled boxes, trays, and lots of other little things.

KENYA

E. Fioravanti and Co. Ltd., P.O. Box 84867, Mombasa, Kenya
22-page brochure, $1. Prices in $.

This export brochure shows reproductions of antique African sculptures and modern Westernized African-style sculptures rather indiscriminately mixed together. The brochure says that Fioravanti borrows works from museums and private collectors to copy them, and does research into the background of these pieces; a little of the research is given in the price list. Most of the pieces cost between $4 and $25, but there are some large wall panels of what they call modern (and I call Westernized) warrior scenes that can be made into doors, and cost $215 each, as does an unusual set of Congolese carved coffee table and chairs.

Kuja Crafts, Ltd., Hotel Intercontinental, Sgt. Ellis Avenue/Uhuru Highway, P.O. Box 9176, Nairobi, Kenya.
Price list, free. Prices in $.

A good selection of things from Kenya, but no pictures. Besides the usual game trophies, skins and ivories, there are things I haven't seen listed anywhere else: batik and tie-dyed fabrics, $2 (each piece is different); two yards of Kitenge material, $6; beaded belts and necklaces, $3 each; beaded hats for ladies, $11; for men, $13; dressed dolls, $2; African decorated walking sticks, $5; musical instruments from different tribes, $19; zebra-skin drums up to $9. Also zebra belts (ladies' and gents' sizes, $5, but teen-ager sizes, rather strangely, $6). Leopard-, lion-, gazelle- and zebra-skin bags, from $36 to $91 according to size. Surface postage: $3 up to 7 lbs.; $5 up to 11 lbs.; and $8 up to 22 lbs.

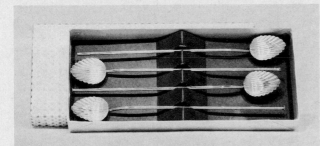

106
Treasures of Italy A set of four 8″ silverplated sip-
through-handle spoons. Just over $3, including airmail
postage
photo Foto Studio Moreno

Sindh General Stores Ltd., P.O. Box 80279, Mombasa, Kenya
Catalogue, free. Prices in $.

This firm has some African-style "typical Java print" dresses
and shirts, made out of very light cotton and machine-sewn.
Sleeveless dresses for women, in American sizes 12, 14 and
16, cost $9; kaftan-sleeved dresses, $13; men's shirts, $8; and
shirts for boys and dresses for girls both cost $6 each, or $10
for two—all those prices include air-mail postage. You can
also buy animal skins, elephant-hair rings, zebra-skin-covered
stools and coffee tables, Masai shields, and, often for under
$1, animal carvings and carved salad servers, paper knives
and walking sticks.

Studio Arts 68, P.O. Box 7904, Nairobi, Kenya
*Price list for African dolls, $1; with photographs, $3. Prices
in $.*
General list, $1; with photographs, $3.

Studio Arts 68 sells carefully chosen crafts made in East
African cottage industries: brightly colored beadwork jewelry
based on traditional ornaments; newly designed, hand-printed
wall hangings, safari tote bags, cushion covers and other
household objects; tie-dyed poplin fabrics (a three-yard dress
length costs about $10); banana-fiber baskets; and a whole
assortment of dolls—some rag dolls and others, collector's
items, carved in wood or molded from clay and decorated
with beads and fabric. Goods are described, not illustrated, on
the lists.

MEXICO

**Vicky, Popular Arts and Embroideries, Apartado 1,
Avenida de las Americas S/N, Pátzcuaro, Michoacán,
Mexico**
*Price lists for clothes, furniture and rugs, all free.
Prices in $.*

An American living in Mexico has a shop which sells three
kinds of goods that are popular with visitors to Mexico.
Unfortunately the lists Mr. Gray sends out for mail order don't
illustrate or describe the goods, although he hopes to have an
illustrated list soon. However, he can supply photographs, for
which he charges.

One list is for colorful Mexican embroidery on handwoven
fabric: shirts, blouses, robes and dresses of all sorts, most of
them for under $15; bags, aprons, potholders and place mats
for under $5. Another list is for Spanish colonial-style furniture
made out of Brazilian walnut (this takes about three months to
make, as it is made to order). There are screens, tables,
writing desks, chairs, bedroom furniture (including
headboards), frames for paintings or mirrors, and also cane
furniture in modern colonial style. Prices are very low and
range from $20 for a gossip chair ("low, comfy") to $216 for a
9′10″-long dining table that seats twelve (dining chairs with
leather seats and ornamental nails cost $30 each). The final
list is for hand-braided and handsewn Henequen rugs in
various designs, colors and sizes of your choice. These cost
$14 per square meter (1 sq. m. = 1.2 sq. yds.).

NORWAY

Husfliden, Vågsalmenning 3, 5000 Bergen, Norway
Knitwear brochure, free. Prices in $.
Rug color brochure, free. Prices in $.

This nonprofit organization fosters Norwegian crafts, selling
all sorts of crafts in their Bergen showroom, and rugs and
knitwear by mail. The traditional Norwegian knits are well
worth buying here—very lovely sweaters for men and women

cost only around $25 each. I've seen the same sort of thing for $45 in New York. Each sweater, jacket, mitten or hat shown is passed by a selection committee, and Husfliden claims they have the largest selection in Norway. The brochure certainly shows more patterns than anyone else's, with the classic Norwegian designs either all over or just around the neck and shoulders. Colors mostly gray, blue, or red on white.

Shaggy Rya-like rugs are designed by professionals and shown in four abstract patterns and several sizes. The smallest, 2' by 4', costs $22 as a complete kit to make up yourself, and $50 ready-made. In the 4' by 6' size the rugs cost $60 as a kit and $155 made up. For the less energetic, woolly cushions in similar styles cost $8 as kits and $20 made up; the kit components—canvas, wool and needles, etc.—can be bought separately.

SCOTLAND

William Anderson and Sons Ltd., 14/16 George Street, Edinburgh 2, Scotland ♛♛
20-page Scottish gift book, free. Prices in $.

This catalogue shows basically the same sorts of things as the Tartan Gift Shops, but not everything is repeated. Anderson's has horn spoons and necklaces around $7 each, deerskin bags, reproductions of seventeenth-century maps, $5, and place mats with reproductions of old prints of Scottish views, $5 each. And instead of illustrating tartan clothes, Anderson's has a special brochure for its made-to-measure skirt service showing nine different styles that can be made up, tweed and tartan samples on request. Knitwear by the most famous makers is sold, and special attention paid to matching sweater shades to skirts.

The Highland Welcome, Golspie, Sutherland, Scotland
32-page brochure, free.

A shop for English holidaymakers with some local products in a "Gifts from the Highlands" catalogue. Several pages of countryish suede and deerskin purses; a particularly nice suede one for $23 is big and square with a buckle fastening; a plain flat shoulder bag with an adjustable strap costs $10.

The silver jewelry is rather more primitive than the usual Scottish jewelry. It comes from Orkney and is based on designs found in excavations and old stonework. Pendants and rings cost about $5.50 each.

The Highland Welcome uses green and red Portsoy marble found in Banffshire, Scotland, and puts it on little gilt boxes, jewelry and gas table lighters, $12.50 (apparently Portsoy marble had its day in the seventeenth century when it was used in the palace of Versailles).

R. G. Lawrie Ltd., 38 Renfield Street, Glasgow C 2, Scotland ♛
16-page "Highland Dress" color catalogue, free. Prices in $.
Handwrought-silver brochure, free.

There seem to be almost as many shops catering to exiled Scotsmen as to nostalgic Irishmen. R. G. Lawrie (By Appointment to Her Majesty the Queen, bagpipe maker) says they have a worldwide reputation as authorities on Highland dress, and put out an extremely informative catalogue with descriptions of correct Highland dress for both evening and outdoor wear, as well as pipe-band uniforms. The catalogue finishes with a list of their most frequently requested books dealing with "things Scottish": clans, tartans, songs, dances and food.

A catalogue for handwrought silver has traditional Celtic

107
William Anderson and Sons Ltd Child's party or wedding kilt. Price according to size.
photo Tony Cleal

108
Tartan Gift Shops Saxony cape available in most tartans. $42.62. Surface postage $3.60.

109
Bangkok Dolls Completely handmade decorative dolls representing characters in Thai classic dance-drama. The White Monkey General and the Black Monkey General (10" high), $15.50 each; Rama, the hero (12" high), $14.

jewelry and some exclusive new adaptations of old silver: necklaces, spoons and forks. A pair of salad servers, for instance, have shafts copied from a fork found in a nunnery on the Isle of Iona, $42.

Paisley Limited, 72–96 Jamaica Street, Glasgow C 1, Scotland
16-page brochure, free. Prices in $.

This catalogue starts with authentic Highland dress and ends, apologizing, with incorrect Highland dress. The incorrect Highland dress consists of four different styles of tartan skirts that can be made to measure (around $22 each), sweaters to match with the chosen tartan, tartan slacks, dressing gown, car coat and Viyella shirts (from $10.50). Prices generally lower than Tartan Gift Shops (below) and William Anderson.

Tartan Gift Shops, 96 & 96a Princes Street, Edinburgh 2, Scotland
28-page catalogue, free; 75 cents air mail. Prices in $. Pringle knitwear brochure, free.

The Tartan Gift Shops, whose order department firmly announces, "This business is owned and managed by a Scottish family, and every order receives their individual attention," puts out the most comprehensive catalogue of these Scottish shops. Jewelry, collector's dolls (Mary Queen of Scots and retinue authentically dressed), Edinburgh crystal, and various Scottish oddities, such as bagpipe bottle tops, model pipers in a bottle, and tartan light switches. In addition to classic day and evening wear (as "correct Highland dress" is called here), there is an abundance of tartan hats, jackets, skirts, stoles, capes and even ponchos; a cashmere tartan shirtwaist dress costs $33, and a floor-length kilted skirt, $34. And hand-knitted Fair Isle sweaters, which none of the other shops show in their brochures, (traditional sweaters knitted out of natural colored Shetland wool or sometimes white, navy, dark brown with a patterned yolk around the neck). And for do-it-yourselfers, but slightly lazy ones, there are knit packs to make a Fair Isle sweater, with the band of intricate pattern already knitted, as well as skirt packs for under $11, complete with zipper and lining, to make tartan or tweed skirts.

SWITZERLAND

Schweizer-Heimatwerk, Rudolf-Brun-Brücke, 8023 Zurich, Switzerland

An official shop for carefully chosen Swiss handicrafts, Schweizer-Heimatwerk has no catalogue. They do have beautifully made goods, however, so write to them if you have something in mind, otherwise here is a list of a few of the many things they stock: cowbells on leather straps, decorated with brass ornaments and colorful wool trimming; gold, red, blue or silver metal Christmas-tree balls that play "Silent Night"; a collection of eighteen different rocks or minerals from Switzerland. Also hand-painted music boxes playing folk music; regional dolls and wooden hand-carved cheese or cake boards.

THAILAND

Bangkok Dolls, 85 Rajatapan Lane, Makkasan, Bangkok, Thailand
Color brochure, 75 cents. Prices in $.

In the distant past, Thai ladies amused themselves making decorative dolls dressed in classic Thai costumes. In 1957

Mrs. Chandavimol, the wife of a Thai government official, revived the world-famous but degenerating craft and started a small business making really beautiful handmade dolls in classic costumes copied from museum displays. Her most sumptuous dolls represent characters from Thai dance-dramas and are dressed in splendid, glittering costumes, but there are also dolls dressed in working clothes of different Thai regions, with handwoven fabrics and baskets made by the people who made the originals. And there is a group of "cuddly" dolls, also in Thai costumes—the only dolls actually meant for children. Dolls are 8" to 13" high and cost between $7 and $18 each.

TUNISIA

Office National de l'Artisanat, Ministère des Affaires Economiques, Den Den, Tunisia.
68-page color catalogue, Vol. I, "Tapis" (Rugs), $4.50.
100-page catalogue, Vol. II, "Divers" (Miscellaneous), $1.50.

The government handicrafts office trains craftsmen, controls quality and sees to it that Tunisian crafts while remaining true to the "purity of their original inspiration" don't stagnate but are allowed to develop freely. Consequently, the crafts shown in the beautifully produced catalogue are a mixture of old and new. Marvelous hammered copper pots and plates, painted wooden chests, pottery, vases, silver jewelry, regional embroidery and lace, and a palatial bird cage all look very traditional, while gold-tooled leather boxes, wrought-iron barbeque sets, hand-painted silk cushions, ceramic lamps, and dolls dressed in Tunisian wedding dresses look definitely modern. However, in spite of the glossiness of the catalogue, no prices or details are given, so determined shoppers must write, preferably in French, and be prepared to receive an answer in French.

TURKEY

Bali Kollektif, Hilton Oteli, Istanbul, Turkey
32-page catalogue, free. Prices in $.

Bali sends out a catalogue full of tempting Turkish crafts, but will sell only some small onyx goods retail (and wholesale quantities are huge). For example, 8" vases are about $6 each, and there are little candlesticks, cups and tumblers, nut bowls, cigarette holders, and three ashtrays. Styles vary from perfectly plain to elegantly ridged and very shaped. Prices between $2 and $8, except for a big 14" plate that costs $17.

WALES

Llyswen Welsh Craft Center, Llyswen, Brecon, Wales
Catalogue, free. Prices in $.

An inexpensive collection of clothes and bedspreads made from handwoven Welsh tapestry and flannel, also those fabrics by the yard. Tapestry is heavier than flannel and is suitable for coats; 56" wide tapestry costs $8 per yard, flannel is lighter and 54" wide flannel costs $4.50 per yard. The basic traditional design of the fabrics is a small honeycomb square woven into wool of another color, but there are all sorts of variations on that pattern, and different color combinations, too: rich new purples and pinks, or blues and greens, or natural-looking browns and seaweedy colors. Tapestry bedspreads cost $22 for single size; $25 for double; $30 for larger than double (measurements not given). Some of the clothes are bargains: tapestry coats for women, $38; flannel skirts, $12; hooded anoraks in tapestry lined throughout in rainproof nylon, $23; capes for children, $15 and up. The center also sells tapestry purses, Welsh socks, tea cozies, sheepskin goods, Welsh dolls and souvenirs.

13 Hobbies

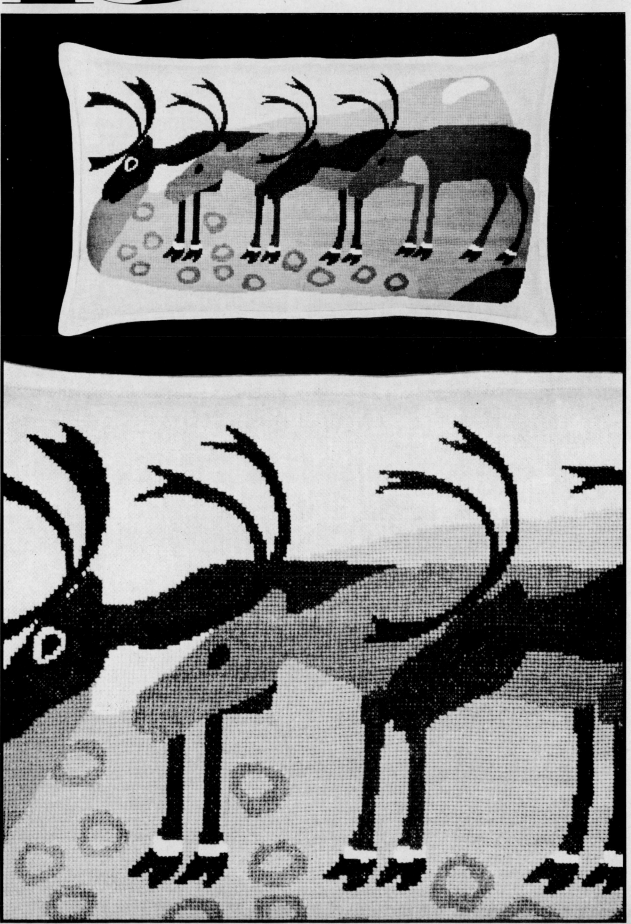

BATIK, CANDLEMAKING AND TIE-DYEING

Candle Makers Supplies, 4 Beaconsfield Terrace Road, London W. 14, England
List of supplies for batik, candlemaking, and tie-dyeing, 50 cents.

Here you can get a beginner's candlemaking kit, which contains acid, dyes, wicks, 5 lbs. of paraffin wax and an instruction booklet, for about $7, including postage. Or if you want to buy things separately, paraffin wax is about 22 cents a pound; beeswax about $1.65 a pound; wicks in all sizes; and perfumes for the candles in pine, lilac, lavender, etc. There is a helpful booklet for 25 cents, *Introduction to the Art of Candle Making*, which, among other things, tells you what to do about all the things that might go wrong.

Another beginner's kit is "Introductory Batik," $12, including postage. A little booklet, *Introduction to Batik*, describes batik as "an old Javanese method of fabric printing." You paint designs on your fabric with melted wax and then dye the fabric. The parts covered by the wax (which is later removed) don't take the dye but keep the original fabric color. You can do it on almost any kind of material and use the results for roller blinds, lampshades, dresses, scarves, wall hangings, etc.

There is no beginner's kit for tie-dyeing, but books and plenty of supplies are available, including the hard-to-get and highly-thought-of French Sennelier silk dyes.

BRASS RUBBING

Phillips and Page, 50 Kensington Church Street, London W.8, England
Price list, 10 cents.

Rather like shading or drawing over a penny under paper, taking "rubbings" from medieval monumental brasses and gravestones has become a popular pastime in England. (Schoolchildren even do it with manhole covers, the result is often a surprisingly decorative design.) Anyone thinking of rubbing brasses in European churches, gravestones in New England churchyards, or even manhole covers on city sidewalks, should write to Phillips and Page first, probably the only shop in the world to specialize in equipment and books for these activities. They have specially made sticks and cakes of "heelball" in colors as well as gold, bronze and silver. Lots of different kinds of paper in all the right sizes and colors, special crayons, erasers, and other useful equipment. Also books about every aspect of the subject, where and how to do it for beginners; history and documentation for addicts.

BUTTERFLIES

Worldwide Butterflies, Over Compton, Sherborne, Dorset, England
36-page catalogues with some color, 36 cents. Spring, winter, plus occasional lists.

Worldwide Butterflies sends live and dead specimens to collectors and schools all over the world, and it is clear that the firm is run by enthusiasts. The wonderfully detailed catalogue not only lists the stock and equipment but is full of extra advice and information on how everything should be cared for and used. The livestock includes stick insects, praying mantises, and eighty-eight kinds of butterflies for breeding. You can get the necessary import permit for live specimens from the Animal Health Division, U.S. Agricultural Research Service, Hyattsville, Md. 20782.

Worldwide Butterflies has a wide variety of entomological equipment: breeding cages, boxes, cabinets and nets, books,

110
Phillips and Page Rubbings taken from English manhole covers.

111
Worldwide Butterflies Danaus Plexippus (Monarch Butterfly), one of the many species bred each summer.

112
Priscilla Lobley Flower Kits Giant poppies made up. Two versions of this kit are available, one in red, orange and pink, the other in blue and green. Just over $3 each.

and various kinds of display cages with or without exotic butterflies. In the summer the Lepidopterists Rearing Outfit, "a complete outfit for the keen beginner," is on sale for about $7.50. And for those who like to go all the way with their hobbies, there are butterfly dishcloths, place mats, table napkins, wall charts, jewelry and carrier bags.

BUTTONS, BELTS AND BUCKLES

Paris House, 41 South Molton Street, London W1Y 2HB, England ☺
15-page jewelry catalogue, free; air mail $1. January and July.
15-page belts-and-buttons catalogue, free; air mail $1. January and July.

Twists and twirls of beads and filigree, leather roses, and braided daisies—all on buttons. This shop is a prize for an ambitious home dressmaker or anyone who likes to change buttons and belts on store-bought clothes for more dressy ones. The buttons are handmade on shank fittings, many available with holes and almost all with screw-on detachable fittings. Each season the catalogue has a page or two of classic shapes and then there are pages and pages of the most exotic and ornate buttons—pleated and gathered, hand-stitched in fabric, leather braid or cord, or made of beads or metal. They can be made in any color, and many can be made in the customer's own fabric.

Classic belts can be made in any width, but there are also very unusual pleated, twisted, fringed belts made out of soft suede or kid, and tied instead of buckled; beaded rouleau tie belts made in gold or silver lamé; grosgrain or ottoman twisted belts tasseled with beads.

The jewelry is heavy and frankly fake, in keeping with the new English extravagance in dress. For about $33 there are "chatelaines"—cascades of chains and beads that hook on the belt of an evening dress; gold or silver neckties with bead tassels that can be used as hair ornaments; chokers of pleated silver and gold lamé with interwoven pearls, $22; and old-fashioned lace-and-satin chokers for $13.

FLOWER ARRANGING

Ikebana International, CPO Box 1262, Tokyo, Japan
Explanatory leaflet, free.

A nonprofit international club for people interested in *ikebana* (Japanese flower arranging) with chapters all over America. If you are interested in joining, write to the headquarters and find out whether there is a chapter near you. If there is, you can join, whether you are a beginner or more experienced. A year's Regular Chapter Membership costs around $8 and entitles members to a yearly magazine, newsletter, and bimonthly postal flower-arranging lesson. Each chapter varies in its activities, but most have flower-arranging classes, demonstrations and study groups. People who do not live near a chapter can become Members At Large for around $5, receive the postal material, and attend meetings if they happen to visit a town with a chapter.

The Ohara School, 7—14 Minamiaoyama and 5-Chome, Minato-Ku, Tokyo, Japan
Price list, free. Prices in $.

The Ohara School, whose flower-arranging style is more traditional than Sango's (below), sells a helpful-sounding book, *Creation with Flowers*, by Houn Ohara (about $10 including sea postage). It covers fundamental styles, color-scheme arrangements, nonrealistic arrangements, tone arrangements and small flower arrangements. For about $1.75 per set, including postage, there are twenty cards, in color, of

arrangements in the Moribana style or the Heikas style by the same author. And in slides, "Ikebana for Beginners" and "Elementary Ikebana," both with step-by-step explanations. Also, an Ohara Study Program is available as a quarterly magazine, about $1.20 per copy. Contents include elementary course and middle course, essays, articles about Japanese traditional art, and a section described as "Things Japanese."

Sango Inc., c/o Sogetsukai, 2—21, 7-Chome Akasaka, Minato-Ku, Tokyo, Japan
8-page color brochure, free. Prices in $.

Sogetsu is the most modern of the leading *Ikebana* schools and through them you can buy everything you need for Japanese flower arranging (or plain flower arranging). A wonderful selection of beautifully simple and unusually shaped containers in restrained colors: black, white, mustard, brick, black and gold. Some expensive lacquerware—a set of five containers that can be piled on top of one another costs $55; also "scissors," which are actually special little shears. Over thirty shapes and sizes in "needlepoint" metal flower holders, and plenty of illustrated, instructional books and magazines in both Japanese and English. Also notebooks, calendars and postcards decorated with photographs or arrangements.

FLOWERS—PAPER

Yvonne Docktree, 28 Mile House Lane, St. Albans, Hertfordshire, England
Illustrated brochure, free.

Yvonne Docktree sells a kit ($2.25 surface, $3.25 air mail) which she designed herself for making five bright and decorative tissue-paper flowers. You can choose between gold, flame, pink, scarlet, turquoise, violet or autumn tints. When you finish the tissue paper and stems provided, you can buy more from her or anyone else, and go on using the instructions and patterns. I made two flowers quite easily with my six- and eight-year-old daughters (they did the cutting and I did the trickier bits).

Priscilla Lobley Flower Kits, Thorpe Lodge, Ealing Green, London W.5, England
Leaflet, 50 cents.

Very refined kits for making lifelike paper flowers to decorate the house: Oriental poppies, mixed roses, and giant sunflowers. The kits have been tested on all ages from "teenagers to grannies," and although some are for beginners, none are for children. Complete with instructions and everything needed except scissors, each kit costs just over $3, including postage. *Flower Making*, a book by Priscilla Lobley, is also on sale, for about $4.

GARDENING

An importation permit is not needed for bulbs or seeds, but it is needed for plants, and should be obtained before plants are ordered. There is no charge. The Permit Section, Plant Importations Branch, U.S. Department of Agriculture, 209 River Street, Hoboken, N.J. 07030, gives out permits and has a circular with information on the details you should give when applying. Ask for "Suggestions to Applicants for Permits to Import Plant Propagating Material under Quarantine No 37."

GARDENING—BULBS

J. Heemskerk, c/o P. Van Deursen, P.O. Box 60, Sassenheim, Holland
Two color catalogues, free. May: tulips and daffodils, etc.;

December: gladioli, dahlias, etc. Prices in $.

Neat little catalogues with lots of illustrations and descriptions of daffodils, narcissi, tulips (eighty-eight varieties, including wild tulips and parrot tulips, etc.), hyacinths, crocuses, lilies, anemones, Dutch irises, and miscellaneous Dutch bulbs. And for $28, including delivery, you can buy a "complete garden collection"—182 bulbs in 19 named varieties with a group to flower in each month from February to June. Half the quantity can also be bought.

Schiphol Airport, Tax-Free Shopping Center, Amsterdam, Holland
Leaflet, free. Prices in $.

Not as interesting for serious gardeners as the other bulb catalogues but good for people who like simple decisions, the Schiphol Airport leaflet includes just a few basic bulbs that come in lots of 50 or 100: daffodils, hyacinths, narcissi and tulips. Prices are $10–$17, including postage.

Tulipshow Frans Roozen, Vogelenzang, Holland
24-page color catalogue, free. Prices in $.

This catalogue is not as convenient as Heemskerk's because the illustrations are larger but fewer, and the plants are only listed and not described. It includes varieties, however, that I haven't seen listed anywhere else, and there are gift selections for sale at $8 and up. Each variety is separately packed, with full gardening directions in each parcel. Bulbs are shipped for planting time in September and early October only.

GARDENING—PLANTS
Quinta Fdo Schmoll, Cadereyta de Montes, Qro., Mexico
Price list, free. Prices in $.

This cactus farm has a mimeographed list of the many cactus plants and seedlings for sale. There are no descriptions, just names and prices, but if the names don't mean anything to you, ask for offers number one or two—both of which are ready-chosen assortments. Prices start at $7 for fifty seedlings, including postage (you can also get smaller quantities). Anyone interested in show plants can write for additional information.

Sunningdale Nurseries Ltd., London Road, Windlesham, Surrey, England ♥
80-page color catalogue, free.

Sunningdale Nurseries belongs to John Waterer, who at the turn of the century did an enormous amount of business with America, but they sell plants, not seeds, which now, following health regulations, must have all earth washed off their roots before leaving England and be inspected on arriving in America. This cleansing procedure is expensive and sometimes bad for the plants. However, Sunningdale's still has a small business with a few dauntless Americans interested in certain plants who are not put off by the rule that there is a $50 minimum for any one order. Stock covers ornamental trees, shrubs, hardy plants, roses and fruit trees.

GARDENING—SEEDS
Allwood Bros. Ltd., Clayton Nurseries, Hassocks, Sussex, England
32-page catalogue, free. Prices in $.

A marvelous shop for carnation and orchid lovers, Allwood specializes in selling by mail. Worthwhile for American buyers, according to Allwood, are carnation, pink and dianthus seeds, many of which are not generally available in America, and their orchid plants, which Allwood describes as

113
Tulipshow Frans Roozen A view of the nursery and show garden, where a thousand varieties of spring flowers can be seen from April 10 to May 15.

114
Thompson and Morgan Ltd Seed and bulb catalogue cover.

"reasonably" priced—Cymbidium seedlings, for example, cost from about $1 each.

Sutton and Sons Ltd., The Royal Seed Establishment, Reading, England ☙☙
98-page color seed catalogue, free.

England's most famous seed company sells a wide variety of flowers, vegetables and herbs in special vaporproof laminated packets. The catalogue contains two pages of sundries—footwear, gloves, etc. Gift vouchers available.

Thompson and Morgan Ltd., London Road Ipswich, 1P2 OBA, Suffolk, England
160-page color catalogue, free. November.

This firm claims to have the reputation of listing more seeds in their catalogue than anyone else in the world, which may be true. Anyway, it is impressively extensive, with some interesting vegetables and unusual flowers.

Flowers are divided into categories such as "The Flower Arranger's Garden," "Everlasting Flowers," and others with seeds I haven't seen at all in America—"Ornamental Grasses" and "Bonsai Trees."

There aren't as many vegetables, but they are worth looking at, too, as strains are different, and there is a "Vegetables with a Difference" selection which includes asparagus-peas, globe artichoke, red brussels sprouts, celtruce (combines the use of celery and lettuce with four times the vitamin C content of the latter!) and scorzonera.

GARDENING—TOOLS
Woodman's of Pinner, 19–25 High Street, Pinner, Middlesex, HA5 5PN, England
96-page catalogue, 35 cents.

England's top garden-equipment store sells "tools to be proud of" by England's leading manufacturers, and specializes in new gardening aids. Enjoyable browsing, I would think, for out-of-action gardener in the winter. Besides standard and new tools for snipping, clipping, digging and weeding, Woodman's carries every sort of garden indoor and outdoor implement from everyday plant supports and greenhouse thermometers to fruit pickers, flower gatherers, little fiberglass pools for aquatic plants, and weather vanes made to order. A pair of standard pruning secateurs costs $2.15, a rain gauge, $2.75.

GEMS

Australian Gem Trading Co., 294 Little Collins Street, Melbourne, Australia
16-page price list, free. Prices in $.

A good catalogue for beginners, with information on the composition of stones sold, detailed descriptions of the different qualities, and instructions for cutting. Not only that, but the catalogue says: "We gladly invite correspondence on gem stones, gemmology, and minerals generally, and if we can at any time advise on technical or other problems, we are only too ready to do so." The catalogue lists many different sizes and types of rough and cut opals, the cheapest being lowest-quality opal chips at $1 per ounce (31 grams), and the most expensive being 1- to 2-ounce finest gem quality selected pieces, at $66 per ounce, from which to cut large single stones. Australian sapphires are also sold in great variety, including Black Star sapphires. Cut and polished star sapphires with guaranteed perfect star in all sizes and colors cost from $5.50 per carat.

Gemrocks, 14–18 Holborn, London E.C.1, England
Minerals and rocks, and books for amateur lapidaries. No catalogue, so write with specific requests.

Keshavlal Mohanlal E. and Sons, 81 Marine Drive, Bombay 2, India
Price lists, 1 retail, 1 wholesale, free. Prices in $.

A list of rough stones for cutting that is appealingly written with explanations and descriptions. Indian star rubies are available at $9 an ounce (about seven stones), Black Star sapphires from Siam at $10 for 50 grams (about twenty stones); these come with special instructions on cutting worked out after personal experience. Color moonstones on sale have been partially cut because in the past customers had trouble cutting them and were unable to get good results. Cut moonstones and agates come in bead, cabochon, egg, and marble shapes. All prices include registered air mail. Other rough stones are handled which are too heavy to go by air, and as they take three months to get to America by sea, customers are advised to buy them locally. However, if you don't mind waiting, Keshavlal Mohanlal is willing to sell them to you.

HERALDRY

Cannocks, Department E, O'Connell Street, Limerick, Ireland
6-page "Heraldry" brochure, free.

Anyone with an ungovernable urge to display their family name should immediately write to Cannocks department store, who can give moderate satisfaction. For at least 200,000 families they have produced crests on door knockers, wall plaques, desk plaques, blazer crests and car shields. An even luckier few with commoner names can go further and equip themselves with crested spoons, charms, key rings, handkerchiefs, tie clips and cuff links.

KITES

Yachtmail Co. Ltd., 7 Cornwall Crescent, London W11 1PH, England
Illustrated price list, free. Prices in $.

Yachtmail sends out an illustrated list of ten impressive cloth and wood kites well described and with flying hints. Start with a 32" by 30" war kite for about $6.50, highly recommended for beginners because it is the easiest to fly. Then advance to a black bat kite, about $5.50, which hovers and dives, or a hawk kite which flaps its wing pieces and looks like a hovering hawk. You can also get reels and string, and a parachute attachment for 30 cents which rides up the string and lets go automatically when it gets to the top. All these prices include surface postage.

KNITTING

R. S. Duncan and Co., 30 Chapel Street, Bradford 1, England
16-page color catalogue with samples, $1.

Each year R. S. Duncan and Co. puts out a splendid catalogue illustrating in color some attractive knitting patterns for children, adults and fatties, with actual samples of three of England's best-known yarns: Falcon, Munrospun and Jaeger at prices that they say are below normal retail prices in the United Kingdom. There are nineteen types of Falcon illustrated, and about three hundred colors and two types (fourteen colors) of Falcon listed. Tweeds to make into skirts, trousers, waistcoats, or whatever, to match with the knitting. There are six Munrospun colors in three-ply knitting yarn with tweeds to match. Five kinds of Jaeger yarn with thirty-six colors. To make things even more convenient, three kinds of buttons in colors to match the yarns and lighting zippers can be ordered at the same time.

Rug kits and needlework kits are illustrated too.

John Lees (Nottingham) Ltd., 24–32 Carlton Street, Nottingham NG1 1NZ, England
Price list, free. Wool samples and catalogue of garment designs, $2 surface mail. Prices in $.

Knitting patterns and a huge assortment of knitting yarns. Most leading English makes are listed: Bairnswear, Emu, Jaeger, Munrospun, Patons, and many more; also Lopi from Iceland. Patons Beehive two-ply, and three- and four-ply baby wool all cost 39 cents per ounce, for instance. John Lees says that English wools are both better and cheaper than other yarns.

Millhaven Knitting Services, Knowstone, South Molton, Devon, England
Catalogue of services, $1.

Help for handknitters in difficulty—if your measurements don't fit standard patterns, Millhaven will adapt the patterns for you. If you spoil your work when you sew it together, Millhaven will fix it for about $2.75, and if you like, will line it too. Or if you decide not to tackle something particularly complicated, Millhaven will do the whole thing (they seem to be especially used to making lacy knitted bed jackets as presents for people in hospital). Send them the pattern and they will quote a price. They also crochet, and make crochet-covered buttons for dressmakers.

MAGIC

L. Davenport and Co., 51 Great Russell Street, London, W.C.1, England
Brochure "Demon Telegraph," free.
98-page catalogue "Children's Magic and Close-Up Magic," $1. Prices in $.

For children, parents and professionals—"tricks of infinite jest that will bewilder the brain." This third-generation family firm (there is a photo of Betty Davenport lifting a white rabbit from a top hat) supplies snappy routines to professional conjurers all over the world, but also manufactures humbler pranks: stinky scent, goofy teeth, dirty nose drops, and squirting chocolate suitable for party favors or "the man who likes pocket tricks (and who doesn't?)" at lower prices than comparable articles in America, they say. There is a small brochure to start you off, with books and popular jokes such as multiplying matchboxes and diabolical dominoes, but anyone who really wants to make an impression should send for the 98-page "Children's Magic and Close-Up Magic" (first in a series of specialized catalogues), which lists tricks with coins and money, dice, matchboxes, and miscellaneous delights such as "Improved Omelet in a Hat," and Chinese Finger Choppers. And for children's parties: spinning balloons, springing sausages, bewildering blocks, whimsical wands, chameleon clowns and, thank goodness, the old favorites, disappearing rabbits and appearing doves.

MOVIES

Portland Films, 45 New Oxford Street, London W.C.I, England
32-page brochure, free.

"Beware those weak hearts! We can only warn you of the unbelievable horror contained in this film, we cannot stop you watching it." Portland Films says that they have the largest 8-mm. home-movie, mail-order house in the United Kingdom, yet manage to reply to letters by return mail. They stock around 2,000 silent and some sound black-and-white and color titles but no pin-up or glamour movies, though there are a few silent little X movies with titles like *Summer Heat* and *Captive Woman* ("Big Jack Devlin was a bully and his job suited him down to the ground. Boss of a women's prison, he used his power to buy himself Love and Lust"). And if you feel like watching with fright as the horrible monster turns on his master and stabs him to death, then holding your breath as the deformed monster carries a girl along the edge of the castle's highest tower, buy *Castle of Death*. However, it must be said that most of the rest of the movies look thoroughly suitable for family viewing and children's parties. Fifty feet Cagneys, Bogarts, Harold Lloyds, Laurel and Hardys, and Chaplins for about $2.20 each. Also lovable Shirley Temple, who in *Polly Tix in Washington* "will bring a grin to every face." Cartoons, travelogues and animal movies. Two-reelers cost about $16.

NATURAL SCIENCES

Watkins and Doncaster, 110 Park View Road, Welling, Kent, England
52-page catalogue, 50 cents.

The letterhead says that this ninety-eight-year-old firm sells "the finest equipment for all the Natural Sciences." R. J. Ford adds that it is cheaper for Americans to buy their products direct rather than through American firms. Of fairly general educational interest are bird, mammal, and "Life in the Oglicene Period" charts for about $1 each, and demonstration cases illustrating different methods of seed dispersal, common objects at the sea shore, etc. Apart from that, there is the necessary equipment for the study and practice of botany, dissection, geology, oology and taxidermy, and being specialists in entomology, Watkins and Doncaster can provide exclusive entomological items such as moth traps, which, they say, they alone manufacture.

NEEDLEWORK

In embroidery a design, often in a variety of stitches, is sewn on a fabric, but the fabric always remains visible as background. In needlepoint (known as tapestry in England) the final surface is entirely covered by small, regular stitches sewn on a canvas. There are four kinds of needlepoint kits available: *charted*—a plain canvas comes with a "chart," or diagram, which you transfer onto the canvas by counting stitches as you sew; *painted*—the design has been painted on the canvas; *trammed* or *trammé*—the design has been understitched on the canvas, and you fill in stitches with the appropriate colors; *part-worked*—the complicated parts of the design have been completed, with only the background left to be filled in.

Art Needlework Industries Ltd., 7 St. Michael's Mansions, Ship Street, Oxford, OX1 3DG, England
Six Aran knitting brochures, $2.50.
Ten English needlepoint brochures, $2.50.
Prices in $.

This is by far the most scholarly and serious of these needlework shops, and the owner, Heinz Edgar Kiewe, has spent over forty years writing books and researching historical designs. He makes a few nasty cracks about "prefabricated bargain basement kits" and says his kits are not for neurotics who want to finish something overnight but require discipline, respect and love from the embroiderer. Anyone who feels up to Mr. Kiewe's standards should write for his very informative brochures, which come with samples of specially dyed wools and describe and illustrate hand-painted and/or charted kits.

Mr. Kiewe says that he has gathered many of his

unpublished designs from customers, including one allegedly embroidered by Mary Queen of Scots, and another said to have been worked on by Marie Antoinette in prison. These two complete kits for chair seats cost $17 each, including postage. Other interesting old designs include medieval French miniatures, Georgian birds, William Morris designs, and a hand-painted seat or panel set for $35 of "The Unicorn Caught," one of the Cluny tapestries at the Cloisters branch of the Metropolitan Museum in New York. And there are several charted needlepoint rugs about 3' by 4' costing about $50, including postage: a Persian "serail" rug, a late Regency rose rug, and a Smyrna hunting rug.

The knitting brochures include wool samples, illustrations and descriptions of Aran sweaters, jackets and hats. Prices, $11–$14 per kit. Also Icelandic, Shetland, camel's-hair and cashmere sweater kits.

Aux Gobelins, 352 Rue Saint-Honoré, Paris I, France
Price list for rug squares, free.

No catalogues are produced by this shop, so it will be a difficult one to order from (and remember that French prices are much higher than English ones), but I am including it because French petit point and wools have such a high reputation. Aux Gobelins sells painted and trammed canvas for armchairs, panels and rugs. They say Americans write and tell them what period work they want, and sometimes specify the color and design (if they want a canvas for a chair, they send a paper pattern), then Aux Gobelins advises them on which model would suit them best.

There is a price list, in French, for rug squares, which vary in price from $12 to $60 and can be bought one at a time.

Klockargårdens Hemslöjd AB, Olsbacka, 795 00 Rättvik, Sweden
Brochure, $1.

Here you can get semiabstract embroidery kits for wall hangings and cushions, as well as kits for Flemish weaving (a small loom is necessary for this), and kits for Rya rugs. Colors are deep and rich—browns with orange, purples with red, and dark blues and greens together.

Luxury Needlepoint Ltd., 36 Beauchamp Place, Brompton Road, London S.W.3, England
Catalogue and wool samples, 50 cents; air mail $1.50.
Prices in $.

According to Luxury Needlepoint, doctors the world over recommend needlepoint, so if you feel you need this "finest form of occupational therapy," this shop will provide explanations (very helpful for beginners) of the ways that canvases come prepared, as well as painted or trammed kits in traditional designs suitable for chairs, cushions, stools, fire screens and carpets with their own special wools, from $5.50. But I like best their Tudor designs of some Chippendale flowers in antique coloring, $20, and four copies of old French pictures, each one showing a rustic boy or girl in a landscape surrounded by a frame of flowers, $20–$38.

The Needlewoman Shop, 146–148 Regent Street, London W1R 6BA, England
68-page color catalogue, 50 cents; air mail $2.
Book list, 10 cents.

The Needlewoman Shop in Regent Street must be the biggest shop of its kind in the world, and the outstanding catalogue for "those who embroider, crochet, knit or sew" should absolutely not be missed. Its virtue lies in its great variety, unlike the other needlework shops, which specialize in one or two styles. The Needlewoman Shop has works of every sort

115
Seldon Tapestries Ltd 5' × 4'1" rug kit, available in nine pieces or in one. Background Chinese blue. $223.20 with the design painted on the canvas, and wools.

116
Clara Weaver 23½" × 17½" Children's Christmas Calendar 8-3027 with rings for small gifts, one for each day from December 1 to 24. Linen, chart, yarn, rings and ribbon, around $7; ready-made, around $35.

117
Clara Weaver 19½" × 15½" Sampler 8-3591. Linen, chart and yarn, about $5; brass rods, about $2.60; ready-made, about $50.

and every style imported from Austria, Denmark, Germany, Norway and Sweden. Tablecloths to embroider, rugs to make, felt appliqué and wool pictures, toys to sew, handkerchiefs to crochet, clothes to crochet and knit, and, of course, a bushel of cushions and pictures to embroider or needlepoint, guaranteed to entrap novices and entice devotees on to new heights. Designs change every year, the catalogue I looked at showed, among other things: Victorian samplers, regional Norwegian designs, London views imitating etchings, silhouettes of famous composers, animals, flowers, hunting scenes, abstracts, and some beautiful German cushions in gold thread on a white background. There is also a needlework-mounting service. Customers' work can be mounted on handbags, velvet cushions, writing cases, stools and various larger pieces of furniture.

In fact, a sewer's every need is covered: accessories, embroidery fabrics, "tools of the trade" are on sale, and what looks like a first-rate collection of inspirational and inexpensive "how to" craft books on tie and dye, patchwork, fashion crochet, flower making, costume dolls, metal-thread embroidery.

Eva Rosenstand A/S, Virumgårdsvej 18, Virum, Denmark
20-page color catalogue, $1.

Edwardian ladies drink tea on a tea cozy, a boy plays a pipe on a telephone-number book, huntsmen ride across a magazine rack, and little girls dance around a mirror. Eva Rosenstand specializes in whimsically designed embroidery kits, mainly to be made into useful objects: glass cases, calendars, coffee cozies, bellows covers and pipe racks. Also bags of all kinds, from needlepoint and cross stitch to silver thread on a Thai-silk background, and beads and gold thread on satin.

The catalogue also shows an appealing collection of cheerful Christmas kits for tablecloths, babies' bibs, cards, mobiles and tree decorations over which cavort bouncy elves, angels, children, snowflakes and stars.

Mounting kits, hangers and sewing accessories are on sale too.

Seldon Tapestries, Ltd., 10 Kings Mansions, Lawrence Street, London S.W.3, England
Brochure, free; air mail 50 cents.

How about a needlepoint picture of your dog, house, hobbies, or favorite landscape? Seldon Tapestries specializes in carrying out customers' own ideas. Write to them with your suggestion and they will quote you a price for a picture on a wall hanging, bedhead, handbag, belt, tray cover, card-table top, rug, etc. They also have an interesting collection of ready-made kits, both painted and trammed.

Clara Weaver, Østergade 42, 1100 Copenhagen K, Denmark
Color brochure, free. Prices in $.

This firm sells pretty fresh Danish designs for embroideries, tablecloths, place mats and tapestries. The designs are light and colorful with only a few traditional designs and with lots of wild-flower bouquets. Unlike most of the other needlework firms in this section, Clara Weaver sells charts instead of trammed or painted canvases, which means you have to count out the design yourself when you are embroidering. If you would like a trammed canvas, it can be done, but will take about three months and cost twice as much. As with all foreign needlework kits, prices are lower than American prices: there are a lot of kits for under $10, and almost nothing for over $20. The pieces can also be bought made up, but at about eight times the price.

Woolcraft, No. 4 Trading Building, Regina, Saskatchewan, Canada
26-page color catalogue, $1. Prices in $.

Delicate little sprays of needlepoint flowers to make into brooches, earrings or cuff links (everything provided) are available here, as are larger bouquets and flowers. Choose between petit-point or wool kits.

This is by far the best place for sentimental pictures—plenty of pekes, poodles, thatched cottages, geese at dawn and moonlit ruins.

POTTERY

Estrin Manufacturing Ltd., 1767 West Third Avenue, Vancouver 9, B.C., Canada
8-page leaflet, free. Prices in $.

A complete range of equipment for potters, including an assortment of wheels with or without motors. Kickwheels cost between $150 and $218, including shipping—which Estrin says is $30 to $100 less than competitors' wheels.

RADIO

H.A.C. Short-Wave Products, 29 Old Bond Street, London W.1, England
Leaflet, free.

H.A.C., makers of the first shortwave kit, now makes two kits for battery-operated shortwave receivers for radio hams. H.A.C. stands for "Hear All Continents," which is what you should be able to do.

The H.A.C. Single Stage, Short-Wave Receiver Model DX, Mark 2, about $10, for beginners, is an improved version of a model which has been on sale for twenty years. It can now be built in an hour by someone with no knowledge of radio, yet the makers say it is ideal for all shortwave reception, especially from amateur transmitters and in Morse code.

The H.A.C. One Valve Receiver Model K, about $14. This model has a completely different circuit, using latest available techniques and modern miniature components. It is intended for people who are not afraid of complications and can solder miniature components. Also it can be made into a two-valve shortwave receiver at a later stage.

Details of the components of both models are given in the leaflet.

SHELLS

Eaton's Shell and Rock Shop, 16 Manette Street, London W1V 5LB, England
Shells, coral, starfish and marine curios from all over the world. There is no catalogue, but if American customers list the shells they want, Eaton's will quote prices.

SPINNING

Ashford Handicrafts Ltd., P.O. Box 12, Rakaia, Canterbury, New Zealand
Leaflet, free. Prices in $.

A very good ready-to-assemble spinning wheel in silver birch costs only about $45, including postage, or even less—$35—if you buy five at one time. Wool is also sold here.

WEAVING

I have talked to a professional and an amateur weaver, both of whom said that weavers should always get their supplies from abroad, as prices are lower and colors better. They claimed that after mailing costs and duty are paid, you save about a $1 per pound of yarn. They recommended the firms (except the one for Finnish yarns, which I found myself).

DYES

Mr. C. D. Fitz Hardinge-Bailey, St. Aubyn, 15 Dutton Street, Bankstown NSW 2200, Australia
Price list, free.

The dyes sold by this firm are produced mainly for use in the firm's own weaving, but they also sell their dyes to customers as a sideline.

World Wide Herbs Ltd., 11 St. Catherine Street East, Montreal 129, Canada
Brochure, free.

A very complete supply of dried-plant material, dyes and mordants, including cochineal at $7 a pound, and indigo root at $2.20.

LOOMS

Vävstolsfabriken Glimåkra AB, 280 G4 Glimåkra, Sweden
Brochure $1. Prices in $.

Lovely traditional Swedish handlooms and accessories at below American prices. Minimum order $100, and everything is sent sea freight.

YARNS

Wm. Condon and Sons Ltd., 65 Queen Street, Charlottetown, Prince Edward Island, Canada
Brochure and wool samples, free. Prices in $.

Beautifully colored wool yarns for knitting and weaving. Weavers should stick to the two-ply and up, as the single-ply yarns do not weave well.

Craftsman's Mark Yarns, Bronberllen, Trefnant, Denbigh, North Wales.
Samples card, $1.

Hand-spun yarn and fleece in lovely natural colors. "Best in the world," says one of my advisers.

Cum Ltd., Roemersgade 5, 1362 Copenhagen K, Denmark
Price list and big book of yarn samples, $3. Prices in $.
Catalogue for looms, $1. Prices in $.

Cum sells looms and weaving accessories, as well as a magnificently wide range of cotton, linen and wool yarns.

Helmi Vuorelma Oy, Vesijärvenkatu 13, Lahti, Finland
Samples card and price list, 50 cents.

This Finnish handweaving firm sells its linen tow yarn in very good glowing and subtle colors, and two thicknesses, no. 4 and no. 8.

The Multiple Fabric Co. Ltd., Dudley Hill, Bradford BD4 9PD, England
Samples card and price list, free. Prices in $.

Camel's hair, horsehair, mohair and wool yarn in natural colors.

WOODCARVING

Ashley Iles Ltd., East Kirkby, Spilsby, Lincolnshire, England
Leaflet $1. Prices in $.

Hand-forged wood-carving tools sold individually and in sets at fairly low prices. For example, a set of six boxwood-handled tools for the beginner costs about $12, while a set of eighteen boxwood-handled tools, including some for "high class" work and fine detail, costs about $34.

118
Clara Weaver 15" × 17" Owl Cushion 1-3864. Linen, chart and yarn, about $7; ready-made without inside cushion, about $46.
photos Koefoed Fotografi

BLANKETS

Wool blankets are heavier and more expensive than synthetic ones, but they have a much nicer texture, and don't mat or pile as much.

W. Bill Ltd., Mail Order Dept., 40 South Molton Lane, London W1Y 1AT, England
Ask for the "Blankets" brochure, free. Prices in $.

Lan-Air-Cel, England's most famous cellular wool blankets, are woven with holes to trap air and give warmth by insulation while being comfortably light. They arc made in all sorts of sizes, including crib size. Single bed, about $14; double, about $20.

Hawick Honeycombe Blankets, Hawick, Scotland
Color brochure, free, and samples on request.

Hawick's makes its own cellular wool blankets for people who hate bedroomy pinks and pale blues. Their blankets are slightly lighter than Lan-Air-Cel (see above), but no other manufacturer has the magnificently violent colors of Hawick's "Boutique Range": Chinese Lacquer (orangy red), Purple Glory, Aztec Gold, Dragon Green, Parrot Blue, and Black Coffee (black, not dark brown). Two sizes only. Single, about $15; double, about $21.

R. N. Peace and Co., 103 High Street, Witney, Oxfordshire 0X8 6LZ, England
Price list, free. Prices in $.

The superb wool blankets sold by R. N. Peace are made by the famous three-hundred-year-old firm Charles Witney of Earley (By Appointment to the Queen). Witney blankets were originally brought over by English settlers who traded them for furs with Indians. (The Indians promptly dyed them blue or red.) Four qualities of blanket are available, each one substantially cheaper than when bought in America. Prices start at $11 for a single blanket in the lightest fabric, and go up to $43 for a king-sized blanket in the very best quality. Each blanket comes in white and about eight other colors, including orange and turquoise.

Westaway and Westaway, 29 Bloomsbury Way, High Holborn, London WC1A 2SL, England
Glen Cree Mohair blanket and rug brochure, free.
General catalogue, free.

Friends who buy their vintage wine from Christie's also buy unbeatably luxurious Glen Cree Mohair blankets from Westaway and Westaway. Made from the wool of Angora goats, the blankets are as light and warm as can be and come in ten solid colors or twenty different checks, and in tartans from bright-yellow-and-apple-green to the inky Black Watch Tartan. Single-bed size, about $37; double, about $52. Travel rugs, $24; knee rugs, $12.

This shop also sells blankets, travel rugs, fabrics and knitwear, and say they are known for having the lowest prices in London.

EIDERDOWNS

These eiderdowns have long been used in Germany and Scandinavia, and have more recently become popular in England, rightly so because they are a great advance—they put an end to bedmaking. The down-filled comforter is zipped into a sheet (rather like a pillowcase) and is used *instead* of blankets and sheets. It doesn't need tucking in, but settles around you as you move in bed. If you put a fitted sheet underneath, there is nothing to do in the morning but give the eiderdown a shake and lay it flat. Anyone who isn't convinced might experiment with their children. Eiderdowns are, of course, perfect for avoiding the agony of trying to tuck blankets into bunk beds.

The German Bedding Center, 26 Connaught Street, London W.2, England
Color "Karo-Step" brochure, free. Prices in $.

The Karo-Step brochure quotes what must be the most banal folksaying ever: "Nobody can fall asleep with cold feet, and he whose feet are getting cold will soon awaken." Prices are higher here (see shops below), starting at $44, plus postage, for a single-bed-sized eiderdown, but there are compensations. Judging by the pictures, the German-style eiderdowns are warmer, thicker and less flexible than the English or Norwegian ones. (However, as American houses are kept so much warmer than European homes, this may not be an advantage.) Many sizes are available, such as crib or king size, and any size can be made to order. The eiderdowns and their covers both come in many colors, and there are pillows and pillowcases to match. Finally, the brochure gives helpful information for anyone choosing an eiderdown for the first time.

Helios Home Supplies, Tytherington Center, MacClesfield, Cheshire, England
40-page catalogue, free.

Helios stocks three brands of eiderdowns, including the most famous English quilt, Slumberdown. In fact, this is a very good place to get eiderdowns for children's bunks, as they have the right size for a 2' 6" mattress. There are many different types of covers to choose from, and everything is well explained. Bunk sizes start at $25; covers at $9.

Also for sale here are Irish linen sheets, twin size, $24 per pair; feather pillows start at $8 a pair. Witney wool blankets start at $12 for double-bed size (less than anywhere else).

Sundt Export Department, Bergen, Norway
6-page quilt and pewter brochure, free. Prices in $.

Sundt, a Norwegian department store, has a list of the "Continental quilts" that they sell by mail to America. Prices, including postage, start at $35 for a lightweight duck-down-filled eiderdown for a single bed. Covers in no-iron crepe cotton, in white or pastel shades, start at $13.25.

FLATWARE

DENMARK

Arti-Forma, Nikolaj Plads 26, Copenhagen, Denmark
8-page brochure, free. Prices in $.

Arti-Forma, whose brochure shows mainly good modern jewelry, have a few household objects, and illustrates three patterns of modern flatware. When I compared the price of one pattern, "Fuja," which in stainless steel cost $12.30 per six-piece setting at Arti-Forma, I found that it costs $22 in a New York department store. Another pattern, "Caravelle,' in silver plate, costs only $12.25 per place setting at Arti-Forma, whereas modern Danish settings in silver plate cost around $23 in the New York store.

GERMANY

Rosenthal Studio-Haus, Dr. Zoellner Kg, Leopoldstrasse 44, 8 Munich 23, Germany

*80-page color Rosenthal Studio Line catalogue, $1.
Rosenthal glass catalogue, $1.*

The big Rosenthal glass-and-china catalogue shows about
ten handsome, modern flatware settings. I compared
prices here with New York prices on one place setting,
"Composition," German price was almost half. They start
at about $12 for a four-piece stainless-steel place setting,
and go as high as $75 for a four-piece sterling-silver place
setting. Pieces all available individually or in sets.

Franz Widman und Sohn, am Karlstor Unter den Arkaden, 8 Munich 2, Germany

*Manufacturers' brochures in German, free: Henkels,
Pfeiffer and Potts stainless-steel flatware; Auerhan and
Reiner silver plate and silver; Othello pocket knives and
horn-handled steak knives; Boker manicure sets*

Germany is well known for its first-rate stainless steel, and the
old family firm of Franz Widman sells the best-known of all
such flatware—sleek and mostly modern Henkels. Prices start
at $4 for a four-piece place setting, "Cardinal." Pfeiffer table
settings are more decorated than the Henkels and start at $5
for a four-piece place setting. They also have baby sets
starting at $5.50 for a knife, fork and spoon.

Both modern and traditional silver and silver plate are
stocked; four-piece silver-plate settings by Reiner start at
$8.50; in silver they start at $25.

If you are energetic, write to Widman's for their brochures
on other German specialties: real horn-handled knives,
carving sets, scissors, manicure sets and Hummel figurines.
But remember, everything is in German, so even though there
are plenty of pictures, it is hard work translating.

HONG KONG

Universal Suppliers, G.P.O. Box 14803, Hong Kong

*30-page color Noritake catalogue, free; air mail $1.60.
Prices in $.*

A full-color catalogue of Japanese Noritake china, glass and
flatware services. Fifty-nine-piece flatware sets for eight
people in 18-8 stainless steel cost $44–$50, and in
electroplated nickel silver, $80. Seventy-four-piece sets also
available, but no individual pieces. Surface-mail postage and
packing cost are an extra $8 per set.

SWEDEN

PUB (Paul U. Bergströms AB), Box 40 140, Export Department, S-103/43 Stockholm 40, Sweden

*Price lists for KF, Gense and Nils-Johan stainless-steel
tableware, $1.50. Prices in $.*

Swedish stainless-steel flatware was one of the first to break
away from traditional shapes and has kept a reputation for
streamlined design. The PUB department store says that their
flatware is one of their most popular mail-order items to
America. They have complete price lists for about twelve
modern table settings with small pictures of the knife, fork
and spoon, or sometimes only the knife. Prices start at $4.50
for four pieces of the fairly conventional Servus: knife, fork
and two spoons by KF, and go up to $7.35 for a knife, fork
and spoon in the slim and angular Saroya by Nils-Johan.
Everything can be bought individually, and prices are
considerably lower than in America.

119
Mothercare (see Clothes section) Reversible wool
blanket.

120
David Anderson (see Jewelry and Silver section) Saga
"408," silver five-piece place setting. About $33.
photo Teigens

121
Rama Jewelry (see Jewelry and Silver section) Bronze
flatware with bronze, teak, rosewood or buffalo-horn
handles. 144-piece sets for twelve in teakwood chest
cost between $35 and $150 each.

THAILAND

S. Samran Thailand Co. Ltd., G.P.O. Box 740, Bangkok, Thailand
10-page brochure. Prices in $.

Bronze tableware is a Thai craft that is very popular with tourists; it is a beautiful light gold color, but like silver, it must be polished. Samran is a leading maker. They sell large bowls decorated with Thai "angels" for about $17; sugar bowls, creamers, salt and pepper shakers for $3–$5. Complete sets of tableware, including postage, cost $48 for six place settings, $60 for eight, and $93 for twelve. There are ten patterns, and handles may be plain bronze, decorative bronze with Thai "angels" on the ends, rosewood or buffalo horn (buffalo horn should not be machine-washed). Tea sets and barbeque sets also for sale.

For more stainless-steel flatware, see Helios Home Supplies (Household Objects) and David Anderson (Jewelry). For silver and silver plate, see Asprey, Carlo Mario Camusso, Garrads, Mappin and Webb, all in the Jewelry and Silver section.

FURNITURE

Furniture is usually so much less expensive abroad that it is well worth sending for. However, if your prime object is to save money, it is not usually worth sending for small single pieces, because shipping charges are disproportionately high. A single coffee table costs about $37 to ship to New York harbor, a three-seater couch between $75 and $110. For instance, Totum's tells me that their three-seater knockdown sofa costs $72 to pack and ship to New York harbor, and their matching knockdown armchair $50—yet the sofa and *two* chairs together cost $115 to pack and ship. The exception to the rule against buying single pieces is when the price difference between what you are buying abroad and in New York is very large. For example, leather couches cost $300 to $1,000 more in New York, and so are almost always worth sending for.

Shipping costs depend so much on where you live and what you are buying that it is hard to give a reliable rule of thumb as to what they will be. Marlau's, which is very experienced in shipping furniture to America, thinks that when you are looking at catalogues you should allow an extra 40 percent of the price if you live in the East, 45 percent if you live in the Midwest, and 50 percent if you live in the Far West. If you decide you are interested in a specific piece of furniture, you can get a better idea by asking the store for the cost of sea freight, and also asking them what the weight will be, as American trucking companies will give you an accurate estimate if you tell them the weight and destination of your load-to-be.

MODERN FURNITURE
DENMARK

These days "Danish Modern" furniture looks almost stately compared to the furniture being designed in Italy and England. It is streamlined, but carefully built to last. Dark rosewood, orangy teak or creamy oak are polished or oiled, and woolen fabrics are still used. The shapes are somewhat austere compared to the knockdown, switch-around, sink-in modules that other countries are experimenting with.

Asbjørn-Møbler, Skindergade 28—32, Copenhagen K, Denmark
80-page catalogue, free. Prices in $.

I have been very pleased with the things I have bought from this efficient store. There is not as much in this catalogue as in Anton Dam's (below), but some of the things are not shown in Dam's catalogue. The handsome Børge Mogensen leather-and-down sofa, easy chair and footstool are here, and the Modus units—a series of square buttoned-leather–and–rosewood chairs, stools and small tables, designed to be moved around. Almost all the furniture can be supplied in oak (which is a lighter color), as well as in teak or rosewood, and a few pieces of furniture are chunkier and less formal than those in the other Danish shops. No light fixtures or rugs in the catalogue.

Anton Dam, Gammel Kongevej 90, Copenhagen, Denmark
100-page catalogue with some color, free. Fabric swatches, free. Prices in $.

A huge, glossy, detailed catalogue illustrating the modern Danish furniture that Anton Dam has been sending to America for the past fifteen years. Page upon page of sleek and now-classic teak and rosewood sofas, chairs with arms and without, dining-room tables, serving tables, sideboards, trolleys, bars, desks, sewing tables, shelves, beds, bunks—anything you can think of and some you can't (bureau-cum-bookcase?). The designers are famous: Hans Wegner, Hans Olsen, Arne Jacobson (as I write, the Jacobson egg chair is available in New York only through a decorator, at a list price over twice Anton Dam's). The fabrics are magnificent: 100 percent virgin wool in brilliant colors. The instructions on how to buy are clear and complete. And the prices, of course, are much lower than in America. A three-seat teak sofa costs $243, and the most expensive sofa is Hans Olsen's four-seat rosewood-and-leather job for $739. A dining table that extends to seven feet costs $135 in teak and $235 in rosewood, while $31 seems to be an average price for a dining chair.

Another handy thing about this store is that they sell smaller items—Rya rugs, lamps, teak ice buckets, etc.—which can be tucked in between the furniture and are thus delivered free of charge.

3 Falke Møbler, Falkonercentret, DK 2000 Copenhagen F, Denmark
30-page color catalogue, free. Prices in $.

This large firm (they have furnished the General Time Corporation Building in Stamford) sells lighting fixtures, carpets, accessories and furniture made in their own workshop. Their designers aren't as well known in America as Anton Dam's and Asbjørn-Møbler's, but the furniture is good and is available in rosewood, teak or ash at the same prices, and there are a few items in steel. (No desks are shown in the catalogue, mainly whole living rooms, including wall units, with a few bedrooms and dining rooms.) Most of the three-seat sofas seem to cost about $480. There is a free-standing bar/cabinet for $180; an extension dining-room table in teak for $230, and upholstered chairs to go with it. $40 each. Rya rugs and lamps are shown, but prices are not given—you have to ask.

ENGLAND

Over the last ten years, young English designers have begun to organize their own firms to manufacture and sell their own designs. In a heroic effort to keep prices down, practically all the furniture that follows comes straight from the manufacturer in knockdown form (packed flat, but completely ready and easy to assemble). Shapes are simple, woods are pale and lacquered or painted in good colors, cushions are bright and removable, and prices are—low.

Pace Furniture Ltd., The Mews, Ravenscroft Road, Henley-on-Thames, Oxfordshire, England
29-page color catalogue, free.

Pace's furniture is agreeably moderate in design and very agreeably moderate in price. Pace's "Profile" line consists of a sofa (about $140 for a three-seater) and a high-backed easy chair (about $65) with birch woodwork, lacquered or painted in white or bitter-chocolate, and smooth cushions that can be covered in brown, gold, orange or blue-green fabric. There is a coffee table to match, and storage units with shelves and doors (a bureau/bar cupboard costs about $68), but the storage units come assembled, so transportation will be more expensive.

For more comfort at a higher price, there is the "Clubman" line (three-seat sofa about $208, armchair $102), looking quite clubbish and solid, with cushioned armrests and same colored woods as the "Profile" line but different fabrics.

There are also two dining tables in the same finishes, and comfortably wide, upholstered dining-room chairs for $39.

Christian Sell and Associates, 45 Camden Passage, London N.1, England
18-page color catalogue, free. Fabric swatches on request.

Christian Sell's "switch-around furniture" is all built in one basic design, thereby solving the problems of people who want a whole room (or house) to match neatly. Everything comes in solid laminated-birch hardwood, either simply lacquered or else painted and lacquered in white to what Christian Sell fondly hopes is a "diamond-hard" finish, and upholstery is in red, orange, navy-blue, dark-brown duck. The main pieces are flattish storage units (each $22 – $33) which can be arranged in various ways to make desks, chests of drawers, coffee tables and stools (with cushions). More conventionally, there are sofas (designed to be used as beds) costing about $152, and beds (designed to be used as sofas); tables, chairs and wardrobes, including a 4'-high wardrobe (about $58) enabling children, for once, to reach their clothes themselves.

Martin Sylvester, Little Clarendon Street, Oxford, England
12-page color catalogue, free.

Martin Sylvester has a hefty "Studio" line of sofas and armchairs made in Finland of laminated beech, and lacquered or painted in any of eight strong colors. Armrests are wooden, and the large, buttoned cushions can be covered in red, orange or navy-blue on white cotton rep or vinyl simulated leather. A three-seat sofa costs about $180, Scoop chairs, quilted cushions on curved bases, $80 each, in a choice of different fabrics. For about $63 there is the

122
Anton Dam Hans Olsen's oxhide and rosewood couch with down cushions, $640; available in fabric for $560.
photo Louis Schnakenburg Reklamefotografi

122

123
3 Falke Møbler Bar table, width and length 39½", height 19½", bar top in black Formica. The bar portion is moved by gas cartridges and automatically lifts when pressed lightly. Prices, including delivery to the port of New York: $180 in teak; $195 in walnut; $220 in rosewood. Prices may be slightly higher after January 1, 1973.

124
Pace Furniture Ltd "Profile" couch and high-back chairs available with beechwood in natural lacquer or white or chocolate glossy paint, and fabric in brown, gold, orange or blue-green. Couch, about $140; chairs, about $65 each. Matching occasional table, about $25.

123

124

125

126

127

129

128

130

125
Pace Furniture Ltd Breakfast set: 48″ × 32″ table, about $55; upholstered benches, about $37. Available in clear lacquered beech or chocolate glossy painted wood, or white Formica. The benches can be covered in brown, gold, orange or blue-green fabric or vinyl.
photo Dennis Hooker

126
Totum Ltd "Alpha" three-seat couch in birch or teak, from about $275.

127
Ikea "Nikka" desk in oak or teak with a plastic lacquer finish. The pedestal on the left has a suspended filing system. About $70.

128
Ikea "Ögla" beechwood armchair in natural or white lacquered finish. About $8.

129
Ikea Chrome-plated tubular chairs upholstered in natural-colored canvas. The one on the left, "Lots," designed by Eric Wørsts, is about $45. The one on the right, "Kroken," designed by Christopher Blomquist, is about $65.

130
Ikea An adjustable light, "Amarant," can be raised to function as a standard lamp or lowered to be a table lamp. About $25.

Gemini Arm-Chair Bed: three foam-rubber shapes clip together to make either an armchair and stool or a 6' 2"-long single bed. All the above can be covered in your own fabric. And in painted wood (purple, if you want), eight square or round dining and coffee tables, one of which is a 6' refectory table for about $78, with benches to match for about $39 each.

Totum Ltd., 19 Bruton Place, London W1X 8HH, England
18-page color catalogue and fabric swatches, free.

Totum's "Alpha" furniture doesn't look as though it could possibly "knock down"; it is large, solid and very cushioned. It is available in teak, just the thing for anyone who isn't sold on light woods and bright colors. There are armchairs, tables and sofas (including a four-seater). A three-seat sofa costs from $275 up (depending on quality of upholstery fabric).

In complete contrast, there is a series of very light chrome-and-canvas chairs called "Design E." The chrome frame comes polished or coated with white plastic, and the sling seats and backs are available in good shades: natural, mustard, orange or purple canvas or black vinyl. $30 and up. (However, these may not be available direct if Totum's finds an American distributor.)

FRANCE

Chapo, 14 Boulevard de l'Hôpital, Paris V, France
Leaflet in French, free.

Just the place for anyone furnishing a Frank Lloyd Wright house. Pierre Chapo, owner of the firm, designs his furniture with a high regard for the natural properties of his materials, and there is lots of talk about function and sincerity in the brochure. Each piece is heavy and solidly made, no nails are used, and the best woods are oiled and polished by hand to show the natural grain. Tables, chairs, chests, beds, bunks, cribs, shelves and sofas—everything's here, and prices are low for this kind of very unusual work, although, of course, you can buy factory made furniture for much less. A thick round table that would look marvelous in a country kitchen costs just over $220, a sofa with big, squashy cushions, about $1,000.

Chapo represented France at the Montreal World Fair and is enthusiastically recommended by friends of mine living in France.

ITALY

Giovanetti, 51032 Bottegone, Casella Postale 1, Pistoia, Italy
Color brochure, free. Prices in $.

Italian designers are turning out the newest furniture designs in the world, and when you find them in America they are horribly expensive. Giovanetti has three models that you can buy direct from them at excellent prices. "Bauhaus" is a knockdown armchair and sofa made of plump but firm cushions which are assembled with the help of chrome fittings in the back which do not show in the front. In the brochure three small children are doing the assembling, presumably to show how easy it is. "Bauhaus" can be covered with fabric (including the customer's own). A three-seat sofa is $250 in shiny imitation leather, or about $415 in real leather. "Petronio" is a square and solid-looking sofa which turns into a single bed; the arms and back go down to form a headrest and a convenient bedside shelf. In fabric $220, in leather $350.

While "Bauhaus" and "Petronio" are modern but not outrageous, for a spot of outrage see "Bazaar"—fiberglass shells which swoop up and curve over the seat, enclosing you in a nest of acrylic "beaver" fur (which is what the fiberglass is covered with). Since it is clearly impossible to sit up attentively in "Bazaar," you are forced to recline languorously, enjoying a back-to-the-womb feeling which can be enhanced by buying several sections and joining them so that they form a circle, or as much of one as you want. Each section costs $180 and is available in white with dark-brown "beaver" fur, or black with fair "beaver" fur.

SWEDEN

Ikea, 343 00 Älmhult, Sweden
200-page color catalogue in Swedish.

Ikea comes *fervently* recommended by Swedes and non-Swedes alike. Apparently this now-enormous business enterprise was started by a man who wanted to make very inexpensive, very good furniture. He managed it with spectacular success, and the big plant and shop outside Stockholm have become a favorite weekend-excursion goal—people drive out, dump their children in the Ikea nurseries, eat in the Ikea restaurant, wander around looking at the chair-and-carpet-torturing machines (everything is tested to see how it will stand up), buy something and drive home with it strapped on top of the car.

There is plenty of everything for the house in the (alas, Swedish-language) mail-order catalogue, including light fixtures and carpets. In general, Swedish prices are higher than Danish, but Ikea's furniture is less expensive than what you find in the grander Danish houses. The range is more catholic, too, because although the prevailing tone is bright and modern (lots of light and painted wood), Ikea happily copies anything popular: "Kolonial" bedroom suites, Louis XVI chests, chandeliers, puffy chrome-and-buttoned "*Italien-inspirerad*" sofas, Spanish and Oriental carpets. Prices: sofas $135 and up, dining-room tables from $55, and a bentwood side chair ("Lena") for $10—which costs $25 in Washington.

This is the place to furnish a child's room. A wooden highchair costs $7.50; a crib that turns into a sofa before and after babies, $27 (I had one of these and it was very useful; it saved storage space and was handy for visiting babies); for older children there are bunks that can also be used as two single beds, about $55 complete; five-drawer desks for $33, or for $55 you can put a top over ten drawers to make a desk; and for the astounding sum of $8.50 there is a desk chair that you can lower as the child grows taller. There are also lots of combinations of shelves, cupboards and toy chests that fit into each other and handy places. *All* the children's furniture is in pale wood or primary colors; not an elf or a flower to be seen anywhere.

REPRODUCTION FURNITURE
Some of these reproductions cost much less than they would in America, notably the furniture from England; others would be very hard to find here. The Spanish and Chinese shops will make pieces in any size you want, and will incorporate your own designs into their models.

ENGLAND

Ashley Furniture Workshops, 3a Dawson Place, London W.2, England
6-page brochure, free. Prices in $.

This offshoot of a large modern-furniture manufacturer sells

131

132

134

133

131
Ashley Furniture Workshops 7'-long Chesterfield with button seat, available in 120 different shades of leather. $575.
photo S. S. Walia

132
C. P. Burge and Son Mahogany campaign desk made with an old top and new legs. $220 and up.

133
C. P. Burge and Son Porter's chair in tufted antiqued hide. About $801.

134
Martin J. Dodge Oval pedestal coffee table (40" × 27", 20" high). About $180.

135
Nord Reproduction Furniture A reproduction of the first steel rocking chair exhibited by R. W. Winfield at the Great Exhibition of 1851.

135

reproduction leather furniture to America by mail, and has what looks like excellent values. All the current and eternal favorites are here: Victorian-style Chesterfield sofas, $550– $650 (these cost around $1,800 in New York); Chesterfield chairs, $365 and up; the Victorian steel-and-leather rocking chair displayed at the Great Exhibition of 1851, for $235 (it is for sale in New York at a higher price and in vinyl instead of leather); a Sheraton tub chair from $180; a Hepplewhite wing chair from $235; a Georgian Winchester chair from $325; an open-sided eighteenth-century Gainsborough chair from $185. You can have most pieces either deep-buttoned or plain with feather-down cushions, and there is an astonishing range of leather. One-hundred and twenty shades in the usual mat leather; twenty-five shades in hand-colored "antiqued" leather; and eighteen shades of fashionable, new, glazed leather which looks very glossy, rather like patent leather. Prices for suede will also be quoted on request.

C. P. Burge and Son, 162 Sloane Street, London S.W.1, England
Brochure, free. Prices in $.

This firm specializes in exporting reproduction furniture at very reasonable prices (the catalogue is in German, French and Italian, as well as English). Unlike any of the other shops, they make tables from old tops with new legs to match, so the tables look antique but are less fragile and less expensive than the real thing would be. In the brochure there is a nice one in "the Regency manner" which costs $185 and up (depending on size). There are usually plenty of tops in stock, so tables can be made according to customers' wishes at prices from $220 to $300.

In straightforward reproductions there are leather chairs, including a hall porter's chair for $801 (a similar chair imported from England costs $1,125 in New York). Also, in pine, yew or mahogany, and in any size you want: butler's tray tables, about $99; folding library steps that can be used as a coffee table, about $105; bedside campaign chests, about $98; campaign Davenport desks, about $190; and spiral library stairs, about $110.

Burge also stocks antiques in the same styles, and carved and gilded pieces, French marble mantelpieces and nautical items, but none of these are in catalogues, so you must write with a specific request.

Martin J. Dodge, The Tin Church, Combe Cabinet Works, Marston Road, Sherborne, Dorset, England
Photographs on request.

Martin J. Dodge, cabinetmakers, makes very fine pedestal tables in classic English styles, though he also has a few chairs. A small, oval coffee table, 40" by 27", costs $180; pedestal dining tables, $460–$920, according to size, with crossbanding around the edges in exotic woods $6.50 a foot extra; Chippendale (Queen Anne) side chairs with leather seats, $216; a child's Victorian chair in walnut, $150. Waiting time for furniture, six weeks.

Nord Reproduction Furniture, 136a Burnt Oak Broadway, Edgware, Middlesex, England
Brochure, free.

A marvelous collection of English leather chairs and sofas, many of them handmade throughout. The frames are hardwood and based on originals. Each piece is hand-sprung with horsehair and hessian filling. The supplest leathers are used, and given antique patina and coloring entirely by hand; wooden parts are hand-polished. There is a very authentic version of the Chesterfield for about $700. It can be made in any size and with several variations. A Georgian-style square-back settee costs from $530; a Chippendale camel-back

settee from $455. Prices for chairs go from $220 for a Hepplewhite-style tub chair to $475 for a buttoned Chippendale-style library chair, and there is a charming Regency-style rocking chair for $265.

Upholstery Workshop, Shorrolds Road, London S.W.6, England
55-page brochure and swatches, free.

The Upholstery Workshop makes and sells its own handmade traditional sofas and armchairs. They say that their prices are high, so they are only able to sell to the "top end" of the market, but I wonder whether their prices will seem so bad in America where anything handmade is terribly expensive. Prices do not include fabrics; swatches will be sent on request. The comfortable-looking "London" for instance, costs $305, and a good-quality Dralon would be about $13.50 a yard. (There are less and more expensive fabrics.) The most luxurious sofa of all, the Berkshire, costs $350 plus fabric. There is a Chesterfield without studs, and generally simpler than the Ashley and Nord versions, a Queen Anne settee, a chaise longue and a Price Regent sofa "sympathetically made" and hand-painted to a client's specifications.

HONG KONG

Cathay Arts Co. Ltd., P.O. Box 5801, Kowloon, Hong Kong
48-page catalogue with some color, free; air mail $3.

This firm sells both wholesale and retail, and publishes a magnificent catalogue with photographs, many in color, of a wide range of teak and rosewood Oriental furniture "for those who appreciate the finest." There is furniture for every room, and some of it is very splendid. Besides sets for living and dining rooms as well as bedrooms, there are bars, hi-fi cabinets, silver chests, ottomans, serving trays, screens and planters. Sizes range from little jewelry boxes (in nineteen different designs) to enormous display cabinets with lighting and scenic inlay decorations.

Prices must be inquired about individually, and are higher than at the firms below.

Charlotte Horstmann Ltd., 104 Ocean Terminal, Kowloon, Hong Kong
50-page brochure, $1.50. Prices in $.

A precise catalogue meticulously describes Charlotte Horstmann's handmade reproduction furniture. Each piece is constructed by only one man from start to finish, and no nails or screws are used on the Chinese pieces. Only tables, desks and chairs are shown, except for a Ming fourposter, a Korean divan and some library steps. Mostly there are restrained Chinese styles: Ming, Chinese Chippendale and Mandarin. But there are about twenty French and English pieces, notably five in the now fashionable "campaign" style: A campaign chest of drawers with brass handles and brass corners costs $240; travel desk, $185; and a coffee table, $170. A Chippendale desk with a slant top costs $175, and a French-style desk with three drawers, $190.

The woods are Burma rosewood and teak, and the weight and moisture of the woods are most professionally described. Shipping information and prices are models of simplicity and clarity. Provided you buy at least three pieces, shipping to your port should add around $25 per piece.

S. Y. Ma, 35 Hankow Road, Kowloon, Hong Kong
Furniture brochure, free; 50 cents air mail. Prices in $.
Coromandel brochure, free; 50 cents air mail. Prices in $.

These brochures are not nearly as neat and informative as Charlotte Horstmann's, but some of the prices here are lower. A rosewood Ming coffee table costs $77, while a similar, though not identical, table costs $105 at Charlotte Horstmann's. Other prices: 22″ end tables, $55 each; a rosewood sideboard, $216; a Winthrop-design desk, $190. The large assortment of Ming and Western furniture (though only forty-three of the most popular pieces are shown in the brochure—photographs can be sent of others) is made from kiln-dried teak or rosewood, and pieces can be made to your own design.

Pewter and brass pots, plates, lanterns, and candlesticks (suitable for lamp bases, the brochure says) also available.

MEXICO

Sala de Artes S.A., Londres No. 141, Mexico 6, D.F.
Catalogue $2.50. Prices in $.

Sala de Artes, in la Zona Rosa, Mexico City's central shopping district, has been shipping furniture and decorative accessories to American homeowners, interior designers and architects for many years. They manufacture and sell "Mexican"-style living-room, dining-room, bedroom and garden furniture, woven and printed fabrics, handwoven area rugs, lamps, ceramics, sculptures and paintings. "Very reliable," say friends of mine whose entire family has been buying huge carved headboards at under half American prices.

PORTUGAL

Fundação Ricardo do Espírito Santo Silva, Largo das Portas do Sol 2, Lisbon 2, Portugal
Photographs on request, free.

This unique museum and school of decorative arts was founded by a Portuguese banker who was anxious to keep alive the arts rapidly being taken over by machinery. There is a museum consisting of Mr. Santo Silva's private collection of furniture and beautifully bound old books, especially collected with this museum in mind. And in twenty-three workshops, experienced craftsmen and trainees copy, rigorously using the original techniques, furniture in the purest styles and periods of the past, mainly French. Wood-carvers, locksmiths, metal engravers, carpet weavers, tapestry restorers and bookbinders reproduce a wide range of decorative objects and luxurious pieces of furniture. A bookbinding department reproduces the "simplest to the most sumptuous" bindings from the sixteenth century to the Romantic period, including mosaic leather work in the style of Padeloup and Le Monier—the Fundação was completely responsible for restoring Madame du Barry's library at Versailles.

As for prices—the Rockefellers, the Rothschilds and the palaces of Fontainebleau and Versailles shop here. If that doesn't put you off, write and tell them what kind of things you are interested in and the Fundação will give you information that "falls upon those."

Sociedade Inglesa Decorações e Antiguedades LDA, Rua da Emenda 26, Lisbon 2, Portugal
Photographs on request, free.

The Sociedade Inglesa reproduces French and English eighteenth-century furniture and decorative objects. They are also decorators and have done the Sandy Lane Hotel in Barbados, and Reid's Hotel in Madeira, in modern styles. Prices are low: an extraordinary, very low country "saddle" chair with velvet cushions, $52 (apparently based on a sixteenth-century seat for riding a donkey); a low, 3′-long carved table with a marble top on gilt or painted base, $59; a black-and-gold-painted Regency chair copied from one left in Portugal by a Marshall Beresford after the Peninsula War, $48. There are also hand-embroidered carpets copied from seventeenth-century carpets in Lisbon museums, or designed especially for the Sociedade Inglesa, costing about $46 per square meter (1 sq. m. = 1.2 sq. yds.).

SPAIN

Abelardo Linares S.A., Carrera San Jerónimo 48, Madrid 14, Spain
Photographs and price list. Prices in $.
(If you don't return the photographs, you are ferociously asked to pay $1.50 for each of them.)

This famous Spanish antique shop in the middle of Madrid makes such authentic-looking reproductions out of old dry walnut, oak and mahogany that one can't help wondering whether they are being passed off as genuine somewhere. (Linares says they have been supplying American dealers for many years.) Most of the pieces are large carved Spanish chests and tables, costing around $700. There are some rush-seated chairs with carved pine backs at about $65 each, and an imposing studded and carved chair upholstered in tooled leather for $188; also a few plain English and French styles. State your interests, and photographs will be sent. Styles not shown can be made.

Perhaps of more general interest are the reproduction lanterns, a few of which are small enough to go by mail and which cost mainly between $16 and $40. There are also mirrors with ornate carved frames gilded in real gold leaf to be made in any size and costing from $65 to $95.

Marlau, Rey Francisco 8, Madrid 8, Spain
Catalogue, $5. Prices in $.

An American couple, the Corcorans, turned a hobby into a business ten years ago, got raves in all the shopping guides to Spain, and have been selling superbly made Spanish furniture to Americans ever since.

The wood is mostly kiln-dried African walnut, which is harder (more durable) than American walnut, and has a more dramatic grain. Everything is hand-carved and can be distressed to look three hundred years old. Only real leather is used, and alcohol-, hot-water- and stain-proof lacquers are polished and rubbed by hand. Almost all the hardware is made especially for Marlau, the brass is solid brass, and the iron is specially finished to prevent oxidation. In other words, the Corcorans are applying American efficiency and enthusiasm to making furniture which, if you could find it anywhere else, would be much more expensive.

The catalogue lists one thousand pieces of furniture, and a lot of "decorative items," such as Spanish floor and wall tiles, and doors. Here are some furniture prices: 24″ square carved coffee table, $112; 5′-long bar, $275; bar stool with leather seat and back, $44; large gun cabinet with hand-carved hunting scenes and automatic light, $740; 6′-high, heavily carved breakfront with customer's *individual coat of arms* hand-carved on center panel, $775.

136

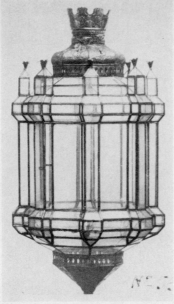

137

138

139

140

141

136
Fundação Ricardo do Espírito Santo Silva "Bonheur du Jour," a reproduction in precious woods of a Louis XVI piece made by the famous ebonist Roger Vandercruse, *dit* Lacroix, named master in 1755. $1,691.

137
Abelardo Linares Handmade wrought-iron lantern. About $70.

138
Abelardo Linares Carved mirror, gilded with real gold leaf (24″ high, 20″ wide). About $78. Can be made any size to order.

139
Marlau Gothic turned headboard: twin, about $362 up; double about $415 up. Bedspread in two colors: twin, about $62 up; double, about $74. End tables, about $141. Hand-carved wooden lamp bases, about $105. Lampshades, about $28.

140
Marlau Carved chest (28″ high, 58″ long), made from very old pine taken from demolished buildings. About $360.

141
Marlau Carved-leg dining table in various sizes. 6′ long, about $300. Side chair, about $65; armchair, about $82.

GARDEN ORNAMENTS AND FURNITURE

ENGLAND

Chilstone Garden Ornaments, Great Linford Manor, Newport Pagnell, Buckinghamshire, England
20-page catalogue, free. Prices in $.

Chilstone already sells garden ornaments to private customers and garden shops in America. Their specialty is handmade reproductions in reconstituted stone of sixteenth-, seventeenth-, eighteenth- and early-nineteenth-century original models. The texture of the stone is specially made to be almost indistinguishable from that of the original, and to be soft enough to pick up mosses and lichens so that it quickly looks old. Prices are reasonable, starting at $17 for an oval Regency basket, and only a few large objects—statues and sundials—cost more than $55. A baluster birdbath costs $23, a mid-Georgian urn with swags of drapery, bunches of flowers and fruit festooning the bowl, $39. (There are fountains, statues, lions, benches, pedestals, urns and even balustrades.) The most expensive thing of all is a fluted urn designed by William Kent for Alexander Pope's garden at Twickenham; it costs $198.

Verine Garden Products, Folly Faunts House, Goldhanger, Maldon, Essex, England
Garden brochure, $1. Prices in $.

Verine makes by hand reproduction plant containers in weatherproof fiberglass—tubs, urns and window boxes—copied from originals, many still being used in stately homes. The containers come in various sizes and are either lead color or white, and are waterproofed for indoor use with plants (or as log baskets) or have drainage holes for outside use.

Styles are admirably varied; some are fairly plain and others very ornate. There is an intricate Burmese urn copied from an old brass original, $44; a tub and a window box taken from originals made during the reign of Henry VIII showing Tudor rose designs costing $33 and $27, respectively; a square and regular Elizabethan tub with a lion's mask on each face; a window box copied from an original molding by the architect Robert Adam; and some simple Grecian-style urns. The original of the most expensive tub of all ($110) was made for King Charles II and has the royal cipher plus nymphs, dragons, water babies, shells and rams.

Prices include delivery to customer's door; all costs are covered except duty. If larger quantities of varying sizes are bought, so that containers can be fitted into one another, then costs go down.

HONG KONG

Kowloon Rattan Ware Company, 4 Hankow Road, Kowloon, Hong Kong
4-page illustrated brochure, free. Prices in $.

This firm seems to sell absolutely all the rattan screens, chairs and stools available in America, and at a third of the price. Curly, fantastic, Victorian styles, classic porch styles, and the smooth modern styles that go for high prices in New York shops. If you are planning to people a porch, garden or house with a forest of rattan, it is worth buying from here, otherwise the savings involved probably won't be worth the trouble. Most prices are from $5 to $15. They have other things not on the brochures—animal laundry hampers and tables, some small enough to go by mail. Ask for photographs of these.

142
Verine Garden Products Fiberglass reproduction in lead color of a 1757 tub with a ship, mermaids, starfish and sea shells in relief. The 18"-diameter size is $60, including postage. Other sizes are available.

143
Kowloon Rattan Ware Company Donkey table, $10.

144
Chinacraft Ltd Royal Worcester "Hyde Park," an Italian Renaissance design raised in 24-carat gold. Five-piece place setting, about $26.

GLASS AND CHINA

No one but a reckless spendthrift should buy imported expensive glass and china in America. Most of it sells for half the American prices in the country where it is made, so with little effort (but some patience), quite a lot of money can be saved, especially by people who are buying large quantities.

Like Scottish knitwear, the glass and china business seems to be one of the best organized foreign-mail-order activities; several of the shops say they have been at it for over twenty years. Goods are expertly packed, and on the rare occasion when something arrives broken, most of these shops will immediately replace the article simply on your say-so.

For some reason, English bone china, which has calcinated bone among its ingredients and is stronger than any other china, carries less duty than earthenware (the softest china) or regular porcelain. Duty on bone china comes to about 15 percent of the retail price, and shipping one five-piece place setting can cost about $5. So, for instance, at this writing on Wedgwood's "Colonnade Black," which costs $21.34 in England and $42.95 in New York, you save about $13 a place setting. And on Wedgwood's "Ascot"—$32.13 in England, $65 in New York—you save about $23 a place setting.

Duty on glasses for the table comes to between 11 and 13 percent of the price you pay, while surface-mail and insurance charges for eight glasses come to about $10.50, so you should add *roughly* $1.75 extra for each glass. High as that sounds, you will still save a great deal on certain glasses—for instance, about $36 on eight "Prelude" water glasses by Orrefors ($2.74 each in Sweden and $8.50 each in New York).

BELGIUM

Cristaux du Val St-Lambert, Etablissements Dubois, 57 Rue des Chatreux, Brussels, Belgium
This firm has many customers in America who buy Val St-Lambert glass directly from them to save money. At the moment there is no catalogue, but if you want to replenish your stock, or have seen the glass already, write and ask for the price of the style you are interested in (preferably giving style number as well).

CZECHOSLOVAKIA

Bohemia Moser, 12 na Příkopě, Prague 1, Czechoslovakia
Leaflets, free. Prices in $.

Bohemian glass has long been famous, and anyone with the faith and patience to wait for six months and with an inclination to join distinguished company can buy complete sets of this glass at prices much lower than its equivalents from other countries. It is sold only in complete sets of seventy-two items: one dozen each of white wine, red wine, port-sherry, liqueur, champagne, and medium-sized tumblers, (sizes are given by grams contained in each size). The leaflets dwell lovingly and very undemocratically on the important personages that own "this glass of kings—the king of glass" (Honoré de Balzac). "Lady Hamilton," a glass with large petal-shaped indentations, is owned by the King of Morocco, Mohammed V, and by the Shah of Iran, yet costs only $215 the set. "Royal 202," a smooth glass with a fine gold rim and a band of small diamond-shaped incisions at the base, has been owned by Edward VII of England, Haakon

VII of Norway, and the Maharajah of Baroda, among others. The very ornate "Splendid," finely cut almost all over, has been owned by Elizabeth II of England, Alfonso XIII of Spain, and the Maharajah of Hyderabad. It costs $700. To the above prices, add about 20 percent for shipping to your nearest port.

DENMARK

Frøsig, Nørrebrogade 9, DK-2200 Copenhagen, Denmark
Manufacturers' brochures: Bing and Grøndahl, Royal Copenhagen, Bjørn Wiinblad, free.

Frøsig has the very attentive Mrs. Buddig looking after American customers, who, she says, have been writing her long and interesting letters for the past fifteen years. The numbers of American customers have increased enormously, not through advertising but through the "mouth to mouth" method—not surprisingly, as you will see. Royal Copenhagen porcelain is sold here in both first and second quality, but the high standards of Bing and Grøndahl makes it possible for them to stock and sell only its second-quality porcelain, for the defects are very hard to see. Prices are consequently splendidly low for their porcelain figurines, misty-colored flowered vases, and pale-blue scenic ashtrays. When I compared prices, "Mary," a small girl in white cap and white flowered dress holding a baby in her arms, cost $50 in New York and $17.25, including postage, from Frøsig. "Reading Children" cost $57.50 in New York and $21.30, including postage, from Frøsig.

Also here are Bjørn Wiinblad's whimsical lovers frisking coyly through the seasons, she growing plumper and finally producing a baby—a series of twelve platters costing $2.25 each, including postage, available in any number from three up.

ENGLAND

Chinacraft Ltd., 499 Oxford Street, Marble Arch, London W1R 2BH, England
80-page color catalogue, free. Prices in $.
Dinner China: John Aynsley, Royal Crown Derby, Royal Doulton, Minton, Royal Worcester, Wedgwood, Coalport, Crown Staffordshire, Royal Chelsea
Crystal: Stuart, Waterford, Tudor, St. Louis, Edinburgh, Thomas Webb, Royal Brierley
China Ornaments and Giftware: Crown Staffordshire, Wedgwood, Coalport, Royal Crown Derby, Aynsley, Royal Chelsea, Royal Doulton, Hammersley, Royal Worcester

Chinacraft shows the widest range of the London shops in their very good and complete catalogue, which includes sample shipping costs and customs duty. They show a little more china than the other shops, and a lot more traditional cut glass. They also have a whole section of giftware with quite a few pieces of Wedgwood's Jasperware illustrated— the famous pale-blue, green or black china, with Greek figures in white relief: earrings and brooches for $12 to $15, two ashtrays or heart-shaped boxes for about $13, three little cigarette cups for $15. Also, Crown Staffordshire flower clusters: eight place-card holders, $11.50; six pairs of tiny salt and pepper pots thoroughly disguised as pink flowers in white vases, $16; Coalport porcelain roses or posies in bowls, and Coalport houses. Finally, much more expensive pieces like the Wedgwood "prestige" pieces, vases and bowls at around $185 each; and Royal Worcester limited-edition figures: "Apaloosa,"$245; "Charlais Bull," $208; and "Napoleon Bonaparte" suitably more expensive at $900.

Gered, 174 Piccadilly, London W.1, England
Wedgwood and Spode 20-page color brochures, free.
Prices in $.

If you definitely want Wedgwood or Spode, write to Gered;
they show more table settings from these companies than
anyone else.

**Thomas Goode and Co., 19 South Audley Street, London
W1Y 6BN, England** ♔♔♔
58-page color catalogue, free. Prices in $.

Bone China: Minton, Royal Worcester, Spode, Wedgwood,
Royal Crown Derby, Coalport, John Aynsley, Hammersley
Earthenware: Wedgwood's Queen's Ware, Simpsons, Spode,
Booths, Midwinter
Crystal: Thomas Webb, Stuart, Royal Brierley

   Thomas Goode produces an elaborate and excellent
catalogue showing a few patterns from each make that they
stock, with interesting short histories of the companies and
their products—helpful for people who are still making up
their minds about what they want. Unfortunately, prices are
only given for five-piece place settings, though others are
given on request, of course. Engravers are available to
decorate crystal presentation pieces, and to put monograms
or crests on glasses.

   Thomas Goode also has a "varied but limited" antique
stock of china which can be sold by mail (and requires no
duty), but information can only be given in answer to
inquiries about specific types of antique china.

The Leach Pottery, Saint Ives, Cornwall, England
2-page leaflet, $1.

Bernard Leach, probably the most famous modern potter in
the world, sells at agreeably low prices pottery designed by
himself and made in his studios by apprentices. The first
Western potter to study in Japan, Leach came back to
Cornwall with Shoji Hamada and developed a classically
simple style both in his own original pots and also in an
appetizing collection of pottery to be used around the house:
stewpots, jugs, coffeepots and baking dishes, soup bowls,
sauce pots, casseroles and coffee cups. Some of them have
an unglazed sandy outside and a smooth glossy glaze inside,
others are glazed on the outside in tenmoko that varies
between black and rust, oatmeal, gray, or pale celadon green.
Prices vary between 55 cents for an egg cup and $4.50 for a
large lidded coffeepot.

**Leather and Snook, 167 Piccadilly, London WIV 9DE,
England**
12-page color brochure, free. Prices in $.
*Royal Crown Derby, John Aynsley, Royal Worcester, Royal
Doulton, Wedgwood, Minton, Coalport and Thomas Webb
Crystal*

Leather and Snook puts out a small and neat brochure
showing just a few of all the patterns they can supply from the
above companies. Prices are only given for five-piece place
settings, but all details and prices can be supplied when you
write.

FRANCE

Editions Paradis, 29 Rue de Paradis, Paris X, France
20-page catalogue with some color, free.

Prices at these French shops seem to be roughly a third lower
than in New York, and there is also a 20 percent export
discount. Editions Paradis has a neat little brochure showing
Baccarat, Lorraine, Saint Louis, Villeroy and Boch glasses, as
well as porcelain starting at about $3.25 a plate and going
up to about $37 a plate for decorated-by-hand-in-gold "Marie-
Antoinette."

   Price list in French and English, but only sample prices are
given for each glass or china table setting, so you have to get
an individual estimate for whatever you are interested in.

**Limoges-Unic, Ventes par Correspondence, 26 Rue de
Paradis, Paris X, France**
120-page catalogue in French, free.

Limoges-Unic puts out a large and luscious color catalogue
for their busy mail-order service. Elegant French Limoges
porcelain by leading manufacturers with impressively literary
names—"Balzac," "Colette," "Corneille," "Gide," "George
Sand," etc. Prices start at $19 for a dozen dinner plates in
plain white (the white version of any shape is usually
considerably cheaper than the patterned versions) and
sometimes go as high as $110 for a dozen dinner plates.
Pieces are available individually or in dinner services, tea
sets or coffee sets.

   Glass by Baccarat, Lorraine, Val St-Lambert, and modern
glass by Daum, including their household objects: fascinating
icelike cracked-glass ashtrays, little ones from $9 up; gas
lighters from $22; clocks from $110; and table lamps from
$25 to $75.

   Also French silver, which is a grayer color than most silver,
and silver plate. But I compared one or two prices on the
famous French "Cristofle" silver plate, and prices seem to be
about the same in New York.

Obéron, 73 Champs-Elysées, Paris VIII, France
*22-page catalogue, $1.50 (refundable with first purchase).
Prices in $.*

A large tax-free store for foreigners, Obéron is an excellent
place to buy crystal gifts. The catalogue is in English and
shows plenty of Baccarat and Lalique objects, some at half
the American prices. A Baccarat squirrel paperweight costs
$21.60 at Obéron and $44 in New York. A Baccarat caviar
bowl is $56 at Obéron and around $100 in New York. Lots of
table items, vases and smokers' sets, and also some Baccarat
crystal stemware, each glass up to $9 less than in New York
(the Baccarat "Harcourt" water jug costs $61 at Obéron and
$100 in New York).

   Obéron also stocks porcelain gifts: Chantilly boxes; swan-
shaped salt and pepper dishes at $6.50 the pair; blue-and-
gold Limoges ashtrays, $2.70; informal Porcelaine de Paris
baking dishes; and Fourmaintraux flowery earthenware.

GERMANY

**Franz Widman und Sohn, am Karlstor Unter den Arkaden,
8 Munich 2, Germany**
This is the place for the renowned Hummel figures, the
chubby children named things like "Little Wanderer,"
"Playmates" and "She Loves Me—She Loves Me Not." Prices
$3–$27, but mostly under $10.

German toy shops also sell Hummel.

145

146

147

148

145
The Leach Pottery Oven-proof stoneware with glazed interiors. Ashtrays, small bowls and lidded soup bowls, around $2; coffeepot and tall jug, around $5 and $7.

146
The Leach Pottery Glazed stoneware in black to rust, gray-brown, pale green or oatmeal. Small pieces at various prices up to $2.50, large pieces around $8.
photos Studio St. Ives

147
Leather and Snook Royal Crown Derby "Olde Avesbury." Five-piece place setting, $26.55.

148
Royal Tara Bone china "Georgian" shape, "Bird of Paradise" pattern. Five-piece place setting, about $12.

Rosenthal Studio-Haus, Dr. Zoellner KG, Leopoldstrasse 44, 8 Munich 23, Germany
80-page color Rosenthal Studio Line catalogue, $1.
Rosenthal glass catalogue, $1.
Leaflet for smokers' sets, free.

A gorgeous, lavish catalogue crammed with Rosenthal's gracefully modern china, glass and flatware by leading European designers (and, from America, there is a space-age tea-for-two set designed by Walter Gropius).

The catalogue I looked at showed tableware in twelve different shapes, each one of which could be decorated with any of several patterns, and each one with glasses and stainless-steel flatware to match, often by the same designer. To compare prices I chose, completely at random, Tappio Wirkkala's "Composition." Four place settings with a "Diadem" pattern (twenty pieces) cost $200 in New York, $93.20 in Germany. The red-wine glass cost $9 in New York, $5 in Germany, and the flatware cost $74 for a sixteen-piece set in New York and only $79.20 for a *thirty*-piece set in Germany.

In addition to tableware there are vases, ashtrays, glass-star candleholders, and three nice little pottery table lamps with molded white or colored bases and bright-colored shades; plates decorated by Bjørn Wiinblad with wide-eyed figures in rich reds, blues and gold. Although this Studio Line catalogue shows drinking glasses as well, the glass catalogue lists only stemware, about twenty-nine patterns.

There is also a little leaflet with china smokers' sets, each set contains an ashtray, lighter and cigarette box. Prices from $40 for a white set with a delicate molded fruit-and-flower design; a set with Bjørn Wiinblad's lovers painted in blue costs $51.

HOLLAND

Focke and Meltzer, Kalverstraat 152, Amsterdam, Holland
Rosenthal catalogue, $1; Christmas gift brochure, September; Christmas and Commemorative Plates brochure, March; other manufacturers' brochures, free. Prices in $.

Founded in 1823, this international glass-and-china shop is visited by over twenty thousand Americans a year. Besides stocking Royal Delft and the best-known Dutch crystal hand-blown Leerdam and hand-cut Kristalunion, they also carry china and crystal from most other European countries: Val St-Lambert, Waterford, Rosenthal, Herend, etc., so if you are looking for something that you can't find elsewhere, try them. If you are interested in Christmas plates, Focke and Meltzer has a brochure showing most of them together with other commemorative plates ("The Moon," "Mayflower" and "Mothers"), all at about half the cost in America. Prices start at $11, including postage.

Royal Delftware, International Mailing Dept., Markt 45, Delft, Holland
Royal Delft brochures, free. Prices in $.

In 1969 this special department was set up to sell genuine Royal Delft (founded in 1653) by mail. Royal Delft was one of the first European earthenwares to show Chinese influence, and the familiar blue flower and bird designs are more robust and less formal than the leading china from other countries. Although plates are shown, the catalogues are mostly full of jugs, mugs, vases, candlesticks, table lamps, and traditional tiles with Delft designs which, this firm says, cannot be found in America at all. Prices are mainly in the $10—$25 range, including postage, with wall plates inspired by Rembrandt paintings costing over $100.

HONG KONG

Universal Suppliers, G.P.O. Box 14803, Hong Kong
30-page color Noritake catalogue, free; air mail $1.60. Prices in $.

A good catalogue showing about seventy-five Japanese Noritake china patterns in a very wide assortment of designs—plain white, flowery, gold-trimmed, etc. Twenty-four-piece tea sets start at $16 (plus $8 for postage and insurance); sixty-seven-piece dinner services for eight start at $47 (plus $25 for postage and packing). Also, plastic dinner services, eight patterns, each $42 for fifty-three pieces, and children's sets and plates.

IRELAND

Stephen Faller, Industrial Estate, Mervue, Galway, Ireland
Manufacturers' brochures: Doulton, Minton, Waterford glass and Galway crystal, any or all of these for $1. Royal Doulton books: figures, $3; character/toby jugs, $2.

The Royal Doulton collectors' book shows more figures, animal models, character and toby jugs, and rack plates than one ever gets to see in a shop. Perhaps of special interest are the Williamsburg figures introduced in 1960, a series of statuettes dressed in the eighteenth-century clothes of Williamsburg, Virginia; a gentleman and lady, $25 each; as well as the blacksmith, the silversmith, the wigmaker, etc. And for dog lovers, a series of hand-painted dogs, some of them modeled from famous championship winners, most of them about $12 each.

Apparently in the 1840s the Duchess of Sutherland had the novel idea of decorating her house with plates on the moldings around her rooms—within a few years the fad had caught on all over the country and has continued off and on ever since. Doulton makes a series of rack plates for people still doing it, mainly representing historic English buildings and famous authors such as Shakespeare and Dickens.

Waterford is available here too, though the export manager complains that the manufacturers don't send enough of the most popular things—it seems that sugar-and-cream sets, honey jars, candlesticks, etc., are most in demand, so you had better get these from another source.

Robert Hoggs and Co. Ltd., 10 Donegall Square West, Belfast BT1 6J, Northern Ireland
Manufacturers' brochures: Selected Royal Doulton figures, character jugs and tableware; Waterford glass; Baleek china; Hummel figures; Old Country Roses; Coalport; Wedgwood Jasperware, free. Prices in $.

In addition to the ubiquitous Royal Doulton and Waterford, Hoggs sells harder-to-find Baleek china—distinctive ivory-colored tea services with molded surfaces in imitation canework and shamrocks, and vases with raised flowers and decorations. A tea cup, saucer and plate cost $10.25, including postage.

The Coalport brochure, which Hoggs can send you, has, as well as the tableware, lots of gift suggestions: little bowls and candy dishes; sugar-and-cream sets; flatware with china handles; a clock; the "floral studies" realistic-looking china-flower posies; and the reproductions of Georgian pastille burners, cottages and castles through whose chimneys smoke sailed up.

Royal Tara Ltd., Tara Hall, Galway, Ireland
10-page color leaflet, free.

Royal Tara has a leaflet illustrating their own bone china, and

149
Cellini's Silver Factory Capodimonte figurine "Small Girl with Dog." $31.20.
photo Bazzechi

150
Svenskt Glas "Original" hand-blown, cut, full crystal by Orrefors. *From left to right:* cocktail tumbler, $4.88; champagne/sherbet, $9.02; wine decanter, $27.16; water goblet, $7.52; red-wine glass, $5.88.

151
Svenskt Glas "Romeo and Juliet" by Orrefors. Hand-blown, engraved, full crystal, 8″ high. $42.53.

if you are longing for delicate old posies and rosebuds, write to them, as a few of their patterns are more romantic and country-cottage-ish than anything made by the better-known English companies. There are also mugs and tea sets decorated with hunting scenes.

ITALY

Cellini's Silver Factory, Piazza Santa Croce 12, Florence, Italy
28-page catalogue, free. Prices in $.

In the middle of this silver catalogue there are two full color pages of Italian Capodimonte figurines—humorous and "world renowned" as the catalogue says. Prices from $11 for "The Dog and the Butterfly" to $123 for "The Musicians"—a couple of down-and-out old men looking very pleased with themselves as they play on the guitar and violin, their pockets bulging with bottles of booze.

SWEDEN

PUB (Paul U. Bergströms AB), Box 40 140, Export Department, S-103 43, Stockholm 40, Sweden
Manufacturers' brochures: Kosta, Orrefors, Skruv glass. Rörstrand china, $1. Prices in $.

This large Stockholm department store sells Swedish glass by mail and also Rörstrand's famous modern china tableware. The most familiar pattern, "Mon Ami"—a regular design of stylized four-petal blue flowers on a white background—costs $3 per dinner plate, $8.50 for a coffeepot, and $22 for a casserole with lid. Flameproof "Koka"—wide blue bands with darker fish painted in—is $2.25 for a dinner plate, $1.40 for a coffee cup and saucer, $4.20 for a pitcher. "Amanda"—shiny brown bands with gray-blue lines and circles—is $1.50 for a dinner plate, and about $3.30 each for serving platters, bowls and casseroles.

Svenskt Glas, Birger Jarlsgatan 8, S-114 34, Stockholm, Sweden
39-page catalogue, free. Prices in $.

A handsome and well-organized catalogue showing an enormous variety of Orrefors and Kosta modern Swedish glass in the grand manner. Besides the gracefully simple crystal tableware (wine glasses cost between $3 and $7), there are lots of decorative household objects: chunky ashtrays and candle holders, $5.50 and up; cigarette boxes; heavy apple- or pear-shaped perfume bottles; thick bumpy bowls; and more delicate vases with engravings of birds, butterflies or children; crystal bells; glass-framed mirrors. For sheer decoration: "ice blocks" by Vicke Lindstrand—pale-green glass blocks engraved with polar bears or dolphins, individually signed, $40–$550—or drinking glasses based on beautiful nineteenth-century Swedish designs, one showing Karl XIV Johan on a royal journey surrounded by an elaborate decoration of stylized flowers and leaves. Wine glass $39, beer mug $95.

HARDWARE

J. D. Beardmore, 3-5 Percy Street, London W1P OEJ, England
Illustrated leaves, free.

You will find twenty thousand different items stocked in this wonderland of reproduction furniture fittings and architectural

152
H. L. Barnett A boxed pair of large Dartington crystal goblets. About $9.50 a pair. Surface postage $1.80.

153
The General Trading Company 9″ polished and laquered brass Dolphin doorstop. $40.36. Surface postage $10.72.

154
The General Trading Company Herend porcelain tea-caddy-shaped lamp base, hand-painted with different "Rothschild Birds." About $33. Surface postage $4.29. Shade to order.

155
The General Trading Company Black-and-white print wastepaper basket, about $12.73; surface postage $4.29. Black-and-white umbrella stand, $20.10.

156

157

156
Halcyon Days 1½″ boxes enameled on copper inspired by eighteenth-century Bilston and Battersea enameled boxes. $15.85.

157
Halcyon Days Enameled cigarette box for twenty-five king-size cigarettes, with a design taken from a François Boucher etching; in antique puce or charcoal on white. $29.

158
Henningham and Hollis Silverplated stirrup cups: 3″ size, $10.20; 5″, $16.50.

158

metalwork in brass, bronze, copper and iron. Prices are not available now and whatever they are, they are clearly not low, though Beardmore's says that they are lower than they would be in America. For top-quality period reproductions of the "great eras in brass," write and tell them what you are looking for and in what style. People who crave just one fabulous door knocker and people who are trying to outfit an entire building in one style should be equally well served, because the range is very complete. There are decorative fittings for electric lights, curtains, bookshelves, cabinets, cloakrooms, clocks. If it is metal—or can be made more elegantly in metal—it is here. You can even have your keys fitted with a variety of grand cast-brass ends to match other period fittings.

Erme Wood Forge, Woodlands, Ivybridge, South Devon, England
Brochure, free.

Hand-forged door knockers, hearth furniture, weather vanes and gates, mainly to customers' orders. Weather vanes start at about $33 and go up to $66; there is a huge choice of models. A 3′ gate starts at about $77, and other gates go up to $550.

Ingersoll Locks Ltd., Regent House, 89 Kinsway, London WC2B 6RZ, England
Illustrated brochures, free.

At the moment, Ingersoll deals only with government and industrial users in America, but they will be happy to sell to anyone else. Each customer is given an exclusive lock combination, and duplicate keys can only be bought by an authorized person. Cost per key: about $16–$22.

Rim locks, mortise locks, window locks and padlocks—the brochures describing them are clear as day with diagrams, measurements, and all the explanations you'd need.

S. C Pierce & Son Ltd., Bredfield Ironworks, Woodbridge, Suffolk, England
General brochure for gates, window grilles, railing, free. List for domestic ironwork and weather vanes, free.

Besides a good selection of larger wrought-iron articles, Pierce has a few miniature weather vanes suitable for summer houses and garages at about $16 each.

HOUSEHOLD OBJECTS AND GIFTS
CANADA

Habitat Toronto, 277 Victoria Street, Toronto 200, Ontario, Canada
Color sheet, free.

A new branch of the English firm Habitat, which burst onto the English scene several years ago with colorful, modern and inexpensive things for the house. Everything here is either made by English Habitat or chosen with a sternly discriminating eye, and Habitat Toronto says they are already being called by American designers who have seen their wares in England (an architect from Texas recently ordered seven hundred of their own flatware place settings). Unfortunately, by the time things reach us via Canada (the English shop only considers orders of over $260), goods are medium-priced instead of low, but they are still attractive. A knockdown sofa costs about $274; summery cotton-and-acrylic bedspreads in hot colors, $49 single, $71 double; do-it-yourself paper lampshade kits, about $3.80; enameled book ends, about $3.80; 3″ stoneware kitchen storage jars with cork bungs, about $1 each; shiny purple-and-black

aprons, about $5 for adults and $3 for children. Also some toys, including very special rag dolls named after the March sisters in *Little Women* and dressed in long old-fashioned dresses, about $17 each.

DENMARK

Den Permanente, Vesterport, DK-1620 Copenhagen, Denmark
Catalogue planned, $2.50. Prices in $.

Everything shown and sold at "The Permanent Exhibition of Danish Arts and Crafts" has been chosen by an independent selection committee to represent the best in Danish applied arts, made both industrially and by craftsmen. The result is a stunning array of top-quality modern pots and pans, glass, cutlery, ice buckets, salad bowls, etc. Some of them are widely exported and familiar to people who like modern design: Dansk, Kastrup-Holmegaard glass, Kaj Bojesen wooden bowls and toys. Others, such as the "Cylinda" line (a superb new range in stainless steel; see the ice buckets, designed with some sort of collaboration from Professor Arne Jacobson) I have only seen in one New York shop. Prices seem to be roughly one-third lower than in America, so whether you save any money depends on postage and duty. A better reason for writing to Den Permanente is to get beautiful things not available locally.

ENGLAND

Anything Lefthanded Ltd., 65 Beak Street, London W.1, England
Leaflet, free. Catalogue, 50 cents.

The owner of this store is left-handed himself and feels keenly the minor, daily miseries of this neglected minority. Mr. Gruby's shop is stocked with gadgets to make life slightly less burdensome. The leaflet gives details of the most essential things; the bigger catalogue describes over ninety others. Some seem to be rather an exaggeration, like special pastry slicers and knives (surely lefties don't have much trouble with ordinary carving knives?). But left-handed scissors and fountain pens are very popular; so are tailor's shears, $8. And there are playing cards that show the pips whatever hand they are fanned in; left-handed address books; a left-handed writing case, $4.50; left-handed pruning shears, $5.15; seccateurs, $5.20; can openers; ironing boards; and many more gadgets of all sorts, including a left-handed sink.

H. L. Barnett, Brunswick House, Torridge Hill, Bideford, North Devon, England
66-page catalogue, free; 72 cents air mail.

A good year-round mail-order service. The catalogue includes the usual gifts from first-rate firms: Smythson leather, Jacquard silk scarves, Fortnum and Mason food hampers, but also quite a few newer ideas. Pretty handmade Austrian kettle holders and oven gloves, about $2.25; framed reproductions of Piranese's Rome, $10; Celtic silver jewelry from $5; scarlet Portuguese embroidered aprons, $5. An assortment of calendars, including a special doodler's calendar with space and suggestions for doodling, $2.25; and a children's ark calendar with animals to be cut out on each page. There are children's toys from Galt, John Adams and Merrit, and for more expensive gifts, clothes from Peter Saunders, mohair tunics from Highland Home Industries, and Langmore sheepskin jackets and coats, $118 and up.

The General Trading Company, 144 Sloane Street, Sloane Square, London S.W.1, England ♉
Export brochure, free. Prices in $.
34-page general catalogue, $2 (refundable).

The General Trading Company is housed in three discreetly converted Victorian residences and looks more like an elegant private home than a shop. They rather extravagantly call themselves "London's most fascinating store"—but you might well agree. Certainly their smashing catalogue is full of beautiful, unusual and decorative things for the home—antiques or in antique styles: pottery pomanders; animal-shaped brass doorstops; creamy Queen Victoria jugs made from an original mold; gold-tooled leather string boxes with gilt-handled Sheffield scissors; and nineteenth-century brass magazine racks. Lots of glass and porcelain, and a small, impeccable collection of reproduction and antique furniture: a buttoned Victorian sewing chair; cherry-wood end tables with brass-handled drawers; a leather-covered brass-studded library ladder that folds into a pole.

The smaller export brochure lists quite a bit of porcelain and other things specially suitable for mailing abroad.

Halcyon Days, 14 Brook Street, London W1Y 1AA, England
2-page color leaflet, free. Prices in $.

Halcyon Days has revived the eighteenth-century art of enameling on copper. In 1753 at Battersea, London, trinkets and curiosities—snuffboxes, scent bottles, bonbonnières—began to be produced and decorated with scenes and sentimental messages. Similar workshops were set up in Bilston, Staffordshire, and although the craft only lasted for a hundred years, "Battersea" enamels, as they are now called, are prized collectors' pieces. These fetching new Bilston and Battersea boxes are similar to the originals in design and coloring. For $13 each there are little 1½" boxes with flower or rose bouquets; eighteenth-century landscapes or messages, such as "Token of Friendship" or "Forget Me Not." For up to $20 there are round 2¼" and egg-shaped boxes with the same sort of designs, plus birds and animals, and one with a portrait of Napoleon. One that is actually useful as well as very pretty is a cigarette box with a picture of angels in charcoal or antique puce on white taken from a Boucher etching, $33.

Helios Home Supplies, Tytherington Center, MacClesfield, Cheshire, England
40-page catalogue, free.

A useful firm that sells an assortment of things, usually for the house, and always of reputable brands. The catalogue shows a fully illustrated collection of Old Hall cutlery and tableware, England's most famous streamlined stainless steel: vegetable dishes, casseroles, sauce boats, butter dishes, hors-d'oeuvre trays; a three-section hors-d'oeuvre tray in rosewood, $8; a four-piece tea set, $23. Fifty-piece flatware sets start at $80, three-piece carving sets at $18.

"Dorma"—Terylene-and-cotton sheets which have flower designs and deep colors like orange, with blankets and bedspreads to match—are much more expensive than American sheets. Twin size starts at $6.50. Twin-size Irish-linen sheets are $22 a pair.

There is also Bridge cut glass, $28 for six water goblets; Taunton Vale flowery kitchen accessories (pastry boards, spice racks, clocks, shopping lists); table mats from $6.50 for twelve: Dutch interiors, English birds, Turpin fruits, London scenes, Oxford and Cambridge colleges. Old prints of Oxford and Cambridge colleges are also reproduced on linen dishtowels, four for $4.50.

Henningham and Hollis, 4 Mount Street, Berkeley Square, London, W1Y 5AA, England
24-page brochure, free.

Here are gifts, mainly in leather and silver plate, with everything looking like something it is not, and probably intended for that famous class of people who have everything. Friends and relations of such people should certainly send for this brochure, as I can't imagine what the people who have everything have: a quill ballpoint pen; a silver-plated string holder that can be used for posy arrangements; a lily ashtray/candleholder (the petals come off and become ashtrays); chessmen bottle stoppers, a beer tankard/ice bucket; a turtle cigarette box; a thermometer in a gilt flower; a beehive message-reminder; a silver-plated apple-shaped jam jar; brass-beetle boot-remover doorstop. Of course, they may not want them either, but they might like the sporty items, which Henningham and Hollis says are most popular with their American customers, especially the silver-plated fox-head stirrup cups, prices about $10.20 each for the 2-oz. cup, and $16.50 for the 9-oz. size. Plenty of gifts below $10, and nothing above $30.

Smythson's, 54 New Bond Street, London W1Y 0DE, England ♉
Gift brochure, free. Proprietary list, free. Writing-paper samples, free.

The English *Harper's Bazaar* called Smythson's "an international status symbol" (along with Hardy's, sports, and John Lobb, clothes). They are famous for their blue writing paper, which, they say, is by far their greatest export to America, and will send samples of their poshly plain blue-and-cream stationery and their address dies. Paper can be bought plain, printed or initialed. Fifty sheets of "Bond Street Blue" with one initial and envelopes cost $2.50.

Smythson's also makes diaries, which are not sold by mail, since they are distributed in America. But other distinguished-looking things for the desk are sold by mail: loose-leaf morocco address books, from about $27; polished pigskin visitors' books embossed with your house name in gold, from about $55; wallets; onyx desk sets; a series of record books in which to make notes in an orderly way about hobbies and special interests: garden, golf, hunting, motoring, music, theater, wine, etc.; and the most expensive of the lot—$5 for one indexed "Blondes, Brunettes, and Redheads." And, in various sizes, indexed notebooks labeled "Christmas," "Gifts," "Menus" and "Guests," or a tycoonish three-city address book—"London-Paris-New York."

The gift catalogue contains lots of leather, and gadgets for fanatical golfers: gold-plated tees, golf-ball table lighters, and a home practice putter with a removable glass ashtray.

Trencherman's Ltd., The Town Mill, Aresford, Hampshire, England
36-page catalogue, free; $1 air mail. July.

Some of my friends who do a lot of their Christmas shopping through Trencherman's describe the service as very good. It is a gift firm that sells mainly sensible household things costing between $3 and $10: ice buckets, cheese boards, copper kettles, gardening sets, head scarves and writing cases. For $55 there is "Teasmade," the ultimate gadget that wakes you up, lights the room, tells the time, and makes tea or coffee.

Good toys too: rainy-day boxes, rope ladders, laboratory sets, magic sets, and a make-your-own-clock kit.

Way in Dodo, Harrod's, Knightsbridge, London W1, England
Catalogue, 25 cents.

159

159
Way in Dodo Cushion covers.

160
Aarikka Wooden candlesticks with candles, at prices between $1.25 and $5. Candles and candlesticks in gold, red, blue, green, orange, etc.

161
Mothercare (see Clothes section) Blender grinds up meat and purées cooked fruit and vegetables for baby food. The transparent bowl at the bottom can be used as a feeding dish. About $4.

162
J. Jolles Studios Gros-point bag with black, beige, red or blue background. About $125.

163
J. Jolles Studios Gros-point purse. About $88.

160

161

162

163

Top pop for the home by Dodo Designs, which produces a witty, inexpensive line of things in '20's–'30's designs and good, strong colors. Trays, tea canisters, signs, posters, alarm clocks, plastered with Union Jacks and jokey scenes. The best are cushions with boldly designed faces of '20's film stars or gangsters, or a picture of Britannia with the suggestive message "England Expects Every Man to Do His Duty." There are also sets of three cushions which, when put together, make a fat-thighed lady in purple-and-red corset and boots, or a mustachioed, tattooed strong man. Dishtowels and aprons in the same vein: one dishtowel shows a vamp with penciled eyebrows looking invitingly over her shoulder saying, "Honey, we're all washing up."

FINLAND

Aarikka, Nokiantie 2, Helsinki 51, Finland
Brochure, 15 cents.

Aarikka makes delightful and original candleholders and modern jewelry which are sold in their own shops in Finland, and a little is exported to America. Unfortunately, the brochure Aarikka sends out doesn't do justice to their goods, as it is illustrated by small (but clear) line drawings and doesn't give the fantastic, glowing color combinations possible with contrasting candleholders and candles. The little gold, stained or glossily painted wooden candleholders and candles cost under $5 each, but there are also marvelous brass mobiles with candles in delicate circles at various heights, $15–$30.

The neat silvery jewelry also uses circles as the main design element. Pendants have circles and half circles with circles, even heart-shaped pendants have cutouts with circular discs swinging in them, prices $6 to $27. Necklaces, bracelets, earrings, rings, brooches and cuff links are all composed of silver balls and circles. Prices for the smaller things generally $11–$22. Bracelets and necklaces, $33–$44.

IRELAND

Look, College Street, Killarney, Co. Kerry, Ireland
Brochure, free. Prices in $.

I haven't seen the Look brochure which Mr. Murphy, the managing director, says will be most unusual—a mixture of line drawings, glamour, and a bit of the old blarney. However, I have in the past seen some of their products which have no blarney about them. They are colorful, modern crafts, with more of a Scandinavian than Irish look. Bright Irish-linen aprons, about $5 including postage; fabrics, place mats and dishtowels in new designs; tablecloths in strong, solid colors; mohair knee rugs and stoles, about $9 including postage; Galway crystal; and Aran knitwear.

KITCHEN

E. Dehillerin, 18-20 Rue Coquillière, Paris I, France
12-page catalogue in French, free.

The world's most famous kitchen shop is in Paris, naturally enough, and sells by mail to America, *but* although they understand written English, they can only reply in French. They also advise customers to get together with friends and family for orders because only orders for merchandise weighing over 44 pounds are accepted (and go sea freight).

The catalogue, which is strictly for serious cooks, shows a workmanlike assortment of copper cooking pots and pans in all shapes and sizes: basic, nongimmicky utensils; good French chopping knives; and a range of classic molds (but no animal shapes or anything like that); Doufou enameled cast-iron cooking pots; and what they call "*fantasie*" copper, including a jardiniere; lovely rustic stewpots; champagne buckets; and *hâtelets*, skewers decorated with fish, birds and animals. Prices are not in the catalogue, and are only given upon application.

J. Froschl and Co., Schwanthalerstrasse 29, 8 Munich, Germany
160-page catalogue in German, free.

Froschl is the largest chain of electrical-appliance shops in Germany, and says they sell all German electrical appliances on the market. They are mostly 220 volts AC and can be used in America with a transformer. So if you are very design-conscious, you can get some sleek German appliances at lower prices than here (when available). Froschl also carries excellent saucepans, including beautiful Silit, enameled in red, blue or green, with circles inside squares in a lighter shade of the same color. Prices are not given in the catalogue; you must write and ask.

Any electric appliance that runs on 220 volts instead of 110 volts will need a transformer, which can be bought through an American electrical supplies store.

LACE, LINEN, EMBROIDERY AND CROCHET

The lace shops in this section say that the art of making lace by hand is dying out, since fewer and fewer young people are learning it. And it is clearly such a specialized and delicate work that while people may continue to embroider as a hobby, few people will have the patience to make lace. So perhaps it would be sensible for people who like the idea of heirloom lace to get it while they still can.

AUSTRIA

J. Jolles Studios, Andreasgasse 6, Vienna VII, Austria
20-page catalogue of gros-point handbags, free.
20-page catalogue of small petit-point articles, free.
Prices in $.

The world's most productive needlepoint producers, the Jolles Studios, won a Grand Prix at the Brussels World Fair. They design, make up and sell an enormous number of petit-point and gros-point purses and some tapestries at their Vienna shop, and for mail order they have two good catalogues. One shows almost eighty different gros-point handbags in variations of traditional flower designs and a few eighteenth-century garden scenes, priced between $55 and $100. The other has the same styles in powder compacts and change purses, $14 and up; cigarette cases, around $38 each; and some small things for under $11: pillboxes, perfume bottles, comb cases.

Madeira Superbia (below) also has needlepoint.
Obéron (see Handicrafts and Special Local Products) has less expensive needlepoint.

BELGIUM

Maria Loix, 54 Rue d'Arenberg, Brussels 1, Belgium

Y. Pieraerts, 55 Rue de la Régence, Brussels, Belgium
Price lists, free.

Belgium is not only thought to produce the finest linen in the world, but is also renowned for comparatively inexpensive lace.

Both these top shops are very well known to American tourists for their "serious" prices and "perfect" service, and they supply unillustrated price lists for mail order. If you see something you like on one of their lists, write to them, and they will send a photograph of it. They stock a vast assortment of handmade lace—Duchess, Flanders, Princess, Venetian, etc.—but by far the most popular and least expensive is Battenberg, which is machine-made lacy tapes sewn by hand into the final lace shape. Prices seem to be roughly equal at both shops. Here are some prices for goods with lace: place mats, either linen-and-lace or all lace, $2–$7 each; 36" bridge-tablecloths with four napkins, $12 and up; tablecloth 90" by 63" with eight napkins, $50; pastel-colored aprons, $4 and $7 (these only listed at Pieraerts'); blouses, $22–$60; baby bonnets, all lace or lined with silk, $2.75 and up; christening dresses, $20–$50.

BERMUDA

The Irish Linen Shop, Heyl's Corner, Hamilton, Bermuda
Leaflets, 50 cents. Prices in $

The price list firmly says: "WE ART NOT COMPUTERIZED—YOUR ORDER WILL BE READ AND DEALT WITH BY HUMAN BEINGS." Other points in favor of The Irish Linen Shop are that they carry imports from lots of different countries and have convenient, fully illustrated leaflets. However, people eager to save money should compare prices with the other shops in this section, as a few prices are higher here. Besides formal embroideries from Ireland and Madeira, you can find novelties like handkerchiefs embroidered with colorful Bermuda flowers, cocktail napkins with golf, tennis or bridge motifs, bright table mats from Italy, and cheerful modern dishtowels from Ireland.

FRANCE

Pache—Aux Mille et Une Nuits, 6 Rue de Castiglione, Paris I, France
France has always taken "heirloom" trousseaus and layettes very seriously, and Pache is one of the few shops left where you can get entirely handmade lace on lingerie, blouses, layettes and tablecloths. There is no brochure or price list, so write only if you know just what you want and are prepared to pay through the nose. A handmade pure-silk crepe de Chine nightgown with handmade Valenciennes lace costs $135. A handmade, hand-embroidered muslin baby dress with machine-made lace costs $70.

HOLLAND

Het Kantenhuis, Kalverstraat 124, Amsterdam, Holland
Het Kantenhuis imports the very best handmade lace and embroidery from all over the world, so they have a marvelous selection. Antique Venetian, Swiss Embroidery, Brussels (Princess) lace and all sorts of other laces and embroideries are attached to anything you might hope to find belaced and embroidered: collars, cuffs, bun cozies, guest towels, bridge sets, tablecloths, table runners, mantillas and bridal veils. No price list, but they answer specific questions very efficiently.

HONG KONG

China Art Embroidery Co., T.S.T. P.O. Box 5811, Kowloon, Hong Kong

A *very* efficient catalogue is put out by this thirty-eight-year-old firm, which sells clothes and linen by mail. They list in detail a wide selection of embroidery and lace, and prices are lower than anywhere else (although apparently purists do not consider some Chinese laces "genuine" even when made in the same way as European laces). A 36" bridge set with five napkins in Irish linen, embroidery and cutwork costs $6. Venetian-lace oval place mats start at $11.50 for four mats and four napkins. The firm can monogram anything you buy at prices ranging from 25 cents for one initial (on a handkerchief) to $4.75 for a 6" by 24" three-initial monogram with decorations (on a sheet or tablecloth).

IRELAND

Brown Thomas and Co., Ltd., Mail Order Dept., Grafton Street, Dublin 2, Ireland
38-page catalogue, 50 cents. Prices in $.

This well-known Irish store, winner of the "Coup d'Or du Bon Goût" (along with Marshall Field, Saks and others), has a thriving mail-order service to America and an excellent catalogue mainly of Irish products.

Their Irish Linen Shop has a good choice of the best Irish linen at prices one-third to half off American prices. Double-damask cloths start at $6.50; dozens of double-damask dinner napkins are 70 cents each; embroidered tea sets with four napkins, $10; ladies' handkerchiefs with crocheted edges, $1.10. Plain, hemmed sheets cost $25 for a pair of single-bed size, and $31 for double (hand-drawn hem stitch is a dollar more). Besides plenty of linen to choose from, there is a selection of some other things that Ireland is famous for: napkins, luncheon sets, mats, mantillas and bridal veils in handmade Carrickmacross lace; china and Waterford glass; and tweeds by the yard or made up into jackets for men, and coats for women; Donald Davies dresses; sheepskin coats; and the dramatic hooded Kinsale cloak copied from a traditional County Cork cloak in black wool with a colored lining.

ITALY

Jesurum, Ponte Canonica 4310, Venice, Italy
Venetian lace, probably the most expensive lace of all, is sold by this famous old shop, and made in its own lace-making school. Prices are high. Jesurum says that their tablecloths and place mats made with precious antique lace are extremely expensive, and with modern handmade lace are rather expensive. With machine-made lace, a napkin and place mat together cost about $5.50, so you can guess that when they say "expensive," they mean it. Tablecloths in batiste, organdy or linen start at $88; queen-size mixed-linen sheets with embroidery, $82 and up; six-piece machine-embroidered bath sets, $99 and up. Write to Jesurum and tell them what you are interested in, the size and price range you would like, and they will send you their "best offer" with a photograph of the item.

MADEIRA

Madeira Superbia, Rua do Carmo 27-1, P.O. Box 303, Funchal, Madeira, Portugal
52-page catalogue with some color, free. Prices in $.

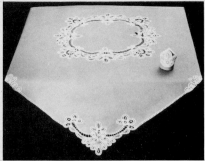

164

165

166

167

164
Het Kantenhuis White or cream linen tablecloth (48″ × 48″) and four napkins, all with Battenburg lace. About $25.

165
Het Kantenhuis White, cream or pastel linen bun cozy with Battenburg lace. About $4.
photo Studio Hartland

166
Madeira Superbia Eight cut-work place mats and eight 18″ square napkins in colored, white or ecru linen. About $55 the set.

167
Madeira Superbia Petit-point picture, canvas size 21″ × 24″, embroidery 11½″ × 15″. About $55.

Madeira Superbia, a large firm with many branches, has a very good catalogue illustrating their famous Madeira embroidery and needlepoint. The embroidery is mostly cut work or appliqué in flower or leaf designs, with an occasional animal thrown in. There are delicately monogramed handkerchiefs, moderately restrained for men, and going off into elaborate profusions of tiny flowers for women. Hand towels in various pastel shades with monograms or designs embroidered in the same or contrasting shade, $1.60 and up. There are place mats, tablecloths, napkins of course, and pretty embroidered cotton pillowcases, $6 the pair, for people who don't want to lash out vast sums for embroidered sheets. Sedate embroidered blouses cost $12, and there is a graceful collection of children's and babies' old-fashioned clothes, including a poplin party dress with cutout eyelets and tucks, for only $5.50.

To switch styles, Portuguese work is also sold here—simple stitches on brightly colored cotton—much more of a folk art. There are extraordinarily cheap hand-embroidered aprons for children, 75 cents; adults, $1.50.

Madeira Superbia is also known for its needlepoint reproductions in' carpets, wall hangings, and pieces for chairs and cushions. A wall panel, "Summer" by Boucher—a voluptuous scene of luscious-looking ladies reclining by a waterfall—costs $158, and flower designs in the style of Dutch masters are worked onto rugs of all sizes. For cushions and chairs there are Chippendale, Regency, Baroque, Louis XV, and "conventional" designs in petit point and gros point.

MAJORCA

Casa Bonet, San Nicolas 15, Palma de Mallorca, Spain ☙

A famous linen shop with a museumlike display of fine old lace and embroidery. One of Casa Bonet's most popular items has been customer signatures hand-embroidered on the corner of handkerchiefs instead of a monogram or an initial. However, if you prefer to stick to monograms, women's handkerchiefs cost from $1.10 up, and men's from $1.65. Both fine white and multicolored Majorcan embroidery is sold here, and a speciality is tuxedo shirts, which can be either simply pleated or elaborately finished with lace and embroidery. But everything must be arranged individually, as there is no catalogue or price list.

MALTA

Gozo 20, Gozo, Maltese Islands
Illustrated brochure, free.

This firm knits, weaves, and crochets—to order, if necessary—and makes crocheted cotton bedspreads at what seem to me to be phenomenally low prices for something almost unobtainable elsewhere: single-bed size, from $36, and double, from $62. They make, surprisingly, all-crochet bathroom sets to match any color scheme—flannels, fringed bathmats, $7, and fringed towels. Cushion covers in island designs, 18″ by 18″, about $10; and Victorian tablecloths, bags, hats, stoles and wraps—all in crochet, and in sober colors such as creamy white, rust, olive green, peacock blue. There are also lace cloche hats and a '20's-style hat, wide or floppy brimmed, $10–$13; and handwoven ties, bags and desert boots in weaves and leather; sweaters in fabric and wool; and hand-embroidered coats and evening boots to order.

168
E. Bakalowits Söhne Hand-cut crystal lamp available in
several sizes, the smallest 22″ wide × 13½″ high. About
$225.

168

169
170
171

169
A.B. Ellysett 10″-high table lamp. Base in polished pine,
and shade in pine splintwood; takes a maximum
wattage of 60w. About $7.50.

170
A. B. Ellysett 11″-high table lamp. Base in polished pine
and shade of frosted glass; takes a maximum wattage
of 60w. About $8.50. 14″-high size takes a maximum
wattage of 75w and costs around $9.50.
photo Hans Agne Jakobsson Ab

171
Fog and Morup Hand-blown glass lamp "Heliotrop";
inside glass white, outside blue or brown. About $45.

172
Fog and Morup "White line," lamps designed by Jo
Hammerborg. About $11 – $28.

173
The General Trading Company (see Household Objects
section) Antique pewter: George IV quart tankard by
Yates and Birch (circa 1820); baluster-shape tankard
(circa 1830); plate by Samuel Duncombe (circa 1745);
sandwich box (circa 1860). Similar pieces are usually
available.

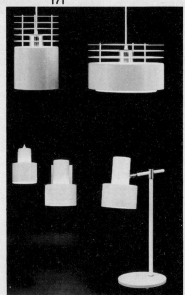

172

173

LIGHT FIXTURES

Any lamp bought from abroad will need an adapter, an inexpensive little gadget on sale at electrical supply stores which enables the plug to fit into American outlets (or, of course, the plug can be replaced with an American one). British lamps don't take screw-in bulbs, so their bulb sockets have to be changed; with lamps from other countries, just make sure the metal tongue at the back of the socket is in contact with the bulb.

E. Bakalowits Söhne, Halirschgasse 17, 1171 Vienna, Austria
Photographs and prices, free.

Austria is a leading producer of fine hand-cut crystal, and this firm makes splendiferous modern chandeliers in what they say is A-1 quality, produced only in Austria. They have made lights for all sorts of theaters, government buildings, and posh hotels in Europe, and in America have supplied, among others, the John F. Kennedy Center in Washington, the House of Congress in Springfield, Ill.—and Alexander's department store in New York.

But all sizes of lights are made: little metal and crystal candlesticks, small wall or table lights, and small to huge ceiling lights. The designs range from fairly classic and unobtrusive compact shapes to dramatic sunbursts of glittering crystal. Prices are high; the candlesticks are about $38 each, and the lamps between $135 and $1,000.

AB Ellysett, Box 82, S-285 01 Markaryd, Sweden
23-page catalogue with some color, free.

A designer, Hans-Agne Jakobsson, thought up these handsome pine lamps made in "darkest Småland," a forresty part of Sweden. Table, wall, floor and ceiling lights have shades made from slivers of natural pine. The lamps give a specially soft, warm light so appealing that the lamps have become very popular, and not only widely exported but also widely copied. Prices start at about $7.

Fog and Morup, Amagertorv 8, 1160 Copenhagen K, Denmark
30-page color catalogue, $1. Prices in $.

A good selection of modern lights for indoors and outside by leading Danish designers. Mouth blown-glass pendant lights in gracefully simple shapes, brass and copper wall and ceiling lights in more complicated shapes (and these are usually especially expensive in America); enameled lights in red, white, blue or yellow from $17; and a whole lot of lights for wall, ceiling or table in one design: a smooth round ball, half light-giving white plastic and half lacquered enamel, $14–$33. Also Royal Copenhagen table lamps in earthenware and porcelain, including a lamp produced to commemorate Copenhagen's 800th jubilee with a delicate blue picture of the old city taken from a copperplate engraving.

Tuzex, Export Department, Rytirska 13, Prague 1, Czechoslovakia
General catalogue, price list and photographs of garnet jewelry, stemware catalogue, crystal chandeliers catalogue, all free.

As the catalogue says, "For more than four hundred years chandeliers of Bohemian crystal have decorated royal palaces, concert halls, theaters and cathedrals throughout the world." But don't be daunted, Tuzex shows twenty-nine chandeliers, most of them ordinary house size. In fact, these hand-cut crystal chandeliers are great bargains in spite of the legendary reputation of Bohemian crystal, and are even less expensive than Waterford. Shapes are more horizontal than vertical (good for low ceilings). Most of the lights are one-tiered, and the dangly bits are short and teardrop-shaped. Two of the chandeliers are an unusual combination of enameled china and crystal.

Small two-light sconces start at $29, including postage; 12" ceiling baskets start at $70; and full-fledged chandeliers at $99 and up, including postage, though with a very few sizes too large or heavy to go by mail, shipping is only paid to the American port.
For more modern lamps, see Ikea (Modern Furniture section); for pottery lamps, see Rosenthal Studio-Haus (Glass and China section); for hand-painted Indian lamps, see Central Cottage Industries Emporium (Handicrafts and Special Local Products section).

PEWTER
ENGLAND

The Pewter Shop, 18 Burlington Arcade, London W.1, England
24-page catalogue, free.

A wide choice of first-rate but expensive English cast pewter made by Crown and Rose, a very old firm that still uses traditional methods: they cast in gun-metal molds (often the original ones) and turn on the lathe by hand. Tankards start at about $14, candlesticks at about $27, and 5" plates are about $11 each.

HOLLAND

Focke and Meltzer, St. Lucien Shop, St. Luciensteeg 18, Amsterdam, Holland
Pewter catalogue, free. Prices in $.

A very good choice of classic and typically Dutch pewter, including a page full of spoons. But ask specifically for the pewter catalogue, because glass and china are also sold here and at Focke and Meltzer's other branch.

A. Tobben, Haven 5–9, Volendam, Holland
10-page brochure, free. Prices in $.

Lead-free Royal Holland pewter in simple classic and modern designs at lower prices than anyone else's. Tankards start at about $7, candlesticks at about $5, and plates at about $5. There are also things like gas lighters, fondue sets, and tea and coffee sets.

MALAYSIA

Selangor Pewter Co., Mail Order Dept., 231 Jalan Tuanku Abdul Rahman, P.O. Box 15, Kuala Lumpur, Malaysia
14-page brochure, free. Prices in $.

Apparently Malaysia, too, is known for its pewter. Selangor is a large old family firm employing over three hundred pewtersmiths in two factories. But unlike Crown and Rose, they use new machinery and methods to make lead-free pewter in modernish styles. You can choose to have your pewter plain, hammered, part hammered, or with a local picture (of, say, a bullock cart) engraved on it. Tankards start at about $5, candlesticks about $5. No plates illustrated, but there are napkin rings, cigarette boxes and photograph frames, among other things.
For antique pewter, write to the General Trading Company, (Household Objects); and Harrods (General).

RUGS

ECUADOR

Folklore, P.O. Box 64, Quitó, Ecuador
10-page rug brochure in color, free. Prices in $.
Price list of handicrafts, free. Prices in $.

Folklore has a staggeringly top-notch list of clients:
embassies, famous people and museums. In New York,
Folklore hand-knotted rugs are owned by the Museum of
Modern Art, the Museum of Primitive Art, the United Nations,
and the Metropolitan Opera House (fourteen of them). The
rugs are designed for Folklore by Mrs. Olga Fisch and cost
about $8 per square foot (with roughly $30–$40 extra per rug
for handling and air-freight charges). They come in several
sizes from 4' by 6' to 12' by 14'. Most designs can be made
to order in special sizes and colors, and color samples can
be matched ("to perfection," they say).

   The most distinctive and original carpets are inspired by
old textiles and cave paintings and are in subtle dark browns,
reds and cream. But there are also more conventional rugs:
"Georgia," a very beautiful colonial carpet with pale-blue,
gray and brown flowers on white; or "Caceria" with a pattern
of people, plants and animals based on Colonial
embroideries. There are several modern designs in
gorgeously rich reds, blues and greens—in fact, this is a
terrific place for unusual rugs.

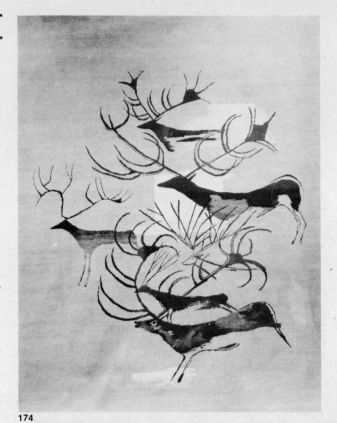

174

FINLAND

Suomen Käsityön Ystävät, Yrjönkatu 13, Helsinki 12, Finland
Color brochure, free. Prices in $.

Rya rugs, the shaggy Finnish carpets, in large, blurry, abstract
designs and magnificent colors: suns in fiery yellow and
orange; squares within squares of magenta and brown;
icicles of gray on white. The rugs here are particularly finely
and subtly colored, but humbler versions can be bought at
the Scandinavian furniture stores at much lower prices. A do-
it-yourself kit here costs about $88 for a 4' by 5' rug (the
same thing made up costs $217, and there is a waiting time
of three months).

*For more Rya rugs, see Anton Dam and Ikea (Modern
Furniture), and Husfliden (Handicrafts and Local Products).*

176

GREECE

A. Karamichos, 3 Mitropoleos Street, Athens 118, Greece
6-page color brochure, free. Prices in $.

Greek Flokati rugs are rather like the Finnish Rya but longer-
haired, silkier and traditionally made in white. Karamichos
make the heaviest and most sumptuous by hand in qualities
not often exported because foreign stores prefer cheaper
versions, though if you buy them directly from Greece the
prices are low, under half the New York prices I have seen.
Made with a 4" pile from sheep's wool and fluffed under
waterfalls, the rugs are available in plain, natural colors or
simple designs—squares, triangles, etc. For a few extra
dollars they can be custom-dyed, *really* custom: you are not
allowed to say airily "red" or "blue," you have to send a color
swatch you want matched. Nine sizes and two qualities.
Prices start at $11 for a 3' by 5' rug; and one, 6' by 9', costs
$61.

178

175

174
Folklore "Cuernos" hand-knotted rug in cream and brown (or any color to order); several sizes. $7.15 per square foot.

175
Folklore "Curiquinge" hand-knotted rug in red, brown, pale blue and pale yellow on beige background (or any color to order). 4' × 6' to any size. $7.15 per square foot.

176
National Welfare Organization Needlepoint rugs, about $46 per square meter (1.2 sq. yds.). Available in several sizes.
"Strawberries," red and green on cream background.
"Birds and Cypress," orange, blue, green, red on cream background.
"Cyclamen," pink, blue and green on cream background.

177
Fernandez Angulo SA "Selecta 152" twin bedspread in black, white and green-gray, about $45.50. Bedspreads in two colors start at $25.50; floor rugs in the same designs start at $4.50.

178
Märta Måås-Fjetterström "Gula Trädet" rug in flossa technique, yellow, red, blue or white-gray, designed by Marianne Richter. $340 per square yard.

179
Märta Måås-Fjetterström "Tuppamattan" tapestry 5'1" × 5'11", designed by Marianne Richter, main color green, blue and red or orange-red. $3,200.
photo Pål-Nils Nilsson

177

179

National Welfare Organization, Handicrafts Dept., 6 Ipatias Street, Athens 117, Greece
48-page carpet catalogue with some color, free. Prices in $. 22-page crafts catalogue with some color, free.

The National Welfare Organization (previously Their Majesties Fund) has encouraged and promoted carpet making by peasants as a means of increasing family income. Instead of trying to compete with Oriental carpets, they have developed unusual and beautiful Greek designs, knotted, woven and embroidered. Based on folk art and Hellenic motifs, styles are simple and graceful, leaning toward small, repeated pictures of stylized flowers, birds and geometric patterns. Prices start at $18 per square meter (1 sq. m. = 1.2 sq. yds.), but are mostly around $46 per square meter. They can be made to order in any size.

HONG KONG

Tai Ping Carpet Salon, 3 Middle Road, Kowloon, Hong Kong
18-page catalogue with wool samples, free. Prices in $. 36-page color catalogue, free.

Excellent, informative catalogue showing the kinds of custom-tailored carpets that Tai Ping has made for firms all over the world, including the Columbia Broadcasting System, First National Bank, Ford and General Motors, the Time-Life Building in New York and Grauman's Chinese in Hollywood. The carpets, manufactured in a large modern factory in Taipo, are made by hand from a blend of New Zealand and Scottish wools in any shape—any design—any size, so this is a marvelous place for anyone having trouble in finding what they want. The catalogues show lots of "contemporary," "periodic," "Chinese" and "Moroccan" designs, but as each carpet is made up to order, there is always a waiting time. Prices for standard designs vary from about $20 to $50 a square yard, with 10 percent extra for custom colors.

MOROCCO

Karmouchi Mohamed, 261 Route de Mediouna, Casablanca, Morocco
Catalogue, $2. Prices in $.

The most widely exported Moroccan carpets are thick-piled, mainly in black, white and earth colors with designs in more or less intricate diamond patterns. The most expensive, from Rabat, are the most complicated—Oriental in style but attractively rougher. Karamouchi Mohamed, wholesale exporters of Moroccan handicrafts, will sell individual carpets but can only correspond in French. The state controls the quality of the carpets, which are classified "*supérieure*," "*moyenne*" and "*courante*" (top, medium and fair), and prices are good: $15–$22 per square meter (1 sq. m. = 1.2 sq. yds.) for the simpler designs, and $33–$46 per square meter for the more intricately patterned carpets from Rabat.

NEW ZEALAND

Antarctic Products Co. Ltd., P.O. Box 223, Nelson, New Zealand
14-page brochure, free. Prices in $.

An informative export brochure shows sheepskin rugs in sizes up to 5½' by 5½' ($68, including postage). Also sheepskin jackets and down-filled jackets.

The Sheepskin Rug Shop, Mail Order Dept., P.O. Box 12-175, Penrose, Aukland, New Zealand
6-page brochure, free.

New Zealand is, of course, known for its sheep, and the manager of this shop chauvinistically says that the sheepskins he has seen on sale in America are poorer quality and two and a half to three times the price. Rugs made out of one or two lamb or sheep skins can be bought dyed in any of fifteen colors. Prices are from $8 to $33, and postage is only about $1.75 per rug. Clipped, rectangular rugs in sizes up to 3' by 6' cost from $22 to $36 in various colors. All are washable.

There is also an imaginative collection of other things in sheepskin: toys, poodle and cat pajama cases, purses, handbags, cushions in all colors (12" by 12", only about $6, other sizes made to order), muffs, hats, all manner of slippers, and even sheepskin-lined, lace-up leather shoes for $10. Sheepskin stools, and car-seat covers—warm in the winter, cool in the summer (they stop you from sweating). Suede clothes, too. Waistcoats and skirts about $18, dresses about $35.

SPAIN

Fernandez Angulo S.A., Calle de Toledo 4, Madrid 12, Spain
30-page color catalogue and wool samples, free. Prices in $.

These brilliant baroque bedspreads and carpets from Spain have been copied all over the world, usually in strong blues and greens or reds and orange. Fernandez Angulo makes them in several patterns and any combination of a hundred colors (although service, which is slow anyway, becomes even slower if you don't choose the standard color combinations). Some of Angulo's products are sold in New York at *three* times the price, and I have seen 2' by 4' rugs for $22 in New York, similar to Angulo's, which are $8 for the same size, and $135 in New York for ones 6' by 9', which are $63 from Spain.

Outside Spain the very fetching bedspread versions seem to be most popular, although in a New York department store prices started at $70 for a twin-bed size. At Fernandez Angulo, twin sizes start at $25 and double at $32. This firm was recommended to me by a friend and both of us have satisfactorily bought rugs. The only hitch is that although the catalogue is in English, English is not spoken (or written), so if you need to ask about anything special, you'll need a translator.

SWEDEN

Märta Måås-Fjetterström, Myntgatan 5, Stockholm C, Sweden
Brochure in Swedish, free.

A weaving studio that makes very beautiful but very expensive original designs in tapestries and carpets. Orders take at least four months to complete, and small tapestries cost $107 and up. Carpets start at $180 per square meter (1 sq. m. = 1.2 sq. yds.).

TUNISIA

Office National de l'Artisanat, Ministère des Affaires Economiques, Den Den, Tunisia
68-page color catalogue, Vol. 1, "Tapis" (Rugs), $4.50.

100-page catalogue, Vol. II, "Divers (Miscellaneous), $1.50.

The Tunisian government has a splendid full-color catalogue published in Paris illustrating sixty-four carpets made by hand in the workshops of the Office de l'Artisanat. Styles vary from very traditional intricate geometric designs to simpler modern versions based on the old patterns. Most carpets come in about eight sizes up to 10' by 13'. Prices on request, but service is puzzling—I wrote two letters in English which were answered in French, and then one in French which was answered in English.

DO-IT-YOURSELF RUGS
Rugplan Ltd., Tivoli Mills, Cork, Ireland
22-page color catalogue, free. Wool samples, 25 cents (refundable).

A nicely designed, full-color catalogue of forty-seven do-it-yourself hook rugs. I would describe the designs as conventional-modern with a lot of floral designs, some clear-cut patterns with squares and diamonds, and two rugs for children's rooms, one descriptively called "Bambi," and the other, "Toytown Express." You can also make a plain rug with no design in any one of fifty good colors. Shapes are rectangular, semicircular, circular and oval. Prices for complete kits, from $16.50 for a 22" by 44" to $44 for a 36" by 70". Even after postage and duty have been paid, prices are roughly a third off similar American kits.

For more do-it-yourself rugs, see the shops in the Needlework section; and Husfliden (Handicrafts and Special Local Products); PUB (General).

TILES

Tiles are expensive, but they can be very decorative and their glazed surface is exceptionally dirt-resistant.

The Portuguese tiles cost from as little as 20 cents, yet in New York I have seen the same tiles for $1 each, and very similar ones for $2. They are fairly compact to ship, and you can save quite a bit of money if you want to tile a large area. But even if you have just a few mailed, you can get a bargain. Fabrica Ceramica Viuva Lamego says that fifty blue-and-white tiles (1 square meter, enough for a coffee table or small counter) would cost $33 to mail to America: $10 for the tiles and $22 for postage and insurance of two parcels. Duty is 24 percent of the cost of the tiles, so you should save about a third of the New York price.

Packard and Ord Ltd., 37 Store Street, London W.C.1, England
Brochure, free.

All sorts of tiles: flowers, fruit and fish in an international-modern style, hand-painted on single tiles or several that join up to make composite pictures. More unusual are the designs based on old tiles: blue-and-white Dutch, flowers from fifteenth-century Damascus, and a series of animal designs for the floor in terra cotta and cream suggested by medieval tiles in the Westminster Abbey chapter house. Prices not available yet.

Fabrica Ceramica Viuva Lamego, Largo do Intendente 25, Lisbon 1, Portugal
7-page color brochure, free.

Blue-and-white or polychrome tiles in traditional Portuguese, heavily decorated Moorish-type styles, also a few modern designs. Tiles cost from 20 cents to 32 cents each, and a square meter (1 sq. m.=1.2 sq. yds.), $10.50 to $16. Any design, plain solid color or otherwise, can be made to special order.

Fabrica Sant'Anna, Calcada da Boa Hora 96, Lisbon, Portugal
52-page catalogue in Portuguese, free.

This large firm has done "*grandes*" works for clients in Portugal and abroad, and finishes the catalogue with a list of them—mostly municipal offices, hotels, embassies and palaces. But don't be daunted; although they show only about twenty different tiles (not as many as Viuva Lamego, above), there are plenty of unusual antique-style ceramic objects for private homes in prices around $10 each: plates, mugs, jugs, jars, name plates, candlesticks and lamps (table lamps at various prices around $16) done in flowery folk-art styles. For more ambitious decorators there are fountains, benches and decorative panels, from a 12-tile, eighteenth-century gentleman on a horse for about $22 to a whole wall-sized view of old Lisbon which is now pleasing guests in a Brussels hotel.

Royal Delft (Glass and China), has Dutch tiles. Marlau (Reproduction Furniture) has Spanish tiles.

180
Fabrica Sant'Anna 20" platter, handmade and hand-painted. About $9.

181
Fabrica Sant'Anna "Artistic Panel." About $22 to $30.

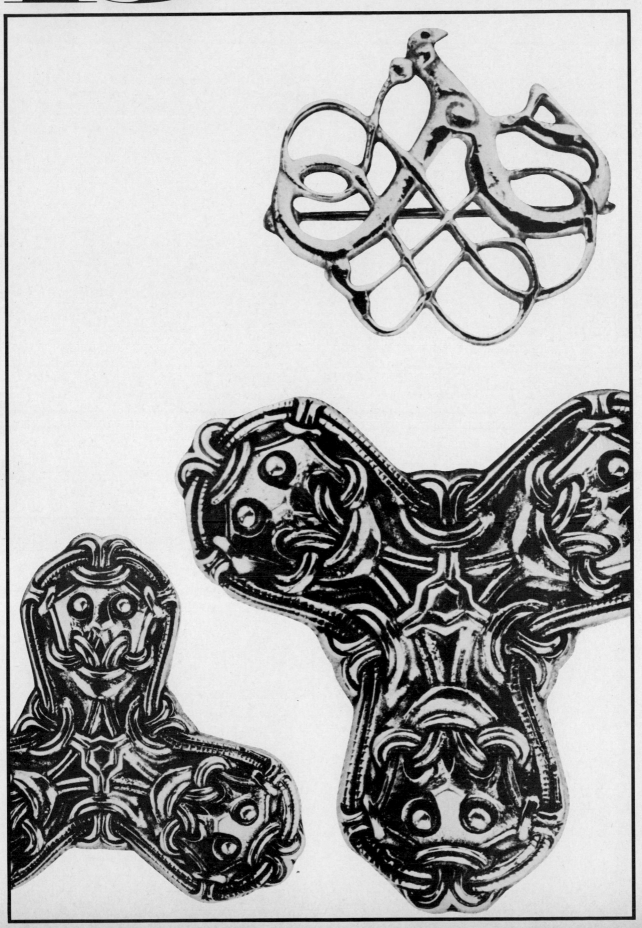

The jewelry is divided into two sections: *International*, for famous jewelers who make fairly classic, conventional and extremely expensive jewelry in worldwide styles, and *National*, for jewelry either made in local styles, or with local stones. Some of the prices in the National section are high, too, but quite a few are not at all. For less expensive and very interesting jewelry, see the Handicrafts and Special Local Products section. For antique jewelry and silver, see the Antiques section.

INTERNATIONAL JEWELERS
AUSTRIA

Heldwein, Graben 13, 1010 Vienna, Austria
18-page color brochure, in German, free. October.

Heldwein makes diamond jewelry and animal brooches, but their specialty is unusual modern jewelry, often to customers' own design. Gold is squashed and ribbed into naturalistic shapes, vaguely petal- or shell-like, usually without stones but sometimes studded with irregularly shaped aquamarines or crystals. Lapis lazuli and coral are worked into golden chains and twisted, tasseled cords for necklaces and bracelets; smooth circles and balls of gold make hanging earrings. This is the only catalogue to show a couple of pages of modern silver jewelry: lighters, boxes, etc.

ENGLAND

Asprey and Co. Ltd., 165–169 New Bond Street, London WIY OAR, England ☙
24-page color catalogue, free. Prices in $.

Asprey's won gold medals at all the famous nineteenth-century exhibitions, and have been "by appointment" to every reigning sovereign since Queen Victoria—but their grand reputation goes back to the eighteenth century when William Asprey started a silver and leather working firm. His descendants have been making dressing cases, fine writing paper, jewelry and silverware for top people ever since.

The gift catalogue is called "The Art of Giving"—an art which must be easy to master with the help of Asprey's and a lot of money. Gifts suggested are classic, and highly expensive, but consummately well made, often in Asprey's own workshops. Diamond jewelry, golden cigar cutters, wine goblets, onyx-marble cigarette boxes, silver nutcrackers, golden-edged crocodile wallets, silver-edged cut glass, and the *Memoirs of Casanova* bound in red calf. There are antique bibelots, and prices go happily over $3,000 (for a mosaic box given by Pope Pius VII to the captain of a British warship, in 1816).

Garrad and Co. Ltd., 112 Regent Street, London, W1A 2JJ, England ☙
33-page color catalogue, free. September.
Regent plate catalogue, free.
Sterling-silver catalogue, free.
William Tolliday at Garrad brochure, free. Prices in $.

Garrad (by appointment to the Queen, goldsmiths and crown jewelers—need I say more?) sends its catalogues to a selected list of important business people in America, but say that they have no mail-order service as at the moment their American customers buy when they come to London. They would, however, be happy to mail catalogues and goods to anyone else.

The gift catalogue shows very expensive modern and antique silver and jewelry. The lowest price I could find was $65 for a pair of cuff links.

The sterling-silver catalogue has interesting handmade and reproduction silver tea sets, candelabra, tankards, wine goblets, (one Charles II reproduction wine goblet, $28), and punch bowls. Six-piece sterling-silver place settings start at about $80.

The silver plate is in traditional designs and is not priced in place settings but by the dozen, as is the English habit. Twelve table forks start at $39. Tea sets to match start at $102 for four pieces.

A color brochure shows pictures made out of gold and jewelry collages by William Tolliday, who exhibits his work only at Garrad's. Prices for signed and limited editions range from $520 to $1,700.

Mappin and Webb Ltd., 170 Regent Street, London, W1R 6JH, England ☙
32-page gift catalogue, free.
Sterling-silver brochure, free.
Mappin plate brochure, free.

On the other hand, Mappin and Webb, silversmiths to the Queen, says that they have many customers in America; perhaps it is because their gift catalogue isn't as glossy and expensive as Garrad's. No antique jewelry or silver; instead glass, leather, dressing-table sets and stainless-steel flatware. There are gold tie tacks and green onyx table lighters for as little as $17.

The sterling-silver brochure shows "the nine great designs" in flatware. Prices for twelve forks, $240–$320, depending on the great design.

The silver-plate brochure has, besides the regular flatware, seven canteens (chests) in veneered oak. Six five-piece place settings in a chest start at $275.

HOLLAND

Bonnebaker, Rokin 88–90, Rokin, Amsterdam C, Holland
18-page color brochure. Prices in $.

Bonnebaker, makers of crowns for William II of Orange, and quoters of Shakespeare ("Dumb jewels often, in their silent kind, more than quick words do move a woman's mind"), makes some neat and symmetrical, conventional jewelry, mainly in diamonds. They also make graceful animal pins (which, instead of being in the usual cute-humorous style, are more realistic than those of other nations) in simple gold with small jewels for eyes: an 18-carat mouse with ruby eyes costs $156, and a rabbit, $130. Also gold tie pins, money bars, key rings in rough gold, and an enamel and gold ballpoint pen for $133.

SPAIN

Grassy, Avenida José Antonio 1, Madrid, Spain
24-page color catalogue in Spanish. Before Christmas.

Flashier jewelry, here, than the northern countries seem to go in for. Animal-head rings—a golden dragon with ruby eyes, a ram with sapphire eyes (about $77) or a lion's head carved out of coral, lapis lazuli or tiger's-eye—for $110 up. Jewelry for men (some of it cheaper than anywhere else): golden belt buckles and pen knives from $66; carved cuff links in gold and jasper start at $110. A tycoon letter opener with gold or silver vermeil blade and lion-shaped handle carved out of precious stones starts at about $75.

Grassy also has departments for rare and decorative antique clocks and Oriental carvings.

HOLLAND

A. Van Moppes and Zoon, Albert Cuypstraat 2—6, Amsterdam, Holland
16-page brochure, free. Prices in $.

Holland and Belgium are the world's diamond-cutting centers. This large and reputable diamond factory in Amsterdam is open to visitors, and thousands of tourists go through the plant every year. Van Moppes and Zoon imports diamonds directly from South Africa, then two hundred employees are involved in the sawing, shaping and polishing. Some diamonds are sold loose, others are made into jewelry, and for that, Van Moppes uses only top-quality diamonds: "blue/white and flawless" is the official grading. They say that their jewelry prices are 30 percent lower than American prices, but I haven't been able to check, as each piece is individual and settings vary, so I leave checking to anyone who considers buying. The brochure comes with a useful leaflet giving general information on cut and quality of diamonds. Prices for rings illustrated, $50—$780; pins, $60—$340; earrings, $225—$666. If you want anything not shown, professional drawings will be sent and you can have pieces made to order. The part I like is that each diamond comes with a written guarantee of the exact quality and weight. The guarantee allows you to trade your purchase for another piece, with no time limit, and full credit of the original price. Van Moppes refunds half of any duty you pay on their goods.

HONG KONG

Hong Kong Jade Center, 20-B Carnarvon Road, Kowloon, Hong Kong
816-page brochure, free. Prices in $.

A big shop selling 14-carat gold jewelry set with jade, diamonds, star sapphires, emeralds, pearls and semiprecious stones. Designs are uninspired and tend to be souveniry (lots of charms), but it should certainly be possible for most people to winkle out something they like, as styles vary and some are respectably plain. Prices are low, specially for jade—jade cuff links cost $33—and opal, moonstone or garnet rings are $22, aquamarine or onyx rings $27, all set in gold.

ISRAEL

Topaz, 121 Dizengoff Street, Tel Aviv, Israel
8-page brochure, free. Prices in $.

This leading Tel Aviv jeweler puts out a brochure showing twenty-four pieces of sterling silver and 24-carat gold jewelry with some extremely low prices—one third of the price of similar pieces in New York. Styles are local, and the best things here are earrings and brooches: a big, jingly gypsy earring set costs $6.50; and filigree brooches set with tiger's-eye, turquoise of Eliat stone (a turquoise-colored malachite stone from King Solomon's Mines, Israel) which is made to match the earrings, $10.

A chain-mail-type bracelet costs $17, and a modern version of an old necklace, squares set with Eliat stones, costs $20. Some things are of special Jewish interest—there are various versions of the Star of David, a modern one in gold for $6, and a watch with Hebrew letters.

ITALY

Giovanni Apa, Torre del Greco, Naples, Italy
46-page catalogue, some color, free. Prices in $.

Since Romans took over the Egyptian craft, Italy has been the place to find cameos, and anyone looking for inexpensive shell cameos will be very pleased with this famous store. A large catalogue illustrates a plentiful selection made in the Apa factories. Mythological scenes, Roman warriors, religious figures, cherubs, women's heads, flowers—they come mounted or unmounted in sterling silver or 14-carat gold and there are all kinds of ornaments for men and women. Prices start at $5 for lockets and rings, and go up to over $220 for plaques of scenes like "The Dance of the Muses" and "Cupids on the Lake" signed by the artist.

Apa also make another Italian specialty: coral jewelry, not rough but polished into beads or carved into roses and fruit. Brooches and earrings mounted on gilded silver cost under $10, heavy necklaces with multiple strands start at $45. "Extra" quality coral mounted on gold costs considerably more; prices start at $33 for earrings.

Cellini's Silver Factory, Piazza Santa Croce 12, Florence, Italy
28-page catalogue, free. Prices in $.

Cellini's makes sterling silver by hand with the same methods and in some of the same styles that were used in the Renaissance by the famous Florentine silversmiths, and have a world-wide mail-order service. It is an excellent place for small, inexpensive objects. There is a page full of tea and coffee spoons; the cheapest, 88 cents, is a coffee spoon with an effigy of Michelangelo's "David" on the handle; an hors-d'oeuvre fork with a Venice lion on the handle costs $1.75. Engraved cuff links, tie tacks, rings and earrings cost under $5. Pillboxes, powder compacts, cigarette lighters—plain or engraved in the curly feathery Florentine style and filigree jewelry—cost not much more. You can also get anything you want in silver for the house in impressively regal shapes—Baroque, Empire, or several Italian styles: coasters ($2.70 up); napkin rings, goblets; dishes, photograph frames; salt and pepper mills; tea and coffee sets; trays; five-piece dresser sets (three brushes, comb and mirror) in Louis XVI or Chippendale style cost only $45 (postage free). Presumably the set is light, as it costs *much* less than anywhere else, but if you are willing to sacrifice some weight in the interests of economy—a terrific buy.

Gherardi and Ghilardi, Lungarno Acciaiuoli 22, P.O. Box 177, Florence, Italy
50-page color catalogue, free. Prices in $.

This well-known Florentine jeweler has a lavish catalogue not to be missed by anyone in search of gold jewelry. Prices for 18-carat gold are comparatively low. The designs can be loosely called "Florentine." Brushed (not shiny) gold is elaborately worked, and when jewels are used, they are very small and worked into, rather than dominating, the design. Take the bracelets—ten pages of them start with bangles, plain ($33), engraved or studded with little jewels, then come chains and twists of all sizes and styles, the bracelets becoming more intricate with each pageful until they become gorgeously complicated, flexible pieces threaded with brilliant enameling and jewels (prices mainly $300—$400), and finally, a page of ferociously colorful, leering snake bracelets. There are exuberant gold-and-enamel or gold-and-diamond pins in the shapes of animals or plants (a rose here costs only $75). Big-domed, ornate rings; pretty, simple necklaces; and earrings with some particularly lovely small hanging earrings for pierced ears, a few tiny ones costing under $25.

G. Nardi, Piazza San Marco 69, Venice, Italy
4-page color leaflet, free. Prices in $.

Nardi shows twenty-two little things: rings, pins and Venetian charms in gold with enameling and jewels. There are three versions of the famous "Othello Pin"—the head of the "Moor of Venice" hand-carved out of black tortoise shell, with crown, earrings, etc., in contrasting gold and jewels; the least expensive version is $220. Also shown is an antique Venetian-style ring and brooch with rose-cut diamonds forming flowers set into dark-blue enamel. Ring, $220; brooch, $350.

JAPAN

Amita Jewelry Corp., Mail Order Service, Kyoto Handicrafts Center, Kumano Jinja Higashi, Sakyoku, Kyoto, 606 Japan
29-page brochure, free. Prices in $.

Amita Jewelry Corp. in the Kyoto Handicrafts Center is visited by thousands of tourists each year and sells little things most of which cost less than $10: silver and gold charms, ivory flowers, heart-shaped crystal pendants, initialed cuff links, silver pen knives, and Damascene jewelry with Japanese scenes or birth flowers worked in silver and gold into a black background. Also for sale are other modern Japanese offerings such as lacquerware, brocade purses and ornamental dolls.

Matoba and Co., Inc., Central P.O. Box 451, Tokyo, Japan
6-page brochure, free. Prices in $.

A shop with a large stock and excellent reputation, Matoba specializes in cultured pearls. As price depends not only on size but also on quality, i.e., thickness of nacre, roundness, smoothness, color, cleanliness and brilliance of luster, mail-order customers write and tell Matoba what price, size and quality of necklaces and bracelets they want, and Matoba does the choosing. Where designs are variable (pins, rings, earrings, cuff links, etc.), there are drawings, but customers can still indicate what size and color of pearl they prefer and what setting. Everything is available in either silver or 14-carat gold. A pendant with a pearl inside a heart costs $9 in silver and $23 in gold; earrings, each made out of seven pearls in the shape of a flower, $12.50 in silver and $28 in gold; a simple circle-of-pearls brooch, $14 in silver and $56 in gold.

K. Mikimoto, Inc., Mail Order Section, 5–5, 4-Chome, Ginza, Tokyo, Japan
48-page brochure with some color, free. Prices in $.

Natural pearls are made when pieces of shell, bone or sand accidentally get into an oyster and the oyster covers the particle with layers of nacre. Cultured pearls are made when a nucleus of shell is put inside the oyster on purpose. The value of a cultured pearl depends, among other things, on the thickness of the nacre formed.

Kokichi Mikimoto invented cultured pearls, and the firm has kept a very high reputation. With a superefficient brochure, they have a worldwide export service of their necklaces and other jewels. Necklaces start *about* (prices for 1972 haven't been decided as I write) $35 for a graduated 5.5 to 5.0 mm., 14" choker with a silver clasp. This year a 17" graduated necklace, going from 8.50 mm. to 5.50 mm., costs $160. Pins, $12–$300; earrings, $14–$80; rings, $35–$350; bracelets, $20–$255; cuff links, $14–$130; tie pins, $7–$69—all shown in conventional shapes, and silver or 14-carat gold.

Queen Pearl Co., CPO Box 1446, Tokyo, Japan
Price list, free. Prices in $.

For their more expensive cultured pearls, Queen Pearl Co. makes individual offers according to what customers want. But for customers who want more than anything to spend as little as possible, there is a list of bargains neatly divided according to price. It starts at $14 for 14" necklaces with round and baroque (off shape) pearls; price includes sea mail.

Besides pearls in standard colors, Queen has black cultured pearls which are not superficially dyed but have gone through some sort of secret chemical transformation. Also South Sea cultured pearls, larger and rarer than Japanese pearls and more expensive.

MAJORCA

Perlas Manacor S.A., Rector Rubi 8, Manacor, Mallorca, Spain
16-page brochure with some color, free. Prices in $.

Majorica is the trademark of the world-famous artificial pearls made by Heutch from "natural essences extracted from marine species in the Mediterranean warm waters." Majorica are generally considered the tops and are often imitated by other manufacturers who give their artificial pearls deceptively similar names. In Majorca, where they are made, Majorica cost well under half what they cost in America. When I compared prices, a 24" necklace in 8-mm. beads (8 mm. is apparently the most popular size) cost $40 in New York and only $16 at Perlas Manacor. Postage is only $1.50 and hopefully you will not be asked, on these small packets, to pay duty, but even if you are, you still save a lot—especially on the long double strands.

There is a price list of necklaces and bracelets by Majorica, and a good glossy and clear little catalogue of rings, earrings and pins in sterling silver with artificial pearls of various makes, including Majorica. None of these cost more than $10, and most are well below.

MEXICO

Sanborns S.A., Avenida F. I. Madero 4, Mexico 1, D.F.
12-page catalogue, free. Prices in $.

Sanborns, a chain of stores, sells Mexican souvenirs and also has a reputation for being large enough to buy in quantity and for keeping their quality up and their silver prices down, though silver prices seem to be roughly equivalent to American prices. Jewelry is modernish in design: geometric bracelet, $12; a large star pin set with topaz, alexandrite, aquamarine or amethyst, $10; daisy earrings set with the same stones, $12.

Silver for the house is gracefully Georgian and seems to be much simpler than the grandiose Cellini equivalents, though there is nowhere near the choice. Sanborns shows "selected conversation pieces": a small instant-coffee container costs $15; baby spoon-and-fork set, $5.84; a glass jam bowl with a silver cover, $25.04.

NORWAY

David Anderson, Karl Johansgate 20, Oslo, Norway
Brochures: Jewelry, Pewter, Silver Flatware, Enameled Sterling Silver, Flatware and other gift items, free. Prices in $.

Norway's top jewelers export widely and are probably best

192
David Anderson Silver coffee set designed by B. S.
Ostern in Museum of Fine Arts, Oslo. Coffee pot, around
$190; sugar bowl and cream pitcher, around $100.

193
David Anderson Silver-and-enamel jewelry. Prices
between $8 and $18.

194
David Anderson Cast-pewter salad spoon and fork,
each 9¼" long. Each about $4.
photo Teigens

known for modern enameled jewelry and silverware, which
they do better than anyone else. Little gilt butterfly pins with
brilliantly colored and ribbed wings start at $4.50. Flower
earrings, leaf necklaces, heart bracelets, clover pins with
ladybugs crawling over them in glowing enamel and gilded
silver are among the inexpensive jewels, while the "Saga"
and "Troll" collections, more primitive and expensive, are
created for the "discriminating" client who is more concerned
with ornamental qualities than brilliance. Spiky pins, pendants
and rings dotted with enameling or set with crystal, amethyst
and jasper cost between $11 and $16.

The glowing enamel colors on larger pieces for the house
contrast beautifully with the silver: unusual demitasse spoons,
salad servers, coffee services and trays, etc., for the table;
and for the desk, "Peer Gynt" silver paper knife with blue or
green enameling and scenes from Norwegian folklore on the
handle, $23.

Besides the enameled silver, David Anderson also makes
pewter decorated with old Norwegian motifs, as well as very
beautiful modern silver and reproduction silver. And, lately, a
program has been started of borrowing silver masterpieces
from Norwegian museums and making careful copies.

PERU

**Carlo Mario Camusso S.A., Avenida Mariscal Oscar
Benavides 679, Casilla, Postal 650, Lima, Peru**
Flatware leaflet, free. Prices in $.
Gift leaflet, free. Prices in $.

Peru is, like America, a leading silver producer. Carlo Mario
Camusso is one of Peru's top silversmiths. Eighteen fairly
classic sterling-silver flatware patterns are shown, and prices
for six-piece place settings vary between $30 and $40. (This
includes a 15 percent discount from the listed prices—part of
Peruvian trading customs, I suppose.) Pieces can be bought
individually or in sets. There are also serving pieces in the
same patterns: sugar tongs, $7.50; bottle can opener, $7.50;
poultry shears, $25.

The gift leaflet shows trays, ice buckets, pitchers, etc., in
various patterns, and Empire pattern plates and platters
starting at $6.25 for 4" ones.

Purchases are delivered ten to sixteen days after the order
and money have been received. They are sent air freight,
which, Camusso says, costs about 5 to 7 percent of the price
of your purchase. You pay for the shipping on arrival.

SCOTLAND

Cairncross, 18 St. John Street, Perth, Scotland
Brochure, free.

Cairncross makes pins and rings with Scottish fresh-water
pearls that have formed naturally inside mussels. Apparently
Scottish pearls are smaller than oyster pearls, have a softer
bloom and vary in color from pale gray to pink. The small and
delicate pins are mostly in the shape of flowers and plants.
Prices start at $26 for two pearls set in 9-carat gold wild-
"blaeberry" sprig and go up to $220 for fifteen pearls in a
branch of heather. Ask about exact sizes—they're not given in
the brochure.

The Iona Shop, 32 Argyll Arcade, Glasgow C1, Scotland
30-page brochure.

Celtic jewelry at modest prices in silver or 9-carat gold. Some
of it, involving thistles and lions rampant, probably only
appeals to Celts, but much is very handsome and can be

universally appreciated. Interlacing—a traditional motif of unending loops that symbolize eternal life—appears in many forms: on charms, cuff links, pins, bracelets and wedding rings. There are circular brooches with a central amethyst or whiskey-colored Cairngorm, originally used for fastening plaids at the shoulder, which cost about $11 each, and reproductions of the Luckenbooth brooch, said to have been the betrothal pin of Mary Queen of Scots.

Scottish pebbles, and green Iona marble, which, according to local folklore, brings good luck, are often used in jewelry and as cigarette boxes, etc. An ashtray of Iona marble costs about $6.50.

THAILAND

Rama Jewelry Ltd., 987 Silom Road, Bangkok, Thailand
Color leaflet illustrating only Princess Rings, free. Prices in $.

Rama Jewelry has been manufacturing and exporting jewelry for the last ten years, and in 1970 expanded into a new seven-story building of their own. They make all sorts of jewelry, including reproductions of traditional Thai jewels, but by far the most popular with tourists is the Princess Ring. A big domed ring studded with multicolored stones, the design is hundreds of years old and is supposed to bring the wearer good luck. Mr. Prapanth, the store manager, says that now when "the world of fancy fashion has taken place," the ring's design is often changed and customers can choose their own stones, sticking to one color if they like. The rings are set in 14-carat gold, and traditionally have nine stones in hierarchical order—diamond, ruby, emerald, topaz, garnet, sapphire, moonstone, zircon, cat's-eye. They cost only $18–$28 each, and air-mail postage for up to three rings is $4.

Bronze flatware and Thai silks are also sold.

195
Rama Jewelry Variations on the Thai "Princess" ring in 14-carat gold which traditionally has nine different stones, but can be made in any combination to order. About $18–$28.

INSTRUMENTS

Lindberg, Sonnenstrasse 15, 8 Munich 15, Germany
51-page color brochure in German, free.

"Das Paradies der Musikfreunde" puts out a jolly catalogue full of laughing groups playing away on pianos and accordions (thirty Hohner models at prices from $35 to $900), "Organettas," "pianets," over thirty kinds of guitars—Western Spanish, electric ("Wanderlust," the least expensive, costs $16)—two electric Hawaiian guitars, six banjos, a ukelele, zithers, saxophones, clarinets, trumpets and horns, drums, violins, and even a lyre. Lindberg says that a lot of folk-music instruments are bought by mail from America, especially concert zithers, Hackbretter recorders, harmonicas, violins, also German sheet music. Unfortunately the catalogue is in German, and it is essential to have someone to translate the technical information.

Firma Kurt Wittmayer, Cembalobau, D-8190 Wolfratshausen, Postfache 1120, Germany
Brochure in German, free.

In their Upper Bavarian workshops, Kurt Wittmayer and his assistants make clavichords, harpsichords and spinets for customers all over the world, including American colleges, universities and professional harpsichordists. Kurt Wittmayer (whose work has been recommended to me by two customers) lectures, writes, exhibits his instruments, and has developed a patented precision shaft action that works in an "irreproachable way" in any climatic conditions.

Apparently the greatest demand nowadays is for small, reasonably priced instruments with modern "backpost construction," but Kurt Wittmayer also copies historical prototypes either to customers' exact specifications or after consultation and advice. Prices for clavichords and spinets are about $390–$780. One-manual harpsichords sell for $1,000 and up, and two-manual harpsichords from $2,250 and up. These are ready for delivery within one to four months after they are ordered. Copies of Baroque and Renaissance instruments take six to eight months and cost $1,650 and up.

PRINTED MUSIC

Blackwell's Music Shop, 39 Holywell Street, Oxford OX1 3SW, England
Catalogues:
General Music Books, free.
Piano and Organ Music, free.
Instrumental Music, free.
Orchestral Music, free.
Operas and Oratorios, free.
Solo, Madrigal and Folk Music, free.
Gramophone Records, free.

A division of Blackwell Bookshop, Blackwell's Music Shop has just expanded into a specially designed new building, and now thinks and hopes that this is the largest shop in the world devoted to books on music and printed music. They stock English, European and American music, and are going to enlarge their antiquarian and second-hand departments.

I am told that although American records are less expensive than any others, foreign records cost less if bought directly from abroad. Blackwell's sells records by all the major English companies, and the complete Erato range from France. They also put out a bimonthly list of recommended recordings of new releases.

William Elkin Music Services, Deacon House, Brundall, Norwich NOR 86Z, England
William Elkin Music Services supplies (promptly, they say) sheet music and books on music from all publishers in the United Kingdom and Europe. No catalogue; write and tell them what you want.

Jecklin and Co., Ramistrasse 30 + 42, 8024 Zurich 1, Switzerland
This firm, which sells musical instruments and hi-fi equipment, also has one of the largest stocks in Europe of records and sheet music, and says they can fill the needs of very specialized customers.

RECORDS

James H. Crawley, 246 Church Street, London N9 9HQ, England
List Vocal Art, one issue, 85 cents; annual subscription, $5.

James Crawley buys and sells rare vocal 78-rpm records, mostly ones that look and sound absolutely new. They also have some rare recordings transcribed onto 12" long-players for about $11 each, and will transcribe others at customers' requests. A selection range of vocalists goes from "French Opera Stars," "Famous Tenors," and great French, German, Italian, Russian singers to music-hall songs and stars like Gertrude Lawrence in the original version of *The King and I* (four records for about $4) or Noel Coward singing "Don't Let's Be Beastly to the Germans." Also a few talkies like Ellen Terry delivering the "Quality of Mercy" speech from *The Merchant of Venice*, and Herbert Beerbohm Tree doing "Antony's Lament" from *Antony and Cleopatra.*

The Swing Shop, 1B Mitcham Lane, Streatham, London S.W.16, England
Being specialists in new and second-hand jazz and blues records in all speeds, The Swing Shop was recommended to me by a New York jazz enthusiast who says that jazz has become so neglected in America that he finds more records in England. Dave Carey, who runs The Swing Shop, says that customers' "want lists" are given careful attention, but as the shop is always frantically busy operating at "full steam" and "battling against the clock," he *wholeheartedly* recommends that jazz fans subscribe to (either or both)

Jazz Journal, 27 Soho Square, London W1V 6BR (monthly)
Storyville, 63 Oxford Road, London E.17 (bimonthly)

which always have a full-page, detailed advertisement of Swing Shop offers and also well-written reviews of jazz issues available in England.

196
Firma Kurt Wittmayer Harpsichord model "Corelli."

French perfume and cosmetics are among the best buys in this book. The shops listed below are beautifully organized to make buying easy, and when you buy by mail the goods are exempt from high French taxes, so they end up costing just over half the American price, even after you've paid the postage and duty. When I compared prices, one ounce of Arpège perfume by Lanvin, for instance, cost $12.50 in Paris, but $27 at my local drugstore. Lancôme's Absolu face cream cost $4.40 and $7 in Paris, but $10 and $13.50 for the same sizes in New York.

See Addresses of Import Information ("Trademark Information") at the end of this book, with hints on what to do about import restrictions on certain brands of perfume.

J. W. Chunn, 43 Rue Richer, Paris IX, France
Price list for perfume, free. Prices in $.

Freddy, 10 Rue Auber, Paris IX, France
Price list for perfume, free. Prices in $.

Grillot, 10 Rue Cambon, Paris IX, France
Price list for perfume and Antoine, Lancôme, Orlane and Stendhal cosmetics, free. Prices in $.

Michel Swiss, 16 Rue de la Paix, Paris II, France
Price list for perfume and Orlane cosmetics, free. Prices in $.

Obéron, 73 Champs-Elysées, Paris VIII, France
Price list for perfume and Orlane and Lancôme cosmetics, free. Prices in $.
General catalogue, $1.50. Prices in $.

Royal-Parfums, 198 Rue de Rivoli, Paris I, France
Price list for perfume and for Dior, Lancôme, Orlane and Stendhal cosmetics, free. Prices in $.

197
Obéron "Step" purse atomizers. Limoges porcelain. About $5 each.

Pets

Harrods Ltd., Knightsbridge, London S.W.1, England
Harrod's pet shop sends lion cubs, pumas, bush babies,
otters, Siamese and Burmese cats, decorative waterfowl,
aviary birds, etc., all over the world. In 1967 they sent an
elephant called Gertie by air to Los Angeles. They will gladly
give a quotation for any animal which doesn't have to
undergo American quarantine, and say that British-bred dogs
are in great demand in America.

A permit is needed to import an animal, for details write to
the Commissioner of Customs, Washington, D.C. 20226, and
ask for the leaflet "So You Want to Import a Pet."

The best place, by far, to get photographic equipment is Hong Kong, a free port which does not pay local taxes and has lower overhead charges. In fact, I first heard about Cinex (below) from a professional Washington photographer who gets his equipment from them because Hong Kong discounts make their prices even lower than professional discount prices available in America. He says that the firm is highly professional and packs superbly. Both Cinex and Cony will send the *Hong Kong Camera Buying Guide*, which contains Hong Kong list prices on all leading makes of still and movie cameras, interchangeable lenses, movie projectors, slide projectors, sound projectors, electronic flash, light meters, fish-eye conversion lenses, tele converters, binoculars and tripods (the guide also contains what looks like useful information on what you need for a basic camera system). However, both firms offer (similar) discounts on Hong Kong list prices, so if you already know what you want, don't wait for the guide, just write and ask the price and mailing charges. Or you can send for the guide, and after deciding what you want, write to one of the firms and ask for their discount price and mailing charge.

T. M. Chan and Co., P.O. Box 3881, Hong Kong
Catalogue, free. Prices in $.

Two of my friends recommend this firm, one of them bought here a Miranda Sensorex Single Lens Reflex Camera f/1.8 for $148 including surface postage and duty. He claims that the lowest American price for this camera is $216, and that it sells for up to $322.45.

Cinex Ltd., General Post Office Box 724, Hong Kong
Hong Kong Camera Buying Guide, free. Prices in $.

I asked Cinex for their discount price on two movie cameras. First, Bauer C3 Cine camera with vario lens f/l.8 10.5–32 mm. lens and case was quoted at $76, for which the *discount* price in America is $109.60, according to *Consumer Guide*. Then, Bell & Howell 375 Filmosound 8 camera with f/2.8 12.5–25 mm. zoom lens is $58 in Hong Kong, whereas the *discount* price in America is $86.65, according to *Consumer Guide* (which is not the same as *Consumer Reports*). This is not as much of a bargain as on still cameras, but you should be able to save up to $22. Cinex said that mailing charges would be $6 surface and $12 air mail.

The Cony Ltd., P.O. Box 5555, Kowloon, Hong Kong
Hong Kong Camera Buying Guide, free. Prices in $.

I asked Cony for their discount prices on several still cameras and found that they were $24 to $65 lower than American discount prices. For instance, there was a great difference between the American price for a Konica Auto. Reflex-T f/1.2 camera and case, and the Hong Kong price. The American discount price is $249.50, according to *Consumer Guide*, and Hong Kong's $185 (plus $4 surface or $19 air mail).

Photo-Rico, Hohe Strasse 160-168, 5 Cologne, Germany
Photo Rico claims to send thousands of parcels a year to America and to sell all the famous German cameras and photo equipment: Zeiss-Ikon, Voitlander, Agfa, Rolleiflex. But the prices I compared with American prices were exactly the same, so don't write to them unless you are looking for something unobtainable elsewhere.

Universal Suppliers, P.O. Box 14803, Hong Kong
Catalogue, free; air mail $1.60. Prices in $.

Universal Suppliers publishes its own catalogue for cameras and accessories, binoculars, telescopes, rifle scopes and spotting scopes, all at the usual low Hong Kong prices. For $1.60 they will air-mail several of their catalogues, but be specific as to what you are interested in, because they have catalogues for many things including stereo equipment, watches, china and embroidered linen.

20 Services

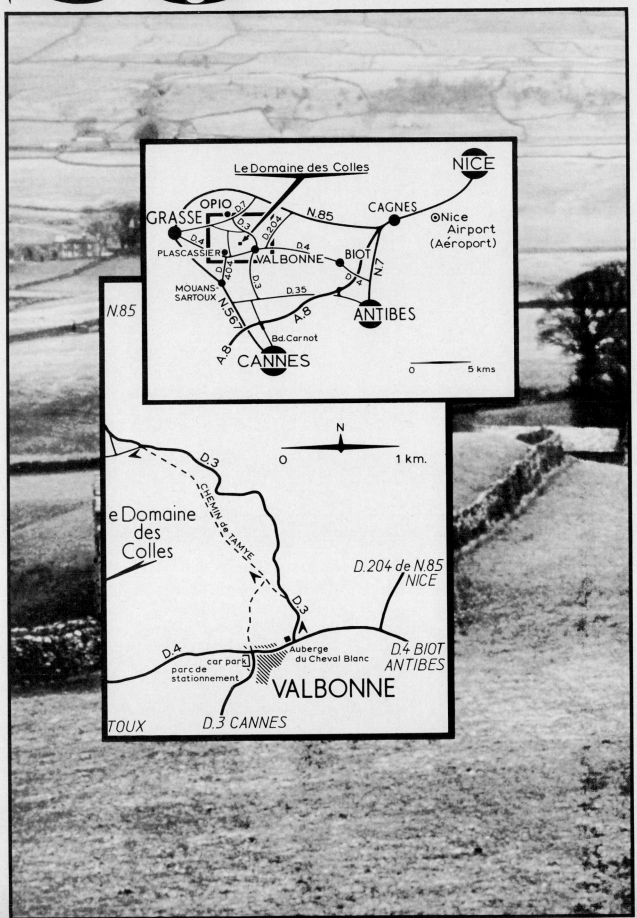

Le Domaine des Colles

NICE

OPIO   D.7
GRASSE   D.3
                      D.204   N.85   CAGNES
                                                        ⊙Nice
                                                        Airport
PLASCASSIER   D.4   (Aéroport)
                              D.4
D.404   VALBONNE   BIOT
MOUANS-   N.7
SARTOUX   D.3   D.35
                                        D.4
N.567   A.8   ANTIBES
A.8   Bd.Carnot
        CANNES

0   5 kms

N.85

N

0   1 km.

D.3

CHEMIN de TAMYE

e Domaine
des
Colles

D.204 de N.85
NICE

D.3

D.4   BIOT
ANTIBES

D.4   Auberge
car park   du Cheval Blanc
parc de
stationnement   VALBONNE

TOUX   D.3 CANNES

BOOKBINDING

George Bayntun, Manvers Street, Bath BAI IJW, England ♡
List of modern reprints bound in leather, free.

A family firm, bookseller and bookbinder, owning a large—possibly the largest in the world—collection of books in new leather bindings: first or fine editions of English literature, standard sets, illustrated and sporting books, poetry, biography and travel.

They also bookbind, mainly for collectors, in leather only, calf or morocco, with gold tooling, and have over ten thousand brass-engraved tools for finishing, many following the designs of important binders of past centuries so that old bindings can usually be copied faithfully. Prices are from $26 upward to any amount.

López Valencia, Bárbara de Braganza 9, Madrid 4, Spain
Price list in Spanish, free.

As both leather and labor are cheap in Spain, bookbinding is astonishingly inexpensive. López Valencia has several American customers and they correspond in English. They will send a brief price list in Spanish, but it is much more useful to write giving them some idea of what you would like done. López Valencia will send a small sketch at the customer's request which serves as a pattern. Prices for a 10″ book start at $3 for a fabric binding and go to $7 for a plain leather binding.

FORTUNETELLING

Roger Elliot, 29 Roland Gardens, London S.W.7, England

Roger Elliot, who calls himself "up and coming" (he should know) and has appeared on the English *David Frost Show*, tells fortunes. He is a graduate of a correspondence course run by the Faculty of Astrological Studies, Burnham-on-Sea, England, comprising two years of study followed by fifteen hours of exams. To tell a fortune he needs $25 and the date, place and, as closely as possible, the time of his client's birth. He also likes a few details about present circumstances, especially if there are problems, e.g. "mother semi-invalid, husband wants to get out of insurance job into something more creative, hoping to move to the West Coast." He then makes a map of the sky as it appeared when the person was born. The map, he says, is really a diagram of the psyche and shows the disposition, character and potential skills of the person, and it also shows when particular facets of the personality will be emphasized or subdued. From this, he says, he can assess the probability of a person behaving a certain way at any time. He tries to cover the following points: basic outlook on life, superficial temperament, inner emotional disposition, chief motivations, potential conflicts within the psyche, major aptitudes and talents, interpersonal relationships, the kind of work that is suitable, the major emotional and spiritual experiences of the lifetime (including partnerships and love liaisons). He also plans each analysis to suit the needs of the client: a brisk, no-nonsense (no-nonsense?) businessman gets a crisp, tabulated report, while a teen-ager gets a more psychologically oriented work-up. Charges: Brief personality assessment and broad forecast for next couple of years, $25. Full personality assessment, $25. Full forecast for a year, $25. Special personality assessment and forecast based on midpoints analysis using IBM computers, $100. Work for business corporations, etc., by arrangement. No mention of money-back guarantee.

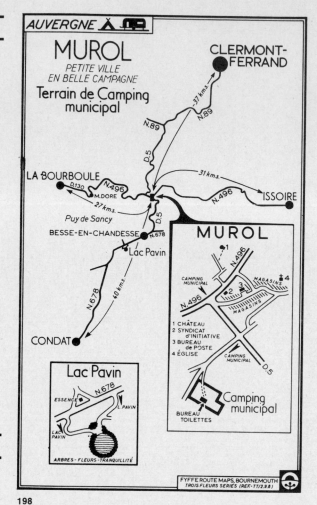

198
Anthony Fyffe "How to Find Us" maps can be made to order in quantities of 200 and up.

LEATHER AND SUEDE CLEANING

Suedeclean Ltd., 30 Baker Street, London W.1, England
Price list, free.

Suedeclean, a large London firm, has an efficient cleaning and alteration mail service for leather and suede. They cleaned a very dirty beige suede coat of mine, perfectly, for which they charged their standard $10. Postage and insurance both ways costs $5.25. There is a very complete list of charges for cleaning and altering suede, leather and sheepskin clothes, hats, bags, belts, ties; and all the prices are low (though, of course, time involved and postage costs make it not worthwhile sending small things alone).

MAP MAKING

Anthony Fyffe, 30 Chantry, Madeira Road, Bournemouth, Hampshire, England
Anthony Fyffe makes "How to Find Us" maps both for businesses and for private homes. Two hundred copies of a 7″ by 10″ functional but not beautiful "social" map cost $95 plus postage. The customer sends the name and address of the place to be pinpointed, and a map of the area, which can be a local map or a rough sketch. The rough sketch is sufficient because Mr. Fyffe has official maps of the United States on a 1:24,000 scale.

Sporthaus Eisult, OHG, Marktgraben 2, 6020 Innsbruck, Austria

No catalogue here, but Sporthaus Eisult says that "since many years" they have been shipping sporting goods to customers in the United States and other countries. The shop stocks skis, ski bindings, poles, Reichle ski boots, parkas, woolen sweaters, cardigans, caps, socks, knickers of corduroy, stretch-material ski gloves, and lederhosen. Nothing exceptional, they say, but by quoting lowest possible prices, finding out the cheapest and most reliable ways of transport, and executing all orders within the shortest delay, they have "succeeded to get many satisfied customers abroad." Sweaters, skis, ski bindings, and poles are the most popular mail-order items (there are special air rates for large quantities). Reichle ski boots cost half to one-third less than in America, and they will arrive three to four weeks after Sporthaus Eisult receives the order. Shipping costs, $5.60.

Correspondence in French and Italian, as well as in English.

GENERAL

Husky of Tostock Ltd., 115 Bury Street, Stowmarket, Suffolk, England
26-page color brochure, 30 cents. Prices in $.

A United States colonel moved to England for a peaceful retirement, but soon found himself making the insulated clothing he had learned about in the Air Force, for his sporty friends battling with the windy and damp English climate. In 1961, as more and more people asked for the clothes, Colonel Gulyas decided to turn the hobby into a business, and now, after more than ten years' work, he has a factory with a staff of fifty, showrooms for personal customers, a color brochure for mail order, and a classy clientele that includes peers, baronets and royalty.

A good and informative brochure describes the waterproof, insulated clothes made of polyester fiberfill and nylon in standard sizes *or sizes to order*. There are specially designed golf coats, $24; fishing jackets, $48; shooting and riding vests, as well as car coats, trousers, underwear and hats for men and women. Also thermoinsulated tweeds which, the brochure says, will make a woman look like a French countess stepping out of a Paris couturier house—well, they won't quite, none of the clothes are highly fashionable but the tweeds do look perfectly serviceable and the insulation is cleverly disguised.

Lillywhite Ltd., Piccadilly Circus, London S.W.1, England ♨
Golf catalogue, free.
Subaqua catalogue, free.
Ski catalogue, free. Only available October to February.

Lillywhite is London's largest sports shop, and stocks equipment and clothes for *all* sports. Their catalogues are excellent—the ski catalogue has some swish outfits, a few from Switzerland and Scandinavia—after-ski wear, hats, goggles, bags, boots and skis—the lot. Prices start at $51 for a one-piece nylon ski suit from Switzerland; a Finnish nylon jacket costs $18. Even though the ski catalogue is only available during the winter, you can buy the contents all year round.

The golf catalogue shows clubs, clothes, shoes and golf gifts—putting improvers, portable golf nets, ball washers, pocket warmers, etc. (No prices at the moment.)

Lillywhite says their subaqua department is the largest in Europe. The catalogue has what looks like everything to me—all the essential equipment and underwater communications sets, cameras, gauges, torches, watches and compasses. Also equipment for water-skiing.

Sports-Schuster, Rosenstrasse 5—6, 8 Munich 2, Germany
100-page color catalogues in German, surface, free; $1 air mail. April, October.

This large sports shop puts out two luscious catalogues a year crammed with famous brands of gear and clothes. An excellent place for anyone who wants to buy ski clothes by mail, because although prices are higher than in Austria, there is a terrific selection: smart sweaters, $23–$34; over fifty glossy jackets, around $45 each; goggles at up to $6; pages of shaggy-fur boots that cost between $25 and $57; and every sort of ski boot; and ski outfits for children.

The summer catalogue shows tennis clothes and parkas, and for camping and the great German pastime—hiking—pages and pages of boots, ropes, rucksacks, picks, sleeping bags, tents and other necessary things. Also skin-diving gear and sailboats with motors.

Alas, the catalogue is in German. However, prices are right next to pictures and Sports-Schuster will answer letters in English *when asked* (otherwise they assume you know German).

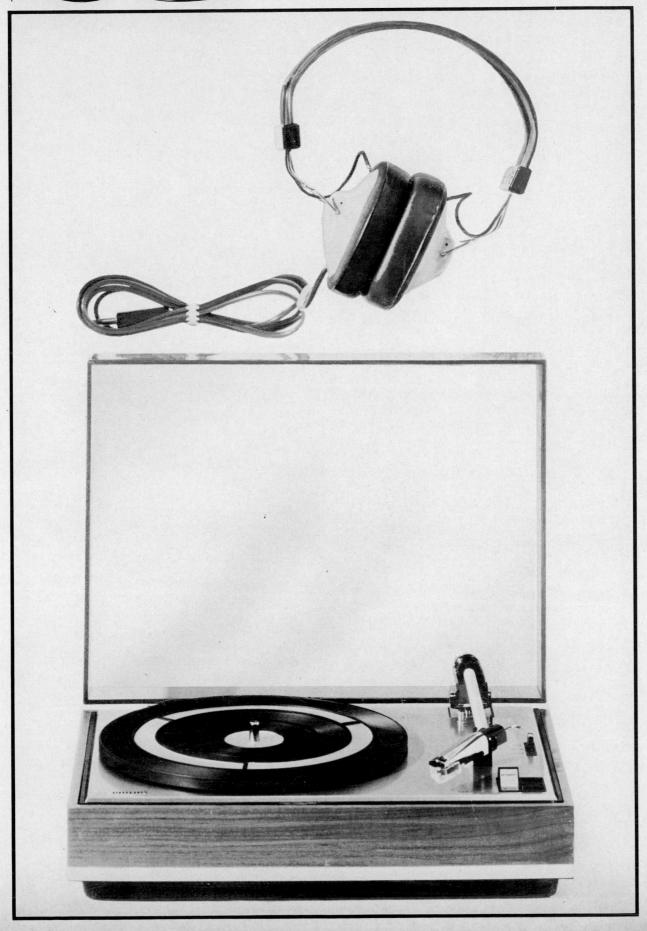

Most stereo belongs to that awkward group of things, just too large or heavy to go by mail and not worth paying sea-freight costs on. However, buying from abroad *is* worthwhile for hi-fi fanatics who are trying to assemble a complete stereo system from the best components made by different specialized firms. You can either send for parts that are small enough to be sent by mail or buy several things at once, so that freight charges are small compared to savings. Hong Kong shops stock an enormous variety of equipment, and are very experienced in mail order. As I write, minimum sea-freight charges from Hong Kong to an American port are $35 to the West Coast and $46 to the East Coast. For that price one amplifier, one turntable and two loudspeakers can be shipped. As Hong Kong prices are only one third or one half of American list prices, quite a bit of money can be saved. But, as always, take into consideration at what prices the same things are actually available to you locally, and whether you can go down and collect the stuff from the port yourself or whether you have to pay someone else a lot extra to see your equipment through customs and deliver it.

ENGLAND

Audio T, Suite 9, 119 Oxford Street, London W.1, England
Price list, free.

Audio T has a personal export department, and feels that the thing really worth buying for American customers is the new Cambridge Audio P.40 amplifier, which has had very enthusiastic reviews throughout Europe (I have seen some of them). The amplifier will probably be available in America by the time this book is published, but Audio T thinks that it will be cheaper direct from England. At the moment it costs about $211, including air freight, to the East Coast.

Michael O'Brien, 226 Worple Road, Wimbledon, London S.W.20, England
Manufacturers' brochures

Michael O'Brien specializes in cut-price top-class hi-fi equipment, and also has a personal export service. He says that these components seem to be of special interest to American customers, prices are very roughly:

	SHIPPING
Quad amplifiers $220	$ 13
SME pickup arms $50	3.25
Tannoy speakers $135	105
Ferrograph tape recorders $366	78

HONG KONG

The Radio People Ltd., 25 Chatham Road, Kowloon, Hong Kong
Audio-equipment price list, free.

The Radio People's price list is in Hong Kong dollars, so if you already know what you want you can avoid the list and write direct asking for the price, including shipping, of what you want. Otherwise write for shipping costs, etc., after studying the list. The Radio People sells all parts and all accessories to do with stereo equipment, and tape recorders, public-address amplifiers, etc., of most leading makes. They also make cabinets to customers' own designs.

Universal Suppliers, PO Box 14803, Hong Kong
Hi-fi price list, free; $1.60 air mail. Prices in $.

207
Klinger hi-fi stereo, beautiful teak cabinet, outlet for the connection of a radio tuner or tape recorder. Available from Fortnum and Mason (see Food section).

208
Stereo cassette recorder in rosewood-veneered cabinet. Maximum playing time twelve hours; with automatic changer and automatic stop at the end of the last tape. Available from Fortnum and Mason (see Food section).

Universal Suppliers has an excellent price list for stereo, but
it is essential to specify that this is what you want, as they sell
glass, china, linen, watches, and goodness knows what else.
In electronics, Universal Suppliers lists amplifiers, tuners,
receivers, changers and turntables, hi-fi systems, tape
recorders, speakers, headphones, color TV (though I checked
Sony and their sets cost the same as in America), radios,
video equipment, electronic calculators. Manufacturers
stocked: Akai, Dual, Garrad, Kenwood, Miracord, Pioneer,
Sharp, Sensui, Sony, Tandberg, Teac, Thorens.

SWITZERLAND

**Jecklin and Co., Rämistrasse 42, 8024 Zurich 1,
Switzerland**
Jecklin's hi-fi and music shop can sell the following superb
Swiss components by mail. These are approximate export
prices, which include surface mail or freight charges:

Revox Tape Recorder

Model A 77	tape deck without amplifier	$330
	tape deck with stereo amplifier 2 × 8 Watt	358
	tape deck without amplifier in walnut case	337
	tape deck with stereo amplifier in walnut case	375
	complete tape recorder with stereo amplifier 2 × 8 Watt and two loudspeakers	475

Thorens Record Player

Model TD 125	with tone arm and wooden cabinet	210
	without tone arm and wooden cabinet	147

Lenco Record Player

Model L75	in wooden cabinet, dust cabinet and tone arm	85

I have bought more toys from abroad than anything else—often in large batches, ahead of time, for birthdays and Christmas, and often chosen by my daughters to give to their friends. Toys are an ideal mail-order buy, easy to choose from a catalogue, easy to ship, and the best toys are less expensive abroad. Many of the most attractive and unusual toys sold in New York stores have been imported, and by going direct to the source, you get a wider choice at lower prices. Take the German Steiff furry animals, for instance—five hundred of them are shown in the German catalogue, far more than you can see in any American shop. On even the smallest you save about $1 each, after shipping, and much more on the larger toys.

Note: Any electric toy that runs on 220 volts instead of American 110 will need a transformer. An American electrical supplies store can order this for you when they know the voltage of the toy.

AUSTRALIA

C. W. Perkins & Co. Pty. Ltd., 70 Sidney Road, Coburg, Victoria, Australia
Leaflet, free.

Beautifully made koala-bear toys in real wallaby or kangaroo fur. I have seen them in one New York store but at more than twice the price. Koala bears start at a very cuddly 4″ high for $1.50 and go up to 17″ high for $10. And only from Australia you can get them with babies on their backs; as pajama sachets, as music boxes, as purses, as muffs, all at very low prices. There are also 18″ kangaroos made out of kangaroo fur with babies in their pouches for only $11. As children always seem to love real fur toys and adore mothers with babies, these must be an unbeatable combination.

DENMARK

Den Permanente, Vesterport, DK-1620 Copenhagen, Denmark
Ask for Kaj Bojesen brochure, free.

This arts and crafts showroom sells Kaj Bojesen's famous wooden toys—his popular teak monkeys have even been copied by the Japanese. The original ones cost about $5 each from Denmark—much less than in America. To go with the monkeys, there are teak elephants, bears and rabbits, but my own favorites are the brightly painted little wooden farm people and animals: a 2″ mum, dad and son cost $2.20, and spotted cows or red horses $1.10 each. You can also get farm buildings, peg men in fire trucks, painted wooden soldiers, boats, and all sorts of things to please young children and parents.

ENGLAND

J. & F. Butler Toymakers, 12 Ebers Road, Mapperly Park, Nottingham NG3 5DZ, England
Leaflet, 30 cents.

A husband and wife make a nice collection of old fashioned toys: rag dolls, peg dolls, wooden dolls and puppets—all wide-eyed and tousle-haired. Also very simple painted wooden planes and boats, and a magnetic fish game. Prices exceptionally low.

Cuckoobird Productions, St. Michael's House, Peckham Bush, Tonbridge, England
Color leaflet, 70 cents (refundable). Prices in $.

A small family firm that manufactures handsome "useful presents" in cotton, at very low prices: some beautiful, big bags for laundry or toys: the bags unzip at the bottom and the one I like shows Punch and Judy in orange, yellow, turquoise and green; also pillowcases with grinning lions or tigers, $3.80; wash packs (washing mitten and hand towel) showing an English guardsman or Dick Bruna animals, $2.20. And a wonderful London-bus shoe bag. I gave one to my six-year-old for Christmas, and somewhat to my surprise, she was delighted with the possibly overpractical gift—and has used it ever since.

Dobbin Designs, Gwithian, Hayle, Cornwall, England
Brochure, 36 cents. Prices in $.

One of the few places left making rocking horses. Dobbin Design's carved hardwood model has been blessed by London's independent and fussy Design Centre, which exhibits in its showrooms the best of British design. The horse comes in two sizes, in dapple gray or palomino with shiny white mane and tail, red rockers, and real leather saddle and bridle. The smaller horse's back is 26″ high, the larger 30″. They cost $108 and $144, respectively. Dobbin Designs has found that freight to America comes to about $65.

James Galt and Co. Ltd., Brookfield Road, Cheadle, Cheshire, England ☺
38-page catalogue with some color, free.

England's leading "educational" toy manufacturer, with a store at the end of Carnaby Street, makes handsome, strong toys, in wood rather than plastic, which are moderately experimental and are generally pleasing to design-conscious parents as well as to many English schools. Prices here are considerably lower than the U.S. equivalents, and the catalogue is excellent. It gives the ages that each toy is suitable for.

I bought from Galt a little bendable dollhouse family—two grandparents, two parents and four children—for about $4.50, and for another $4.30 you can get sturdy wooden dollhouse furniture, a thirty-three-piece dining- and living-room set. If you want one, Galt has a doll with a penis. A similar doll, "Little Brother," is on sale in America, but he costs $17.90 (instead of about $6.50) and is not as handsome.

For decorating walls and inculcating a bit of geography on the side, a 40″ by 29″ color map of the world shows the people and animals that inhabit the various regions. In the same series of charts are wild birds, wild animals, horses, and Wanderland, which is crowded with scenes from nursery rhymes and stories. All these are about $2.25 each. Galt has a good collection of jigsaw puzzles, starting with picture trays for eighteen-month-olds at about $2.25. With these, single objects can be removed in a picture of a busy highway; you lift off the outside of the cars and see all the people inside.

Hamleys, 200—202 Regent Street, London W.1, England ☺☺
Hamleys is the F. A. O. Schwarz of England—a huge toy store selling every kind of traditional toy and most leading brands. It also has many catalogues:

General catalogue, 27 pages, free.

Selections from each floor including art, books, games, puzzles, kits, planes, dolls, crafts, music, science, mechanical toys, sports, and very helpful for parents, a back page full of aids to party giving: novelties, favors, magic tricks, disguise outfits, surprise ball and snappers.

209
Cuckoobird Productions Washpacks designed by Dick Bruna containing one mitt and one hand towel. Each pack $2.20, postage 50 cents. "Teddy" is in yellow, red and white; "Miffy" (rabbit) is in red, white and blue.

210
Cuckoobird Productions Pocket tidy in red, white and blue. Holds eight pairs of children's shoes. $4.35.
photo Council of Industrial Design

Britain's Toy Models, 31 pages illustrated with colored drawings, 10 cents.

A huge range of these tiny plastic animals and people at war and peace. Confederate and federal gun teams, which I have seen in New York for $7.50 each, costs $4.35 at Hamley's, and a farm set imported and sold by a New York department store for $10 costs $3.75 at Hamley's.

Triang, Hornby and Minic Motor Racing and Model Railways, 44 pages in color, 25 cents.

British trains: electric, clockwork and battery. Bridges, stations, scenic materials and people. Also electric car-racing sets and scale-model plastic construction kits. Transformers for electric toys should be bought locally.

Scalestric Home Motor Racing, 32 pages in color, 15 cents.

Cars, tracks, track accessories, buildings, figures to be painted, and kits to build stands, etc. Also some electric steeplechasing sets.

Philips Young Engineer Kits, 8-page leaflet, free.

Seven kits. Electronic engineer, mechanical engineer, interphone engineer, and radio construction kits, ranging in price from $11 to $18.

Homebound Craftsmen, 25A Holland Street, Kensington, London W.8, England
Leaflet, 30 cents.

A good cause that one can support very agreeably. This small shop in Kensington sells fetching soft toys made by disabled workers—rosy-cheeked rag dolls cost about $3.55; mohair teddy bears start at $4; soulful panda families; cheery Humpty Dumptys; and some adorable little mice in long skirts or aprons and jackets which cost only 66 cents each—these seem to appeal to older children as well as to little ones. Puppets are very inexpensive: a penguin, a donkey and a bear, $1.50 each, and unusually sweet-faced Punch and Judy, $2.30 each. But do be sure to add enough postage. Homebound Craftsmen only gives local internal English costs, and they say that their American customers often forget to allow $1 for small parcels and $2 for larger ones.

John Paige, The Manor House, Kings Cliffe, Peterborough PE8 6XB, England
Brochure, 50 cents. Prices in $.

John Paige, a free-lance graphic designer, publishes and sells his own animal and train friezes. The paper friezes are sophisticated, in restrained realistic colors, and can be joined together to stretch right across a wall. The British trains are just the thing for a train buff. Bought by the carriage, entire walls can be covered with them. John Paige suggests that until he publishes some (which he is planning to do), customers can add their own lineside features by making drawings or pasting up photographs of signal boxes, bridges, stations, smoke or anything else. The train friezes are 3″ high, and engines cost 38 cents each, carriages 25 cents. Also two complete trains: the Silver Jubilee, which is 8′6″long, is hauled by a Silver Fox engine and costs $1.30, and the Coronation, 10′ 9″ long, is hauled by a Dominion of Canada engine and costs $2.30.

There are three animal friezes: mustard-and-dark-brown giraffes galloping across a toast-colored background; black-and-white zebras galloping across a blue background; brown-and-green lions standing and lying on a white background. These are larger—11″ high and 44″ long, and cost $1.10 each. Postage for any amount of friezes is 33 cents surface, 80 cents air mail.

211
Dobbin Designs Carved wooden rocking horse in dapple gray or palomino, red rockers and leather bridle and saddle (back 26″ high).
photo Green Lane Studio

212
James Galt and Co. Ltd Brightly colored "See Inside" jigsaw puzzles for children one and a half to three years old. Around $3 each.

213
Tridias Felt jack-in-the-box in a wooden box painted red, blue, green, orange or yellow. About $4.75.

214
Tridias Wooden farm building with a gray removable roof, blue doors and green base, about $6.75. One of a set of three farm buildings, made in scale with Britains farm animals, about $16 the set.
photos Photography West

215
Obletter Spielwaren Arnold Rapido model train. Engine without motor, about $3.90; carriages, about $2.50 each.

211

212

213

214

215

Pollock's Toy Museum, La Scala Street, London W.1, England
Brochure, free.

An old toy-theater maker, now well known for reproductions of its original wares. For about $12 including postage you get "The Regency," a reproduction in plastic and plywood of a theater printed in 1834 measuring 15" by 12" by 12". For about $2.25 you can get the smaller "Victoria" in cardboard. You can add lighting, and fairy-tale scenery and scripts with characters, not to mention the Shakespeare pack of three plays for $2.50. Also on sale are a few decorative old wooden peg dolls, too fragile to be played with, at $1.60 each (undressed) including postage; and "Pearlies," peg dolls dressed in the traditional Cockney royal costume of black velvet and pearls. These cost about $14, including postage.

Tridias, 8 Savile Row, Bath BA1 2QP, England
14-page catalogue, free.

Another good-taste toy shop, well worth looking at. Tridias sells mostly carefully chosen English and Continental toys by other manufacturers, but when driven to it, because they can't find something they like, they make their own. They have made a nice musical carrying box with a handle. It can be used for things like pencils and comes plain with a set of transfers so that the owner can decorate it himself, $6. They also have their own beautiful Georgian dollhouse for $34, good for anyone returning from England by boat, but otherwise disproportionately expensive to ship, as it is too large to be sent by mail. Also their own wooden trucks, trains, forts, farms, etc.

Compared to Galt's (above), Tridias tends to go for more old-fashioned toys and are less "educational." I bought a big box of party favors from them—animal and bird transfers, furry mouse pins, magnetic ladybugs, whistling birds in cages, cutout farms—it was *much* easier to find novel things at Tridias than in my neighborhood.

Ask for the fascinating "Spellbinder" puzzles—elephants, cars, trees, etc., break up into pieces that spell their names, and you can also get Sasha and Gregor, the wistful-faced soft plastic dolls designed by Sasha Morgenthaler. Sasha costs $18 in America, and her clothes $8 for each set. A friend of mine bought Sasha and three sets of clothes from England for a total of $27 including postage (she was not charged duty), and in New York exactly the same things would have cost her $42.

Victoria and Albert Museum, Publications Section, South Kensington, London, S.W.1, England
Lists of cutout paper dolls, cutout rag dolls, jigsaw puzzles, free.

Old-fashioned toys at astonishingly low prices. Nineteenth-century and early-twentieth-century line fashion drawings on white card to be cut out and colored, each one has the doll and three costumes, and costs 45 cents. There are 15" dolls printed in six colors on calico sheet for cutting out and stitching; Alice, a little girl in her underwear (c. 1916), 90 cents; four little-girl dolls of the same date, $1.45. Jigsaws of John Constable's "Salisbury Cathedral," "Chelsea Pensioners Reading the Waterloo Dispatch," model of a butcher shop in the Bethnal Green Museum, and other similar subjects, $2.75 each. All the above prices include surface postage to America, believe it or not. But if you pay with a personal check it is *essential* to remember to add enough to cover bank charges on these small amounts, or the museum will end up in debt to the bank.

GERMANY

Germany produces vast quantities of superb toys, and the leading toy shops below are all quite used to sending them abroad (Spielzeug-Rasch says they have over a thousand foreign customers, and answer letters in French and Spanish as well as in English). Many of the toys are 50 percent less expensive in Germany than in foreign stores—electric trains in O, HO or N gauge, Schuco mechanical toys and Steiff plush animals, for instance, all of which are very popular German mail-order buys. The shops below, in addition to a general catalogue, will send, if you ask, brochures produced by the famous German manufacturers. The full lists of manufacturers' brochures available are in the general catalogues and include model trains by Trix, Fleischmann, Marklin and Arnold Rapido; lineside buildings by Faller and Kibri; mechanical toys by Schuco, soft toys by Steiff (about five hundred in the catalogue), card toys by Ravensburger (see below), figurines by Hummel.

All the catalogues are in German, but they are illustrated by full-color photographs with the prices in Deutche Mark (often written DM) right next to the toys.

Spielwaren Behle, Kaiserstrasse 28, Frankfurt/M, Germany

Spielzeug-Rasch, Gerhart-Hauptmann-Platz 1, Hamburg 1, Germany
Special models catalogue in German, $1.75 (Spielzeug-Rasch only).

Spielwarenhaus Virnich, Luitpoldstrasse 6, 85 Nuremberg, Germany
70-page color catalogue, free, in German.

These three shops all send out the same very good general catalogue, showing colorful German versions of most toys. (Spielzeug-Rasch also puts out a very serious and professional catalogue of specialized models.) Germany is particularly strong on all sorts of models: little wooden villages and the model buildings that are so expensive in America—castles cost about $13, old-fashioned gabled farmyards about $12, a ranch about $10, and "Fort Texas," $7. German construction sets are shown: Baufix, Fischertechnik, and Plasticant; cars and garages; Schuco; Gama; Faller; and a few of the model trains. Plenty of cozy doll cradles, pretty tea sets and some very distinguished dolls (though no cheaper than American dolls)—a delectable ash-blond one costs $16.

Egon Wiedling, Theatinerstrasse 13, 8 Munich 2, Germany
List of model ships, free. Egon Wiedling only.

Kinderparadies, Neuer Wall 7, Hamburg, Germany

Obletter Spielwaren, Karlsplatz 11–12, 8 Munich 2, Germany
40-page color catalogue, free.

These three shops send out the same general catalogue. The difference between them is that Egon Wiedling says his service is slow because he has a shortage of personnel! He is also a model-ship collector and has a list in English of 1:1250 scale model ships from all countries.

The catalogue has, among other things, a pageful of doll furniture in dark blue painted with red, white and yellow traditional bird and heart designs; a pullable cradle, $8; a table and two chairs, $16; and dollhouse furniture "*im modernen Stil*," with tiny toys for the dollhouse children;

216
Charlotte Weibull Handmade dolls 8″ high: bride from
Skåne, about $9; bridegroom, about $7.50; fiddler,
about $6.50.

217
Charlotte Weibull Handmade dolls, peasant children
Åsa Gåsa Piga and Nils Holgerson on a bench. About
$13.50.
photo Alice Strid

rocking horses; tricycles; wagons; and sandboxes. A plain
little wood schoolroom with desks, and benches, bookcase
and blackboard, costs $8. Besides the doll furniture, the
catalogue shows other popular German toys that are just
different enough from American toys to be interesting. A
fascinating marble racer in primary colors and transparent
plastic, $8; painted wooden animals and people that hang on
the wall and move their legs when you pull a string, $2. And
the nesting Russian dolls that I have never found in New York,
$7.
*Ask any of the above shops for the Ravensburger
catalogue.*
24-page color catalogue in German, free.

This catalogue is in German and unnumbered, but the boxes
are partially printed in English and it is well worth the trouble,
as Ravensburger makes widely exported and beautifully
printed board games and hobby kits. The designs and colors
are excellent and most of the games have instructions in
English (you can tell by the pictures in the catalogue whether
they do or not). "Picture Lotto" is about $2.25, and a big
"Animal Lotto" with gorgeous color photographs is about
$2.80. "Memory" costs $1.65, and "Flower Postcards" to be
painted, $1.75. For older children there is a series of "Big
Cities" jigsaw, including New York, at $1.75 each. Excellent
for saving for rainy days, sickness, boredom and other
disasters are the hobby packs at $1.75 each: cards for
pasting; mobiles; napkin rings; telephone directory covers;
leather needlecases; leather picture frames, etc., all to make
and all attractively assembled and presented.

HOLLAND

Dovina, Hollandsestraat 18–22, Rotterdam 25, Holland
Color postcard, free.

Beautifully made plastic dolls 11″ high, dressed in eighteen
different regional Dutch costumes; doll and surface postage,
about $8 each.

SWEDEN

Charlotte Weibull, Box 4042, 203 11 Malmö 4, Sweden
7-page brochure in Swedish, free.

Charlotte Weibull has a seventeenth-century house at Leila
Torg, Sweden, which is a doll shop and puppet theater, and
she hopes to add a doll museum. Tourists already make
special trips to see her well-known collection of lovely
souvenir dolls in good Swedish taste—handwoven fabrics
and hand-painted faces. There are dolls in the costumes of
every Swedish province, dolls from Swedish fairy tales, doll
bookmarks, and dolls to hang up. Some are about $3.50 and
others are about $6.50, and now there is a little folding theater
for about $8 with hand puppets at $3.75.

Watches are easy to buy from abroad, being light and small to air-mail, but you have to be careful with duty, which depends on various things such as thickness of watch and number of jewels—watches with over seventeen jewels are charged $4 extra. Shannon Airport, for instance, says that one seventeen-jewel $57 Hamilton watch is charged with $3.85 duty, while you would have to pay $9.40 for a Hamilton watch with thirty jewels, although it is $5 cheaper.

HONG KONG

T. M. Chan and Co., P.O. Box 3881, Hong Kong
116-page catalogue, free. Prices in $.

Seiko watches for between $30 and $60; Omega and Rolex for between $58 and $215—roughly what they sell for in Switzerland, about a third less than in America.

Universal Suppliers, GPO Box 14803, Hong Kong
Rolex and Seiko watch leaflets, free; air mail $1.60 for both. Prices in $.

Seiko Japanese watches are being heavily advertised in America, where they sell for $55–$100. Universal Suppliers has them for $20–$60, mostly $25–$35; prices include air-mail postage and insurance. One of the watches, a Chronograph Diver, looked to me identical with a Seiko advertised in the *New York Times* for $95; at Universal it cost $45.

IRELAND

Mail Order Department, Shannon Free Airport, Ireland
60-page catalogue with some color, free; air mail 60 cents. Prices in $.

Goods sold in free-port areas (such as Hong Kong, the Caribbean Islands, airports, etc.) are not taxed locally, and although things bought by mail are exempt from local taxes anyway, there is still an advantage in buying from free-port areas because they are highly competitive, and sell even imports at prices as low as or lower than anywhere else. The Shannon Airport shop has a few respectable Nivada and Hamilton Swiss watches for between $27 and $66.

SWITZERLAND

Collet, 8 Place du Molard, 1204 Geneva, Switzerland
Audemars Piguet brochure, Omega brochure, Tissot brochure.
Jewelry catalogue, published in the fall—all free.

Collet sends out manufacturers' brochures in English for these excellent watches. Tissot prices start at around $38, Omega at around $54. I notice a $38 difference between one Omega Chronostop at my local jeweler and at Collet, and the Omega Speedmaster, "the first watch on the moon," costs $62 less in Switzerland.

Itracho Watch Co. Ltd., P.O. Box 289, 8027 Zurich, Switzerland
Catalogues 37 and 41, mainly fantasy watches, $1 each including surface postage. Prices in $.
Catalogue 42, more expensive, plainer watches, $1 including surface postage. Prices in $.

Bedazzling, bejeweled and very inexpensive fantasy watches in rings, bracelets, pins, cuff links and cigarette lighters. Watches inside and outside gilded donkeys, pearly turtles,

218
Heldwein (see Jewelry and Silver section) Jeweled pendant watch by Piaget.

219
Heldwein (see Jewelry and Silver section) Piaget wrist watch with turquoise dial and diamonds.

ruby-eyed flies, enameled cats, green Buddhas, John F. Kennedy and Pope Paul VI. A pendant watch with a zodiac sign on the back costs $7.50; a watch hidden in a ring covered by a gilded bird's nest and pearl egg, $12; an invisible watch in a diamond-and-turquoise studded bangle, $13.

These watches are Roskopf escapement and pin-lever watches, "drugstore" quality, and the kind of thing my watch mender refuses to fix on the grounds that it will break again immediately—so they must be bought only with the understanding that they have a short life expectancy.

Jelmoli S.A., Mail Order Dept. 8021 Zurich, Switzerland
General catalogue in French and German, free. Spring, fall.

The large department store Jelmoli has a general catalogue that shows about twenty inexpensive and medium-priced watches, starting at about $10.

A. Turler, Paradeplatz, 8001 Zurich, Switzerland
Audemars Piguet, Eterna-Matic, International Watch Co. Longines brochures, free.

Switzerland's largest retail watch stores say they have been sending watches to America since the first GIs came by. Eterna prices start at about $80, International Watch Co. at about $110—and Audemars Piguet, which are *very* de luxe, at about $320.

Appendices

CLOTHING SIZE CHARTS

As clothing sizes vary according to the manufacturer, always add measurements.

LADIES

Dresses, Coats, Suits, Skirts
Junior

American	7	9	11	13	15	17
English	9	11	13	15	17	
Continental	34	36	38	40	42	44

Misses

American	10	12	14	16	18	20
English	32	34	36	38	40	42
Continental	38	40	42	44	46	48

Women

American	38	40	42	44	46	48
English	20	22	24	26	28	30
Continental	46	48	50	52		

Blouses and sweaters

American	34	36	38	40	42	44
English	36	38	40	42	44	46
	42	44	46	48	50	52

Stockings and gloves are standard.

MEN

Suits, Overcoats and Pajamas

American and English	34	36	38	40	42	44	46	48
Continental	44	46	48	50	52	54	56	58

Shirts

American and English	$12\frac{1}{2}$	13	$13\frac{1}{2}$	14	$14\frac{1}{2}$	15	$15\frac{1}{2}$	16	$16\frac{1}{2}$	17
Continental	32	33	34	35-36	37	38	39	40-41	42	43

Sweaters

	Small	Medium	Large	Extra Large
American English	34	36–38	40	42–44
Continental	44	46–48	50	52–54

Hats

American	$6\frac{7}{8}$	7	$7\frac{1}{8}$	$7\frac{1}{4}$	$7\frac{3}{8}$	$7\frac{1}{2}$	$7\frac{5}{8}$	$7\frac{3}{4}$
English	$6\frac{3}{4}$	$6\frac{7}{8}$	7	$7\frac{1}{8}$	$7\frac{1}{4}$	$7\frac{3}{8}$	$7\frac{1}{2}$	$7\frac{5}{8}$
Continental	55	56	57	58	59	60	61	62

Shoes

American	$6\frac{1}{2}$	7	$7\frac{1}{2}$	8	$8\frac{1}{2}$	9	$9\frac{1}{2}$	10	$10\frac{1}{2}$	11	$11\frac{1}{2}$
English	5	$5\frac{1}{2}$	6	$6\frac{1}{2}$	7	$7\frac{1}{2}$	8	$8\frac{1}{2}$	9	$9\frac{1}{2}$	10
Continental	38	$38\frac{1}{2}$	39	$39\frac{1}{2}$	40	41	$41\frac{1}{2}$	42	$42\frac{1}{2}$	43	$43\frac{1}{2}$

ADDITIONAL IMPORT INFORMATION

Office of Information and Publications, Bureau of Customs, Treasury Department, Washington, DC 20226 give out several free leaflets:

"Duty for Popular Tourist Items" lists current rates for about eighty items, and is revised whenever necessary. Telephone or write your nearest Customs Office or District Director of Customs for anything not covered.

"Know Before You Go" gives general information about what is and is not allowed into the country. It is intended for tourists but most of the information also applies to shopping by mail.

"Trademark Information." This leaflet lists those foreign articles bearing "prohibited" trademarks recorded in the Treasury Department, such as certain perfumes, cameras, watches, stereo equipment, which must not be brought into the country with the trademark on. However, it is perfectly legal to bring in the articles with their trademarks removed, and if you want to bring something in that has a registered trademark, you can do one of two things: you can ask the shop you buy the article from to remove the trademark, or you can wait until it arrives and is inspected by American customs officers. If they feel it is necessary, a form will be sent for you to sign declaring that you agree to remove the trademark yourself. After signing the form, you mail it back and the goods will be forwarded to you in the normal way.

CONVERSION TABLES

United States Dollars (U.S.$)	.10	.15	.25	.50	.75	1.00	5.00	10.00	12.50	15.00	20.00	50.00	75.00	100.00
Great Britain Pound Sterling = 100 New Pence	.04	.06	.09½	.19	.29	.38	1.91	3.83	4.79	5.75	7.66	19.15	28.73	38.31
France Franc = 100 Centimes	.51	.77	1.28	2.55	3.83	5.11	25.55	51.10	61.32	76.65	102.20	255.50	383.25	511.00
Austria Schilling = 100 Groschen	2.32	3.49	5.81	11.63	17.44	23.25	116.28	232.56	290.70	348.84	465.12	1162.80	1744.20	2325.60
Germany German Mark (D.M.) = 100 Pfennig	.31	.47	.78	1.56	2.34	3.12	15.63	31.25	39.06	46.87	62.50	156.25	234.37	312.50
Spain Peseta = 100 Centimos	6.43	9.64	16.07	32.15	48.22	64.30	321.50	643.00	803.75	964.50	1286.00	3215.00	4822.50	6430.00
Switzerland Swiss Franc (S.F.) = 100 Rappen	.38	.57	.96	1.92	2.87	3.83	19.15	38.30	47.87	57.45	76.60	191.50	287.25	383.00
Hong Kong Hong Kong Dollar (H.K.$.) = 100 Cents	.56	.84	1.40	2.80	4.20	5.60	28.00	56.00	70.00	84.00	112.00	280.00	420.00	560.00
Sweden Swedish Krona (S.KR.) — 100 Öre	.48	.72	1.20	2.40	3.60	4.81	24.05	48.10	60.12	72.15	96.20	240.50	360.75	481.00
New Zealand New Zealand Dollar (N.Z.$.) = 100 Cents	.08	.12	.20	.41	.62	.82	4.11	8.22	10.28	12.34	16.45	41.12	61.68	82.24
Portugal Escudo (ESC.) = 100 Centavos	2.72	4.08	6.81	13.62	20.43	27.24	136.20	272.40	340.50	408.60	544.80	1362.00	2043.00	2724.00
Denmark Danish Krone (D.KR.) = Øre	.70	1.04	1.74	3.48	5.22	6.96	34.80	69.60	87.00	104.40	139.20	348.00	522.00	696.00
Norway Norwegian Krone (N.KR.) = 100 Øre	.66	.99	1.65	3.31	4.96	6.62	33.10	66.20	82.75	99.30	132.40	331.00	496.50	662.00
India Indian Rupee (I.RP.) — 100 Paise	.73	1.09	1.82	3.64	5.46	7.28	36.40	72.80	91.00	109.20	145.60	364.00	546.00	728.00
Netherlands Holland Guilder (HFL) = Cents	.32	.48	.80	1.61	2.41	3.22	16.10	32.20	40.25	48.30	64.40	161.00	241.50	322.00
Tunisia Tunisian Dinar (T.D.) = 1000 Millimes	.05	.07	.12	.24	.36	.48	2.42	4.84	6.04	7.25	9.67	24.18	36.27	48.35
Turkey Turkish Lira (T.L.) = 100 Kurus	.71	1.07	1.78	3.57	5.35	7.14	35.70	71.40	89.25	107.10	142.80	357.00	535.50	714.00
Italy Italian Lira (LIT) = 100 Centesimi	58.00	87.00	145.00	290.00	435.00	581.00	2905.00	5810.00	7263.00	8715.00	11620.00	29050.00	43575.00	58100.00
Japan Yen = 100 Sen	31.00	46.00	77.00	154.00	231.00	308.00	1540.00	3080.00	3850.00	4620.00	6160.00	15400.00	23100.00	30800.00

Based on rates prevailing as of March 1972.
Exchange rates fluctuate within a trading range of 4½%,
established by the International Monetary Fund.
Subject to change.

Compiled by:
Perera Airports Corporation
J. F. Kennedy International Airport
New York, N.Y. 11430

LIST OF CUSTOMS CHARGES

ANTIQUES made at least 100 years before date of entry   free
AUTOMOBILES, passenger   3%

BAGS, hand, leather   10%
BINOCULARS
   prism   20%
   opera and field glasses $8\frac{1}{2}$%
BOOKS
   foreign author   free
   foreign language   free

CAMERAS
   motion picture, over $50 each   6%
   still, over $10 each $7\frac{1}{2}$%
   cases, leather   10%
   lenses $12\frac{1}{2}$%
CANDY
   sweetened chocolate bars   5%
   other   7%
CHESS SETS   10%
CHINA
   bone $17\frac{1}{2}$%
   nonbone, other than tableware $22\frac{1}{2}$%
CHINA TABLEWARE, nonbone, available in 77-piece sets
   value over $10 but not over $24 per set   10¢ doz. + 55%
   value over $24 but not over $56 per set   10¢ doz. + 36%
   value over $56 per set   5¢ doz. + 18%
CIGARETTE LIGHTERS
   pocket, value over 42¢ each $22\frac{1}{2}$%
   table   12%
CLOCKS
   value over $5 but not over $10 each   75¢ + 16%
   value over $10 each $1.12 + 16%

DRAWINGS (works of art)
   original   free
   copies, done entirely by hand   free

EARTHENWARE TABLEWARE, available in 77-piece sets
   value over $7 but not over $12 per set   10¢ doz. + 21%
   value over $12 per set   5¢ doz. + $10\frac{1}{2}$%

FIGURINES, china $22\frac{1}{2}$%
FUR
   wearing apparel $8\frac{1}{2}$% – $18\frac{1}{2}$%
   other items made of $8\frac{1}{2}$%
FURNITURE
   wood, chairs $8\frac{1}{2}$%
   wood, other than chairs   5%

GLASS TABLEWARE, value not over $1 each $22\frac{1}{2}$% – 50%
GLOVES
   wool $37\frac{1}{2}$¢ + $18\frac{1}{2}$%
   fur   10%
   horsehide or cowhide   15%
GOLF BALLS   6%

HANDKERCHIEFS
   cotton, plain   25%
   other vegetable fiber, plain   9%

IVORY, items made of   6%

JEWELRY, precious metal or stone
   silver chief value, value not over $18 per dozen $27\frac{1}{2}$%
   other   12%

LEATHER
   pocketbooks, bags   10%
   other items made of   4% – 14%

MOTORCYCLES   5%
MUSICAL INSTRUMENTS
   music boxes, wood   8%
   woodwind, except bagpipes $7\frac{1}{2}$%
   bagpipes   free

PAINTINGS (works of art)
   original   free
   copies, done entirely by hand   free
PAPER, items made of $8\frac{1}{2}$%
PEARLS
   loose or temporarily strung (without clasp)
      genuine   free
      cultured $2\frac{1}{2}$%
      imitation   20%
   permanently strung (with clasp attached or separate)
      12% – 27%
PERFUME   8¢ lb. + $7\frac{1}{2}$%

RADIOS
   transistor   10.4%
   other   6%
RATTAN
   furniture   16%
   other items made of $12\frac{1}{2}$%
RECORDS, phonograph   5%

SHOES, leather $2\frac{1}{2}$% – 20%
SKIS AND SKI EQUIPMENT   8% – 9%
   ski boots   free to 20%
SLIPPERS, leather   5%
STERLING FLATWARE AND TABLEWARE
   knives and forks   4¢ each + $8\frac{1}{2}$%
   spoons and tableware $12\frac{1}{2}$%
STONES, cut but not set
   diamonds not over $\frac{1}{2}$ carat   4%
   diamonds over $\frac{1}{2}$ carat   5%
   other   free to 5%
SWEATERS, of wool, over $5 per lb. $37\frac{1}{2}$¢ lb. + 20%

TAPE RECORDERS $5\frac{1}{2}$% – $7\frac{1}{2}$%
TOILET PREPARATIONS
   not containing alcohol $7\frac{1}{2}$%
   containing alcohol   8¢ lb. + $7\frac{1}{2}$%
TOYS $17\frac{1}{2}$%
TRUFFLES   free

WATCHES, on $100 watches duty varies from $6 to $13
WEARING APPAREL
   embroidered or ornamented   21% – $42\frac{1}{2}$%
   not embroidered, not ornamented:
      cotton, knit   21%
      cotton, not knit   8% – 21%
      linen, not knit $7\frac{1}{2}$%
      man-made fiber, knit   25¢ lb. + $32\frac{1}{2}$%
      man-made fiber, not knit   25¢ + $27\frac{1}{2}$%
      silk, knit   10%
      silk, not knit   16%
      wool, knit $37\frac{1}{2}$¢ + 20% – 32%
      wool, not knit   25¢ – $37\frac{1}{2}$¢ lb. + 21%
WOOD
   carvings   8%
   other items made of   8%

Index

Index

ABOUT THE AUTHOR

MARIA ELENA DE LA IGLESIA was born in Madrid in 1936, and attended Dartington Hall School and Newnham College, Cambridge, England, from which she was graduated with honors and where she also received her M.A. degree. She has written articles for *The Times* (of London) and is the author of two children's books, *The Cat and the Mouse* (1966), and *The Oak That Would Not Pay* (1968), both of which were published by Pantheon Books. She is married to publisher André Schiffrin and they live in New York City with their two daughters, Anya and Natalia.